BUMPERBOY

AND THE LOUD, LOUD MOUNTAIN

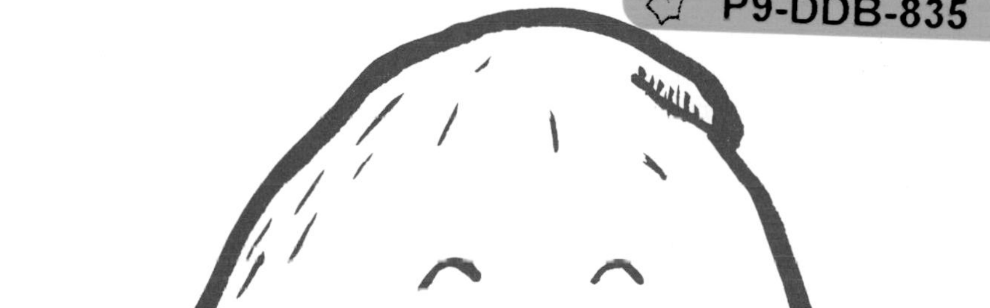

BY DEBBIE HUEY

BUMPERBOY AND THE LOUD, LOUD MOUNTAIN
All content © 2006 BUMPERBOY

Published in association with AdHouse Books
The AdHouse logo is © 2006 AdHouse Books
www.adhousebooks.com

www.bumperboy.net
debbie@bumperboy.net

ISBN: 0-9766610-1-2
10 9 8 7 6 5 4 3 2 1

First Printing, June 2006
Printed in Canada

SPECIAL THANKS TO:
Mom, Dad, Pam, Scott, Cindy, Mike, Sean, Vicky, and Ben:
You all mean everything to me!
Also, many thanks to Chris Pitzer for his continuous support,
to all my friends for their valuable advice,
and to Bumperboy's fans for their encouragement and kindness.

OTHER BOOKS BY DEBBIE HUEY:
Bumperboy Loses His Marbles: ISBN 0-9766610-0-4

PART ONE

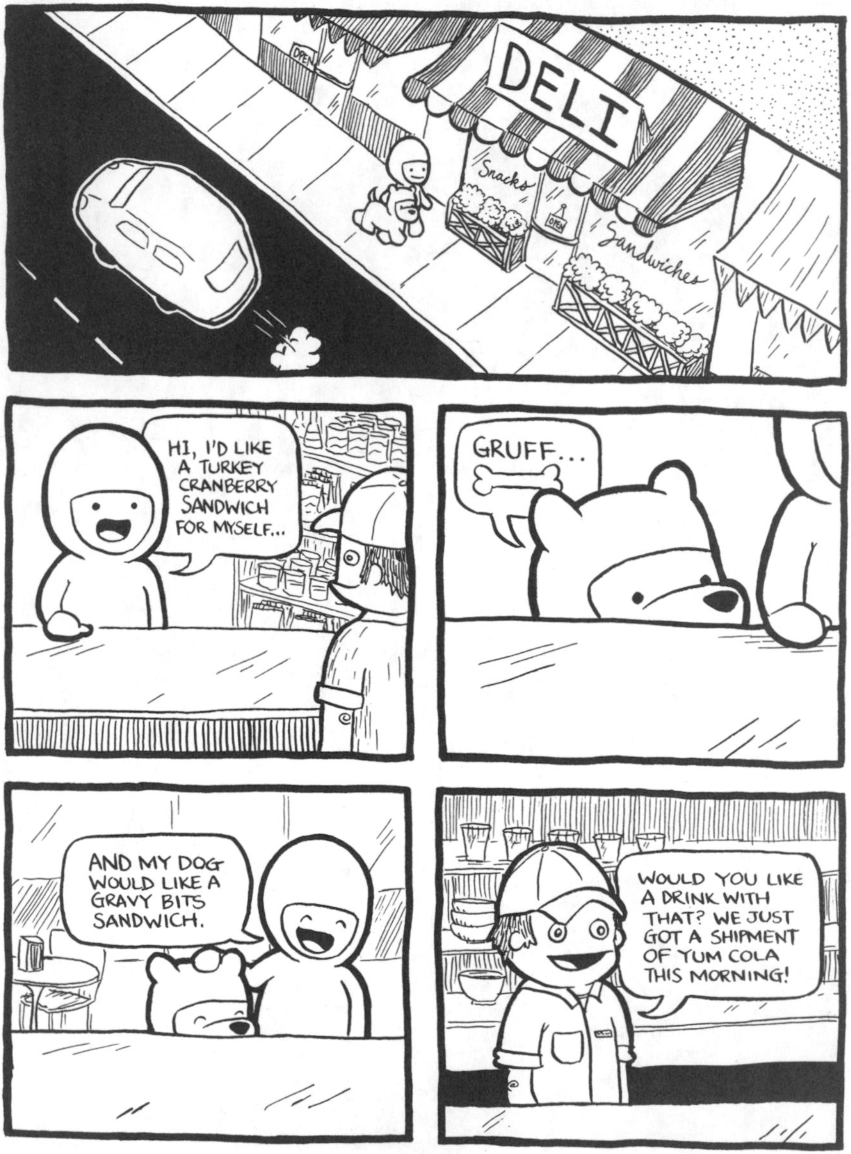
DELI
OPEN
Snacks
OPEN
Sandwiches
HI, I'D LIKE A TURKEY CRANBERRY SANDWICH FOR MYSELF...
GRUFF...
AND MY DOG WOULD LIKE A GRAVY BITS SANDWICH.
WOULD YOU LIKE A DRINK WITH THAT? WE JUST GOT A SHIPMENT OF YUM COLA THIS MORNING!

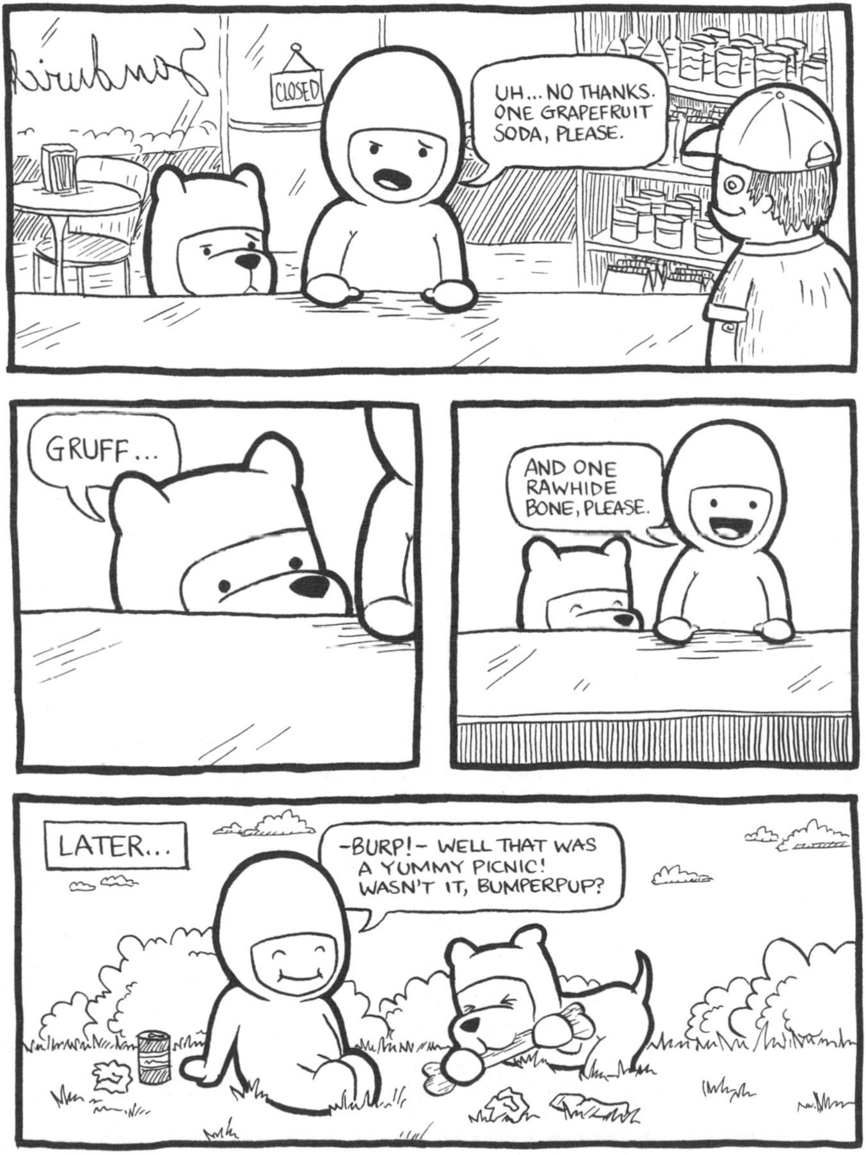
CLOSED
UH... NO THANKS. ONE GRAPEFRUIT SODA, PLEASE.
GRUFF...
AND ONE RAWHIDE BONE, PLEASE.
LATER...
-BURP!- WELL THAT WAS A YUMMY PICNIC! WASN'T IT, BUMPERPUP?

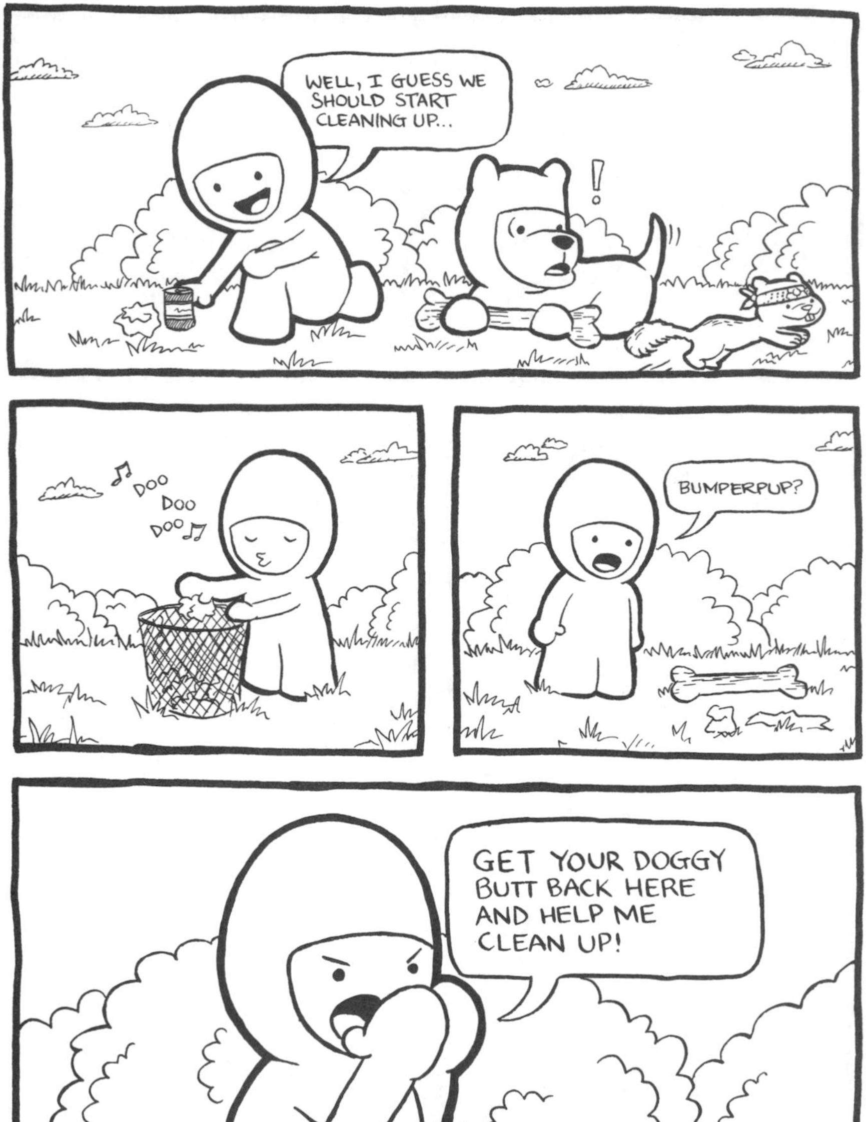
WELL, I GUESS WE SHOULD START CLEANING UP...
!
DOO
DOO
DOO
BUMPERPUP?
GET YOUR DOGGY BUTT BACK HERE AND HELP ME CLEAN UP!

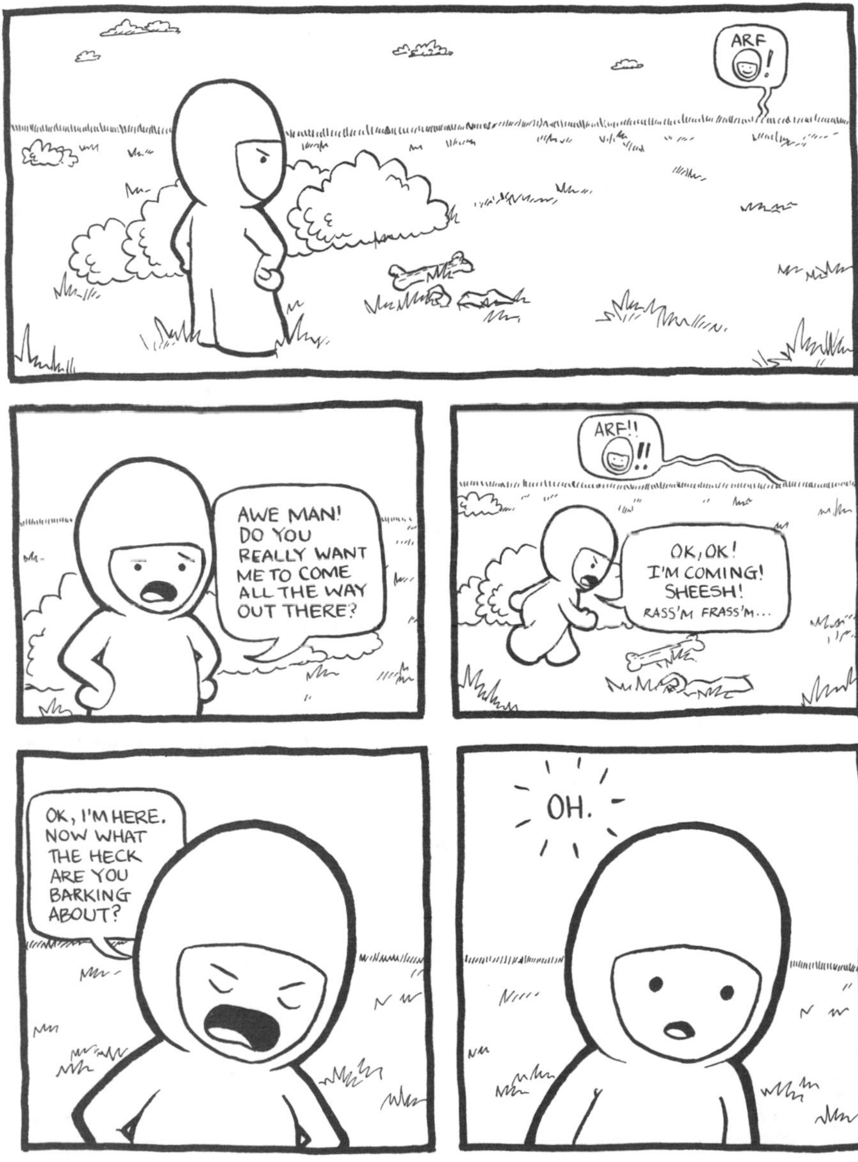

ARF
!
AWE MAN! DO YOU REALLY WANT ME TO COME ALL THE WAY OUT THERE?
ARF!!
!!
OK, OK! I'M COMING! SHEESH! RASS'M FRASS'M...
OK, I'M HERE. NOW WHAT THE HECK ARE YOU BARKING ABOUT?
OH.

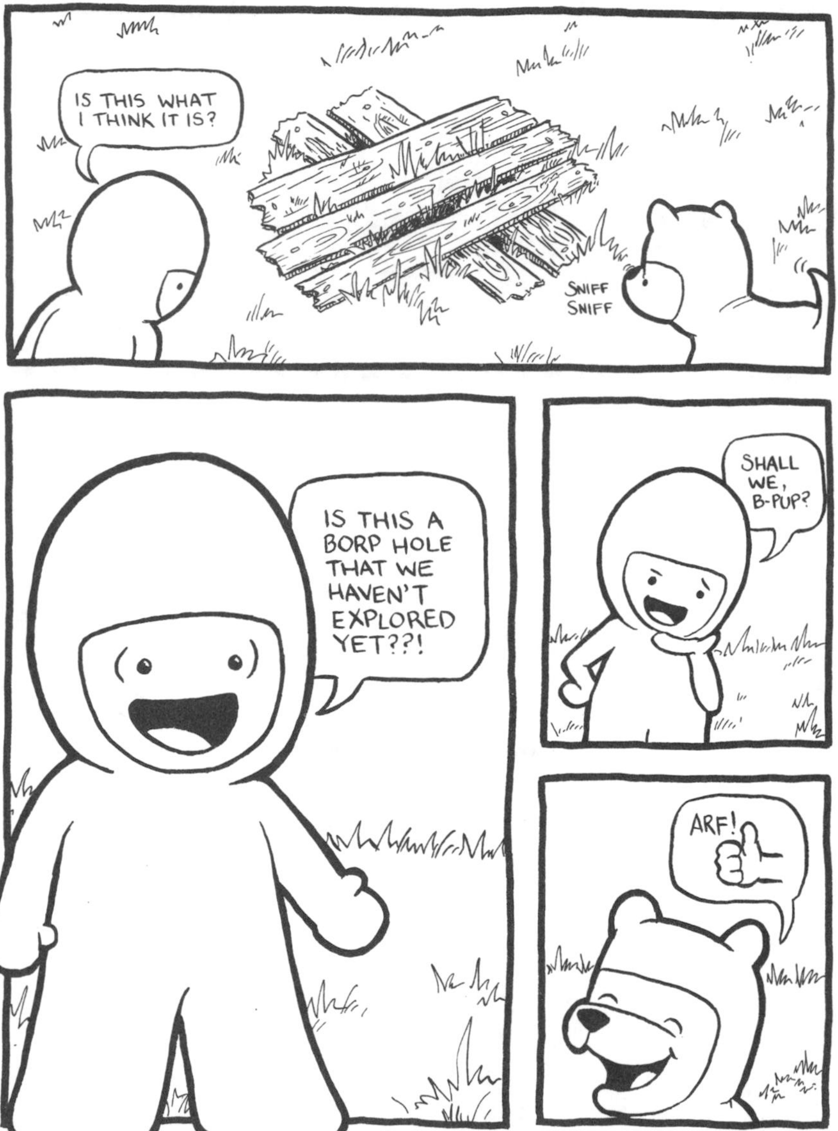
IS THIS WHAT I THINK IT IS?
SNIFF SNIFF
IS THIS A BORP HOLE THAT WE HAVEN'T EXPLORED YET??!
SHALL WE, B-PUP?
ARF!

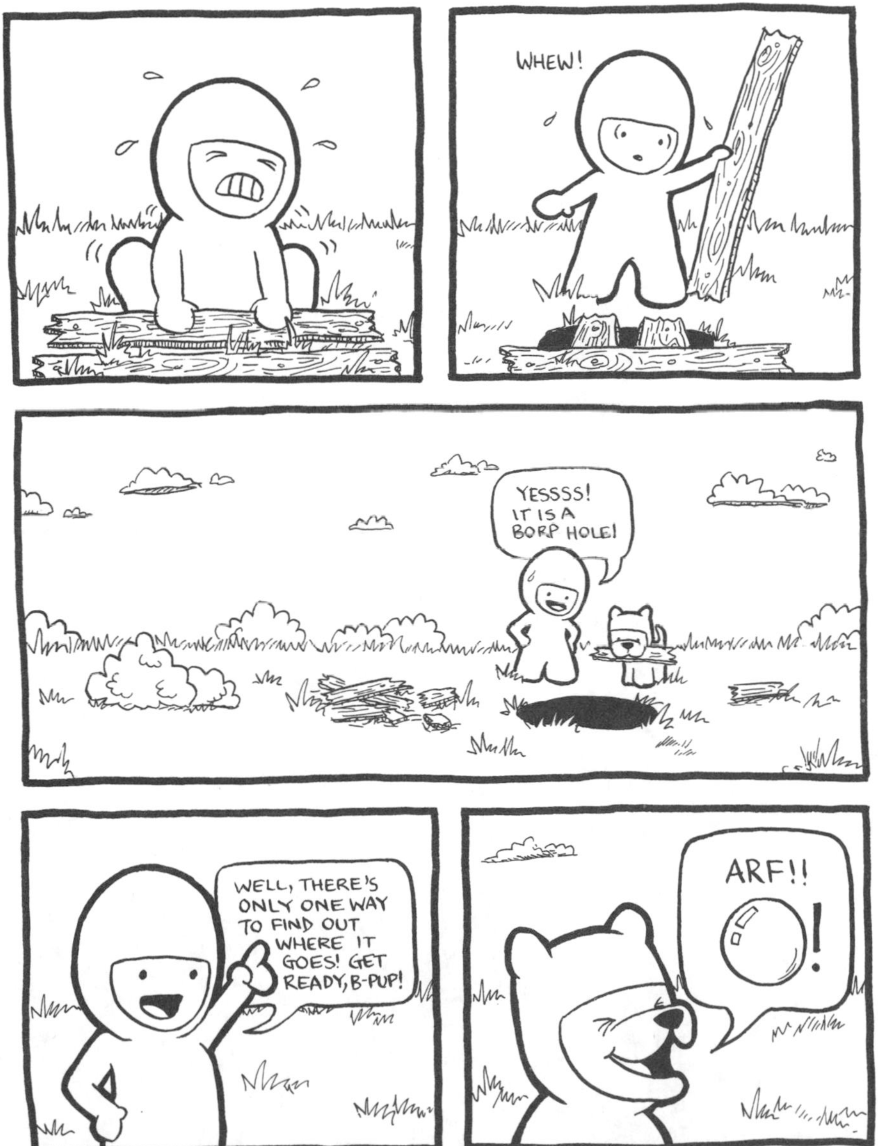
WHEW!
YESSSS! IT IS A BORP HOLE!
WELL, THERE'S ONLY ONE WAY TO FIND OUT WHERE IT GOES! GET READY, B-PUP!
ARF!! !

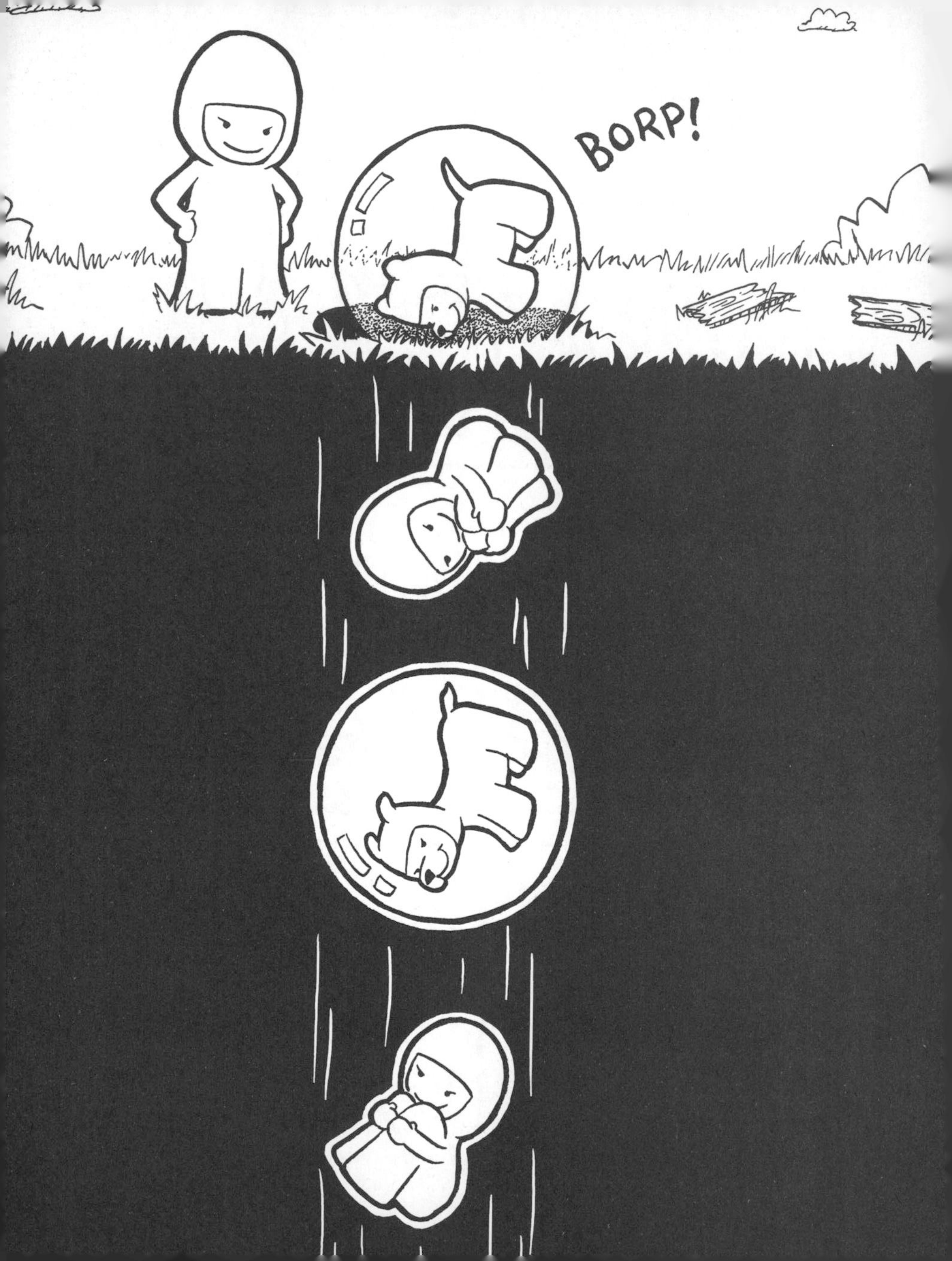
BORP!

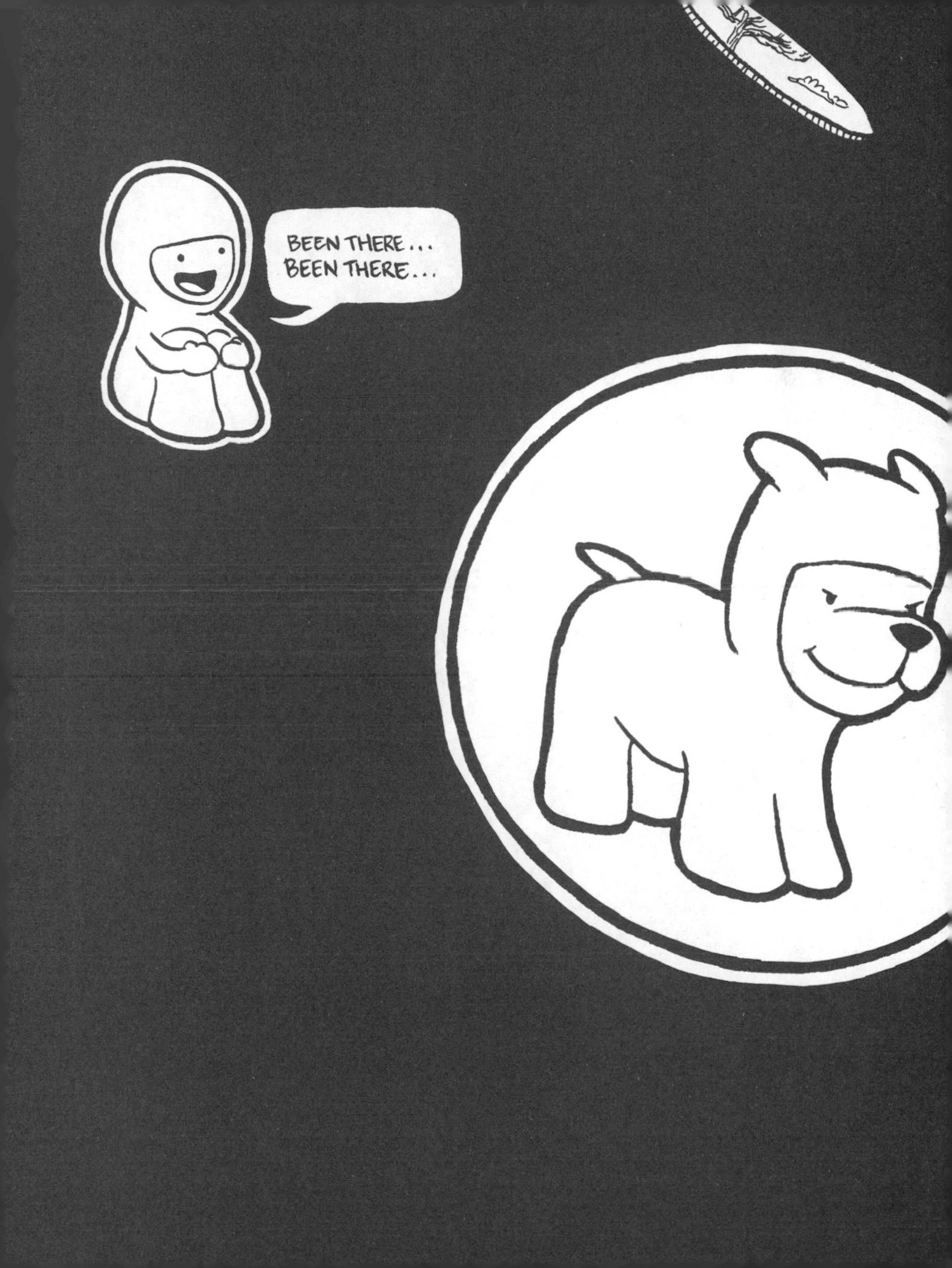
BEEN THERE...
BEEN THERE...

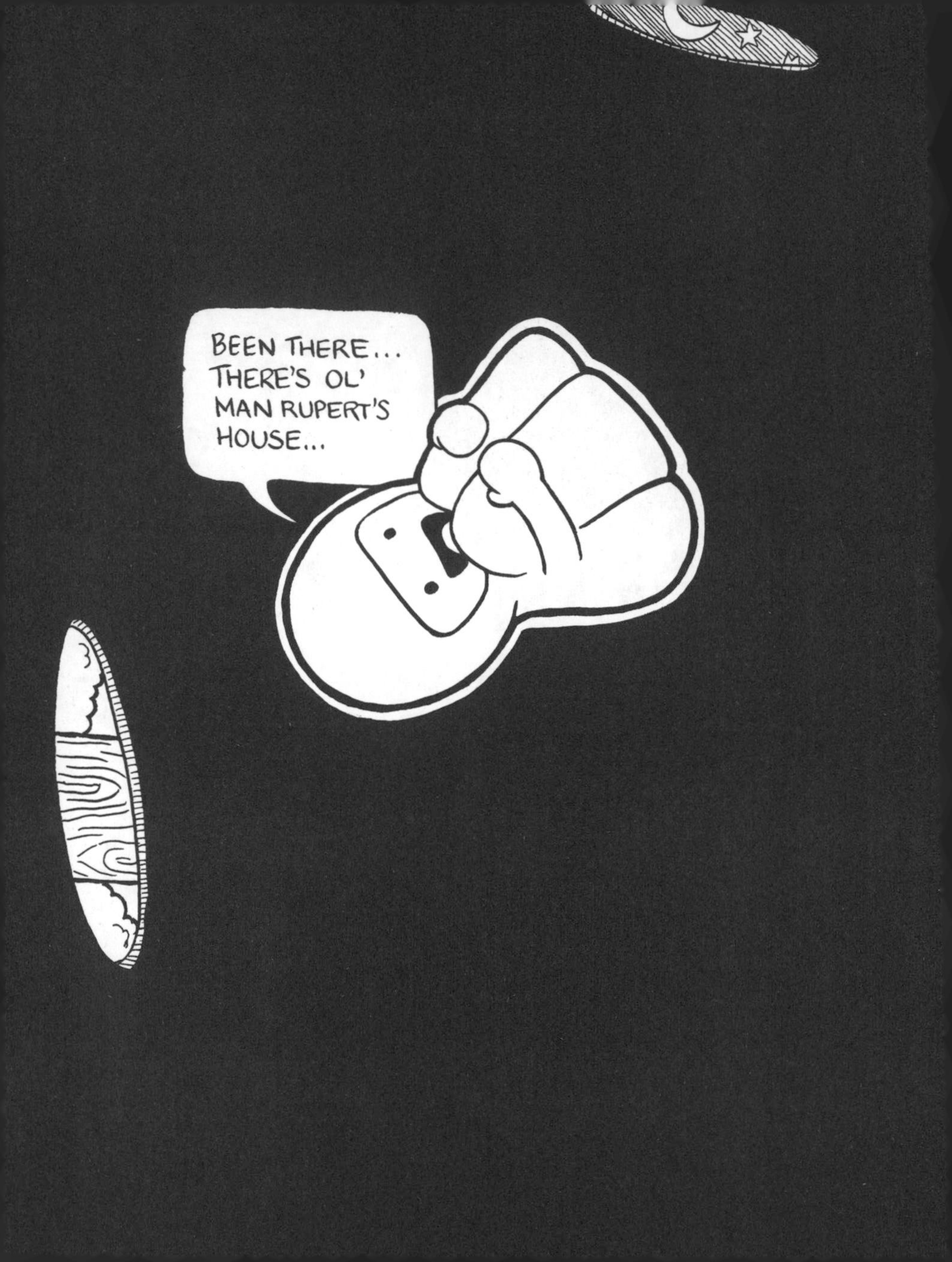
BEEN THERE... THERE'S OL' MAN RUPERT'S HOUSE...

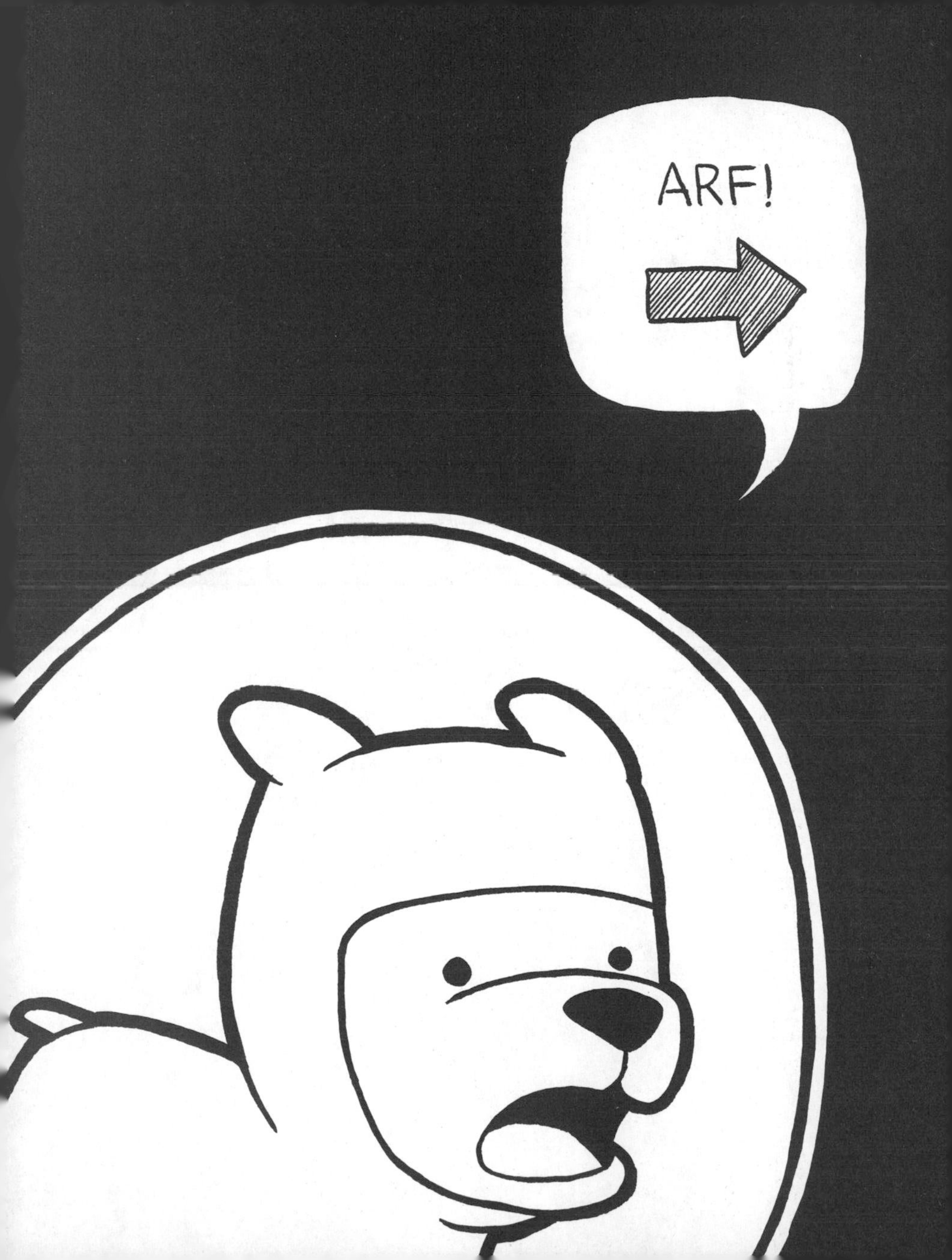
ARF!

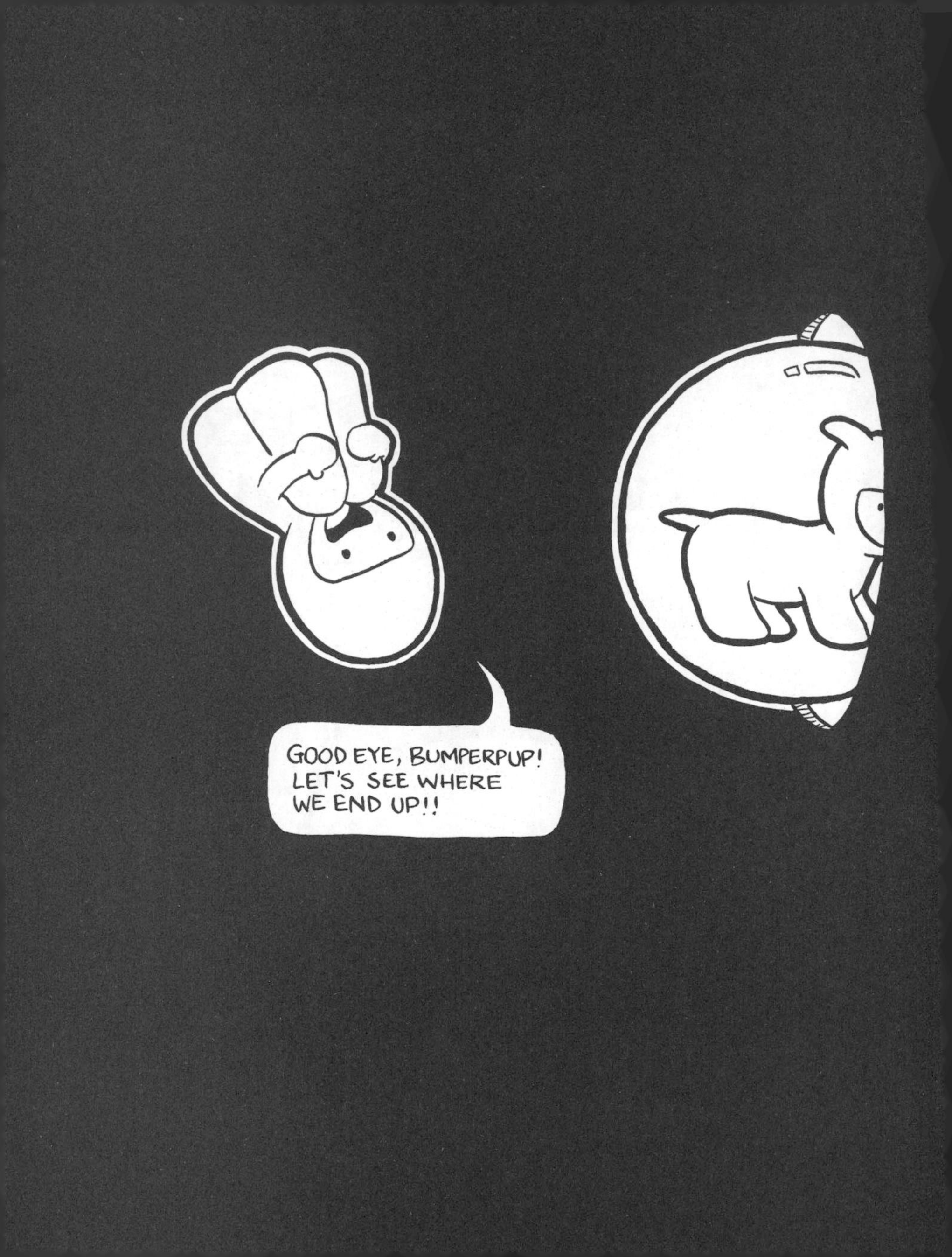
GOOD EYE, BUMPERPUP! LET'S SEE WHERE WE END UP!!

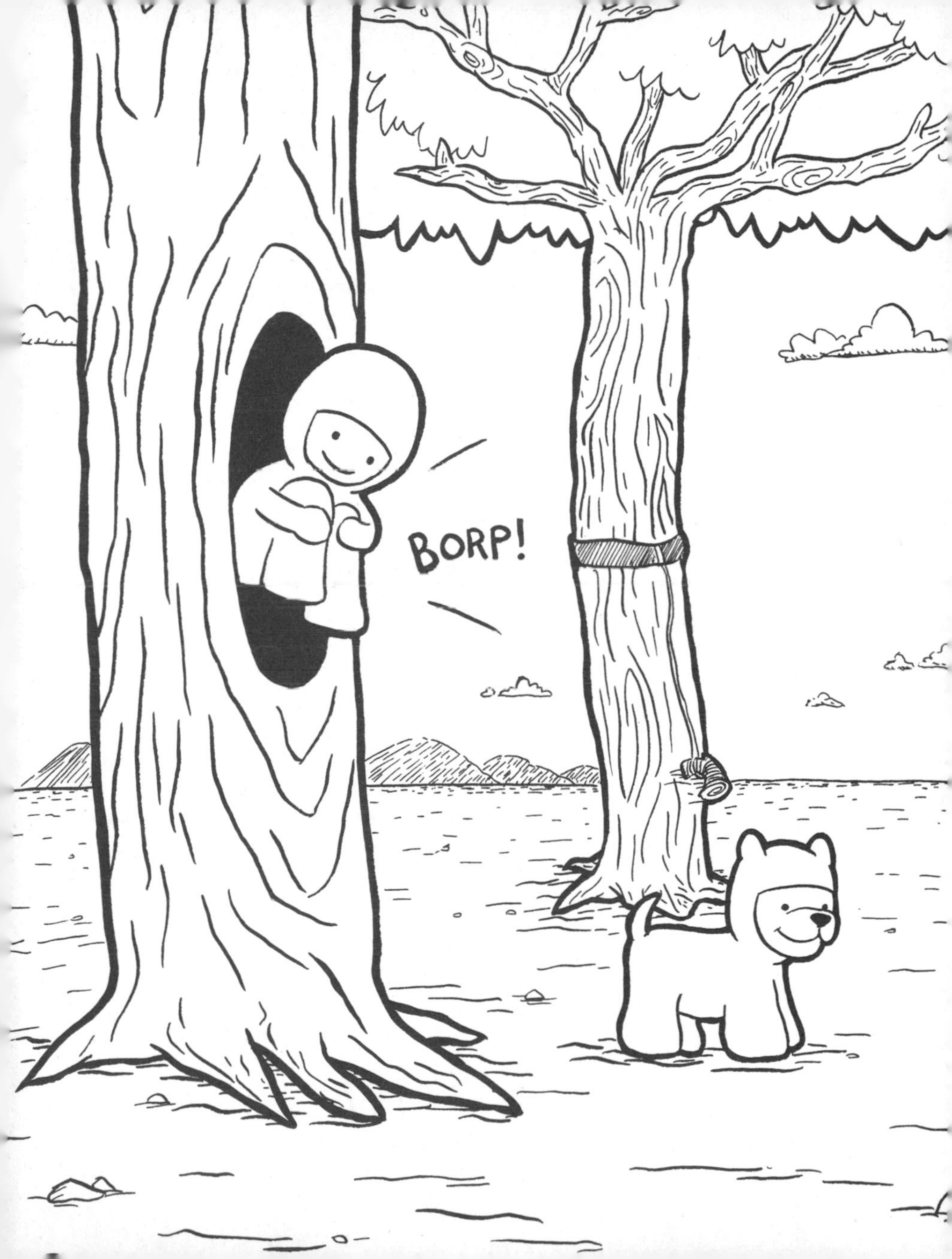
BORP!

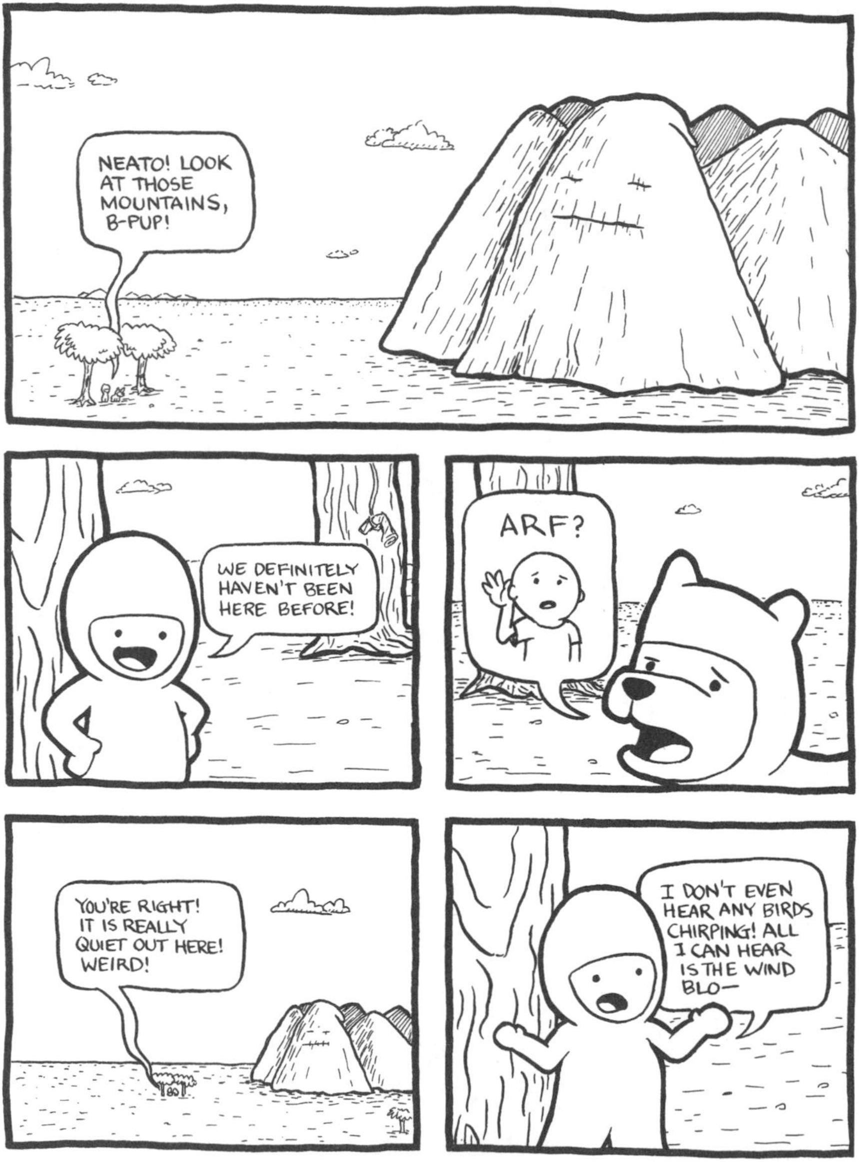
NEATO! LOOK AT THOSE MOUNTAINS, B-PUP!
WE DEFINITELY HAVEN'T BEEN HERE BEFORE!
ARF?
YOU'RE RIGHT! IT IS REALLY QUIET OUT HERE! WEIRD!
I DON'T EVEN HEAR ANY BIRDS CHIRPING! ALL I CAN HEAR IS THE WIND BLO—

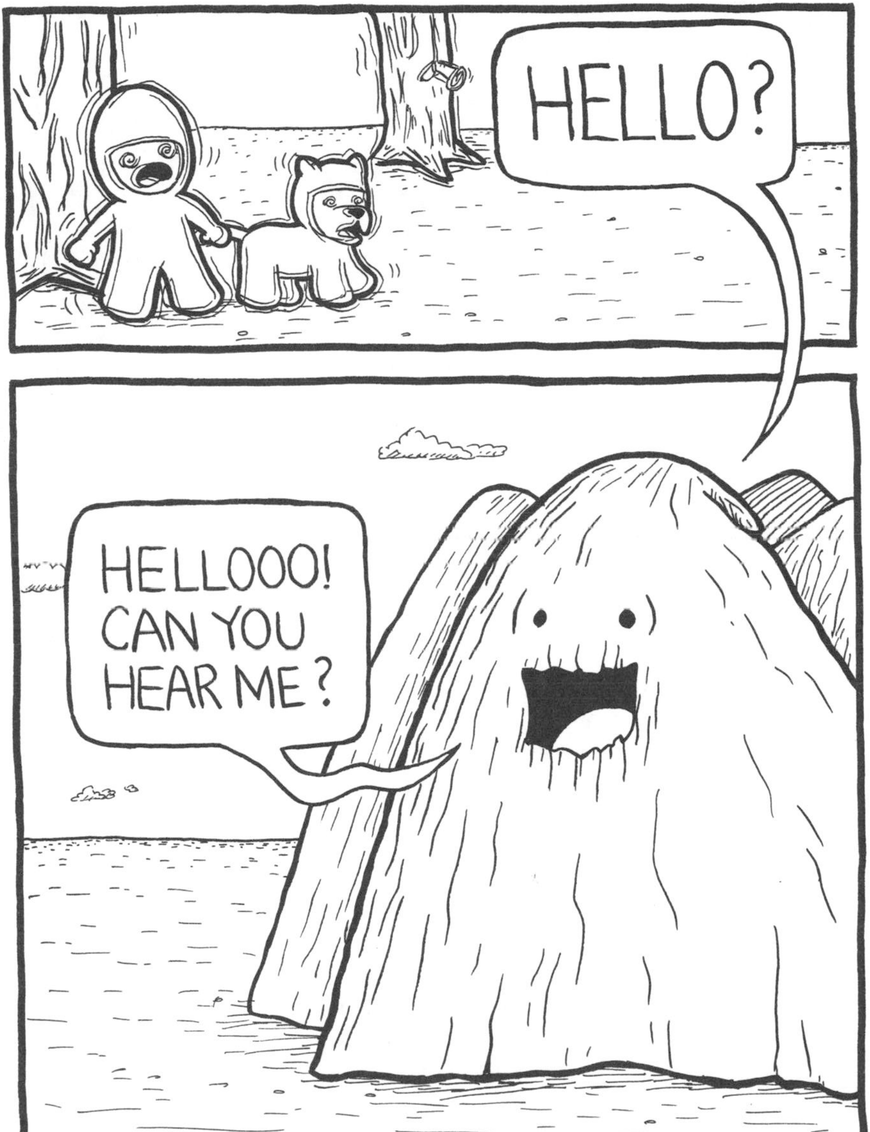
HELLO?
HELLOOO! CAN YOU HEAR ME?

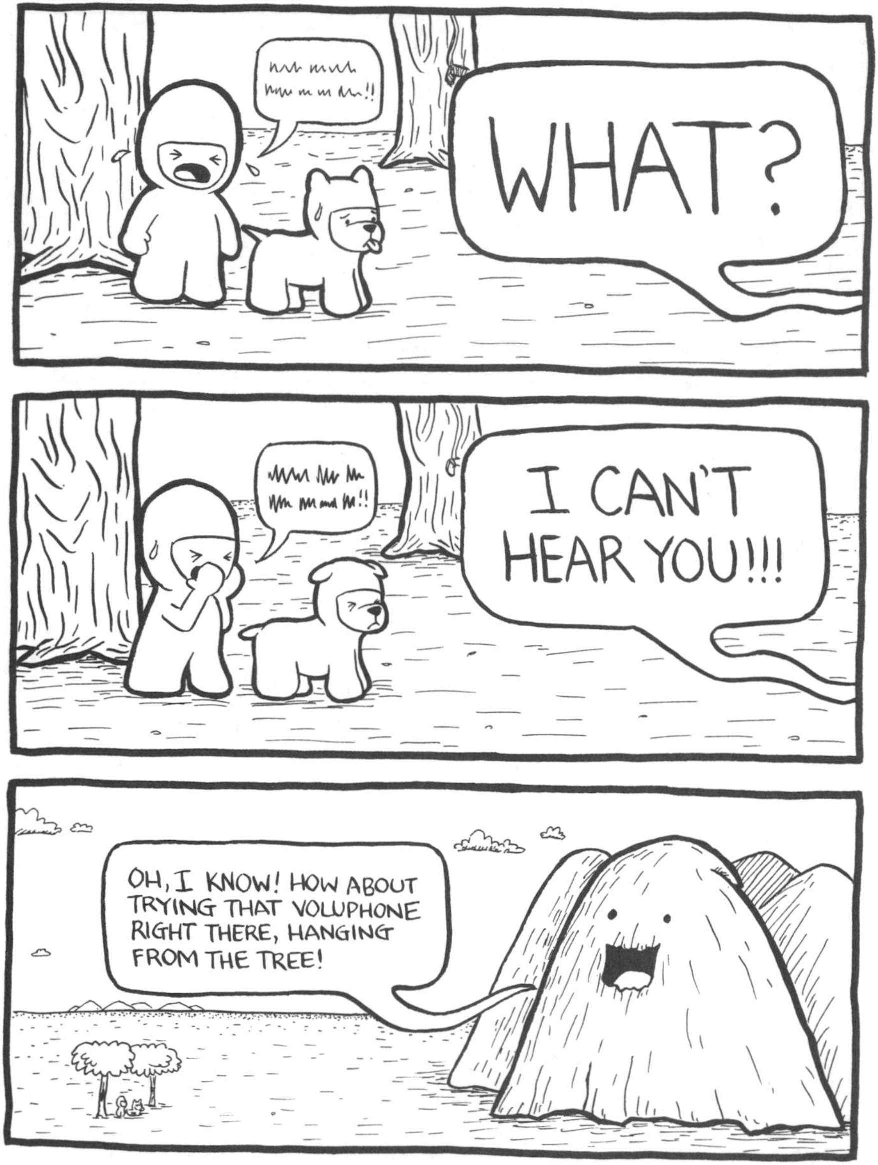
WHAT?
I CAN'T HEAR YOU!!!
OH, I KNOW! HOW ABOUT TRYING THAT VOLUPHONE RIGHT THERE, HANGING FROM THE TREE!

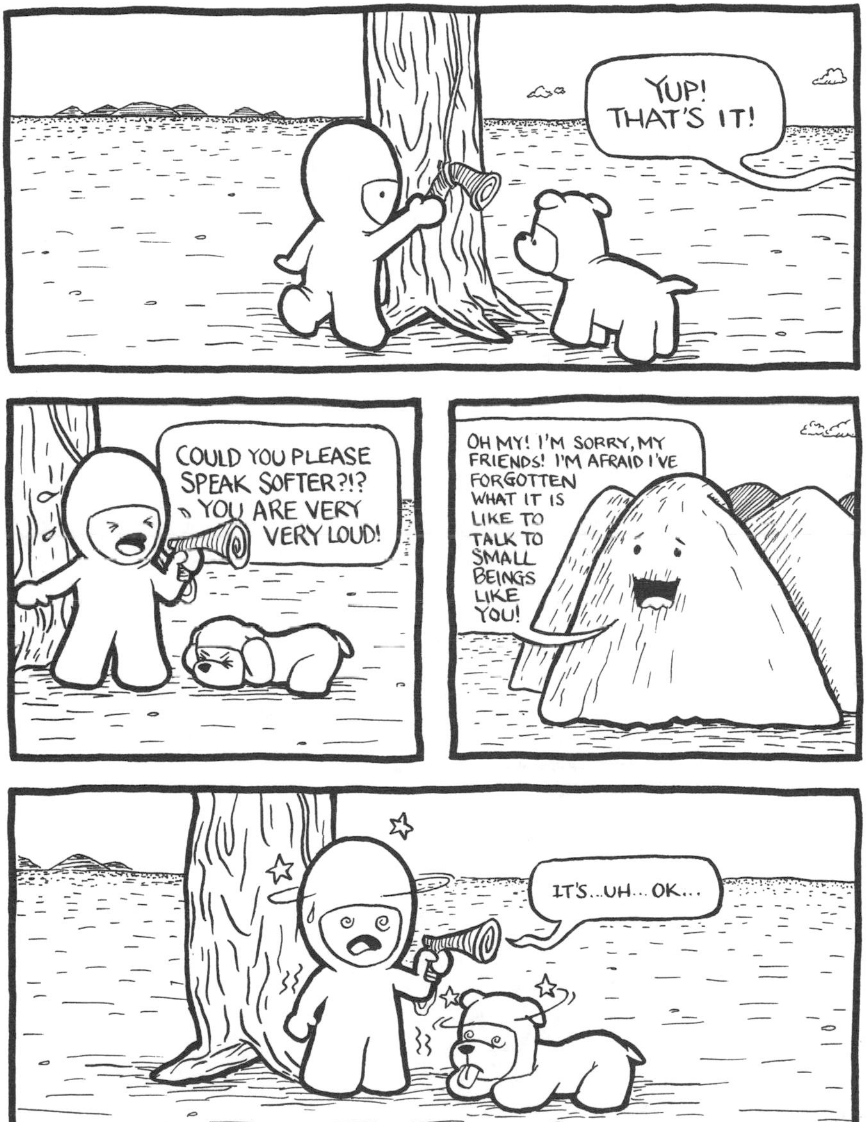
YUP! THAT'S IT!
COULD YOU PLEASE SPEAK SOFTER?!? YOU ARE VERY VERY LOUD!
OH MY! I'M SORRY, MY FRIENDS! I'M AFRAID I'VE FORGOTTEN WHAT IT IS LIKE TO TALK TO SMALL BEINGS LIKE YOU!
IT'S...UH...OK...

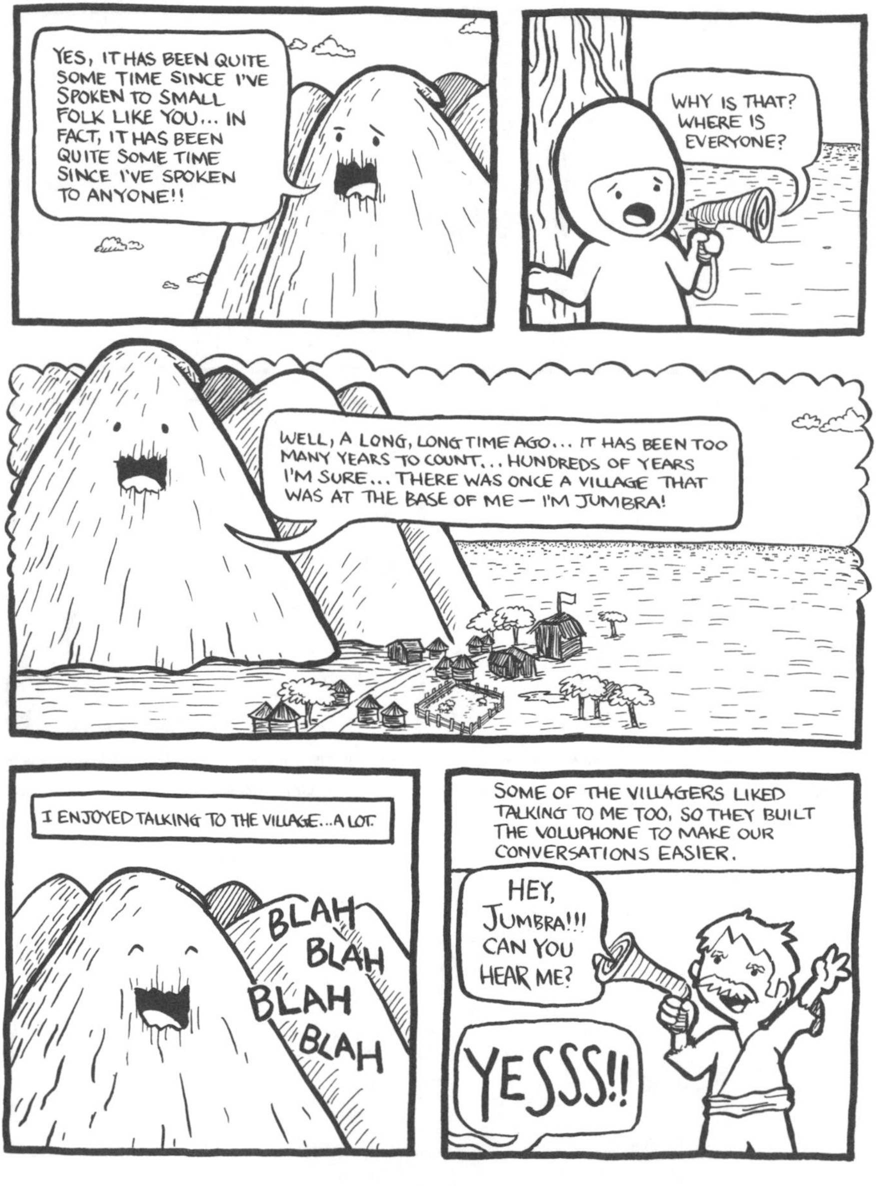

YES, IT HAS BEEN QUITE SOME TIME SINCE I'VE SPOKEN TO SMALL FOLK LIKE YOU... IN FACT, IT HAS BEEN QUITE SOME TIME SINCE I'VE SPOKEN TO ANYONE!!
WHY IS THAT? WHERE IS EVERYONE?
WELL, A LONG, LONG TIME AGO... IT HAS BEEN TOO MANY YEARS TO COUNT... HUNDREDS OF YEARS I'M SURE... THERE WAS ONCE A VILLAGE THAT WAS AT THE BASE OF ME — I'M JUMBRA!
I ENJOYED TALKING TO THE VILLAGE...A LOT.
BLAH BLAH BLAH BLAH
SOME OF THE VILLAGERS LIKED TALKING TO ME TOO, SO THEY BUILT THE VOLUPHONE TO MAKE OUR CONVERSATIONS EASIER.
HEY, JUMBRA!!! CAN YOU HEAR ME?
YESSS!!

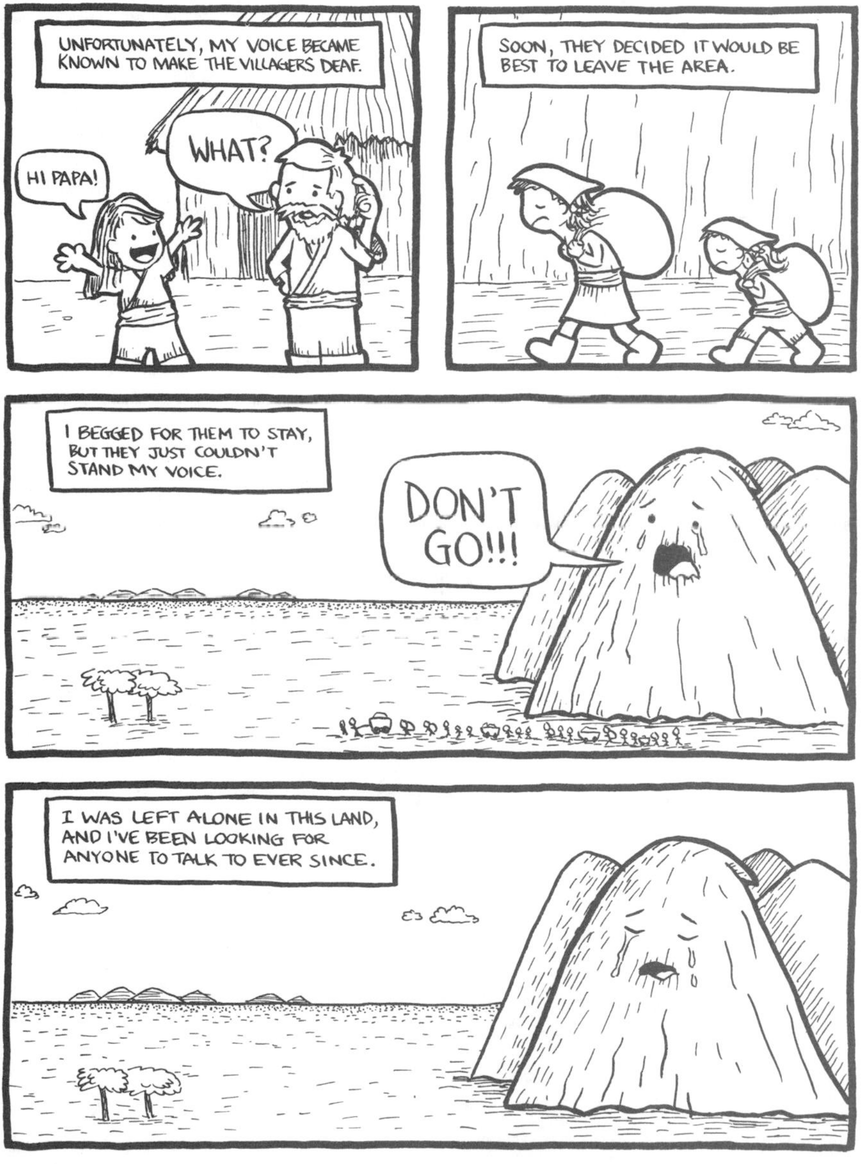
UNFORTUNATELY, MY VOICE BECAME KNOWN TO MAKE THE VILLAGERS DEAF.
HI PAPA!
WHAT?
SOON, THEY DECIDED IT WOULD BE BEST TO LEAVE THE AREA.
I BEGGED FOR THEM TO STAY, BUT THEY JUST COULDN'T STAND MY VOICE.
DON'T GO!!!
I WAS LEFT ALONE IN THIS LAND, AND I'VE BEEN LOOKING FOR ANYONE TO TALK TO EVER SINCE.

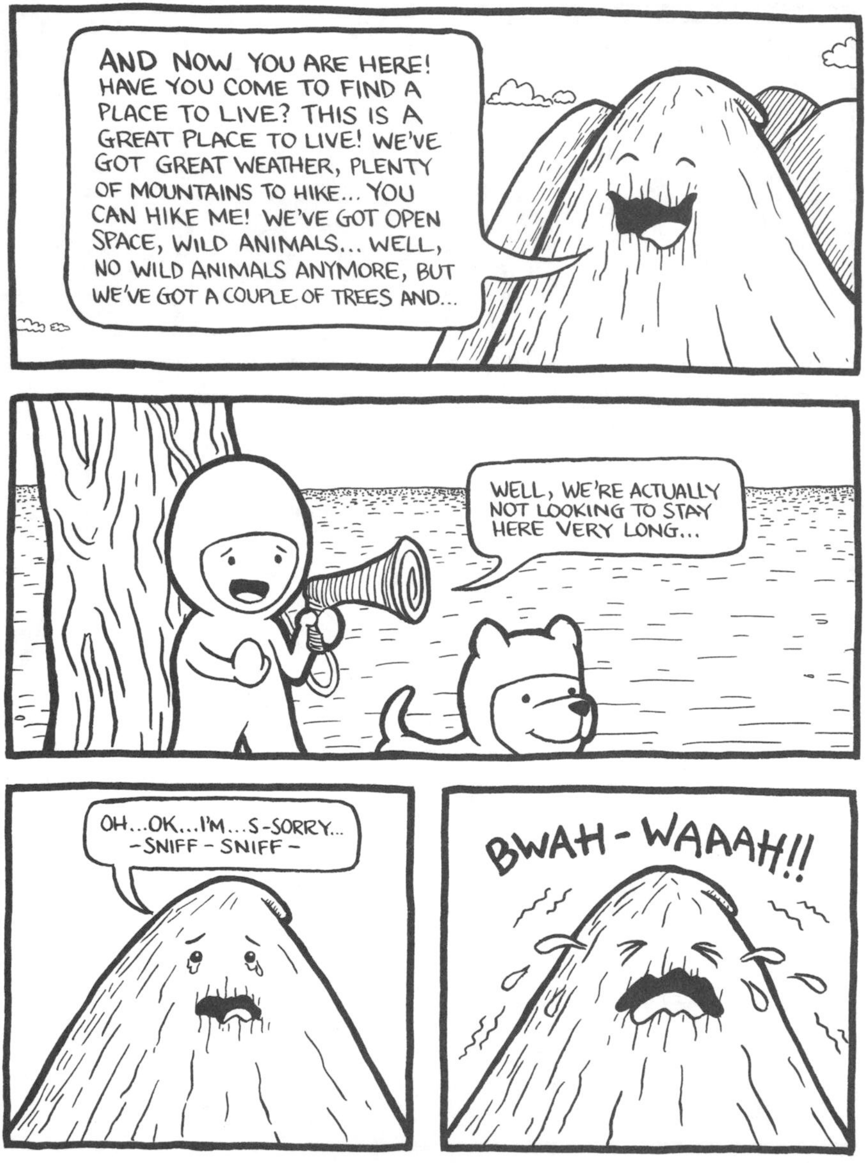
AND NOW YOU ARE HERE! HAVE YOU COME TO FIND A PLACE TO LIVE? THIS IS A GREAT PLACE TO LIVE! WE'VE GOT GREAT WEATHER, PLENTY OF MOUNTAINS TO HIKE... YOU CAN HIKE ME! WE'VE GOT OPEN SPACE, WILD ANIMALS... WELL, NO WILD ANIMALS ANYMORE, BUT WE'VE GOT A COUPLE OF TREES AND...
WELL, WE'RE ACTUALLY NOT LOOKING TO STAY HERE VERY LONG...
OH...OK...I'M...S-SORRY... -SNIFF - SNIFF -
BWAH - WAAAH!!

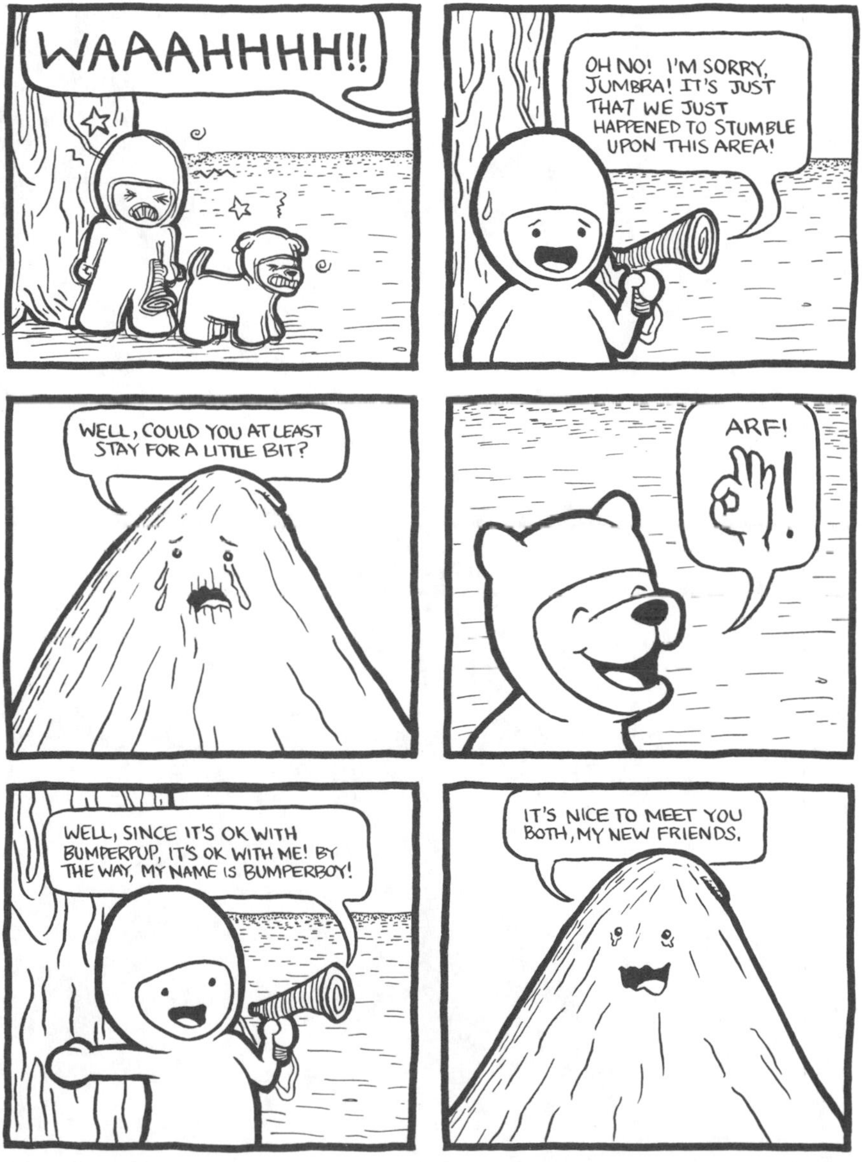
WAAAHHHH!!
OH NO! I'M SORRY, JUMBRA! IT'S JUST THAT WE JUST HAPPENED TO STUMBLE UPON THIS AREA!
WELL, COULD YOU AT LEAST STAY FOR A LITTLE BIT?
ARF!
!
WELL, SINCE IT'S OK WITH BUMPERPUP, IT'S OK WITH ME! BY THE WAY, MY NAME IS BUMPERBOY!
IT'S NICE TO MEET YOU BOTH, MY NEW FRIENDS.

PART TWO

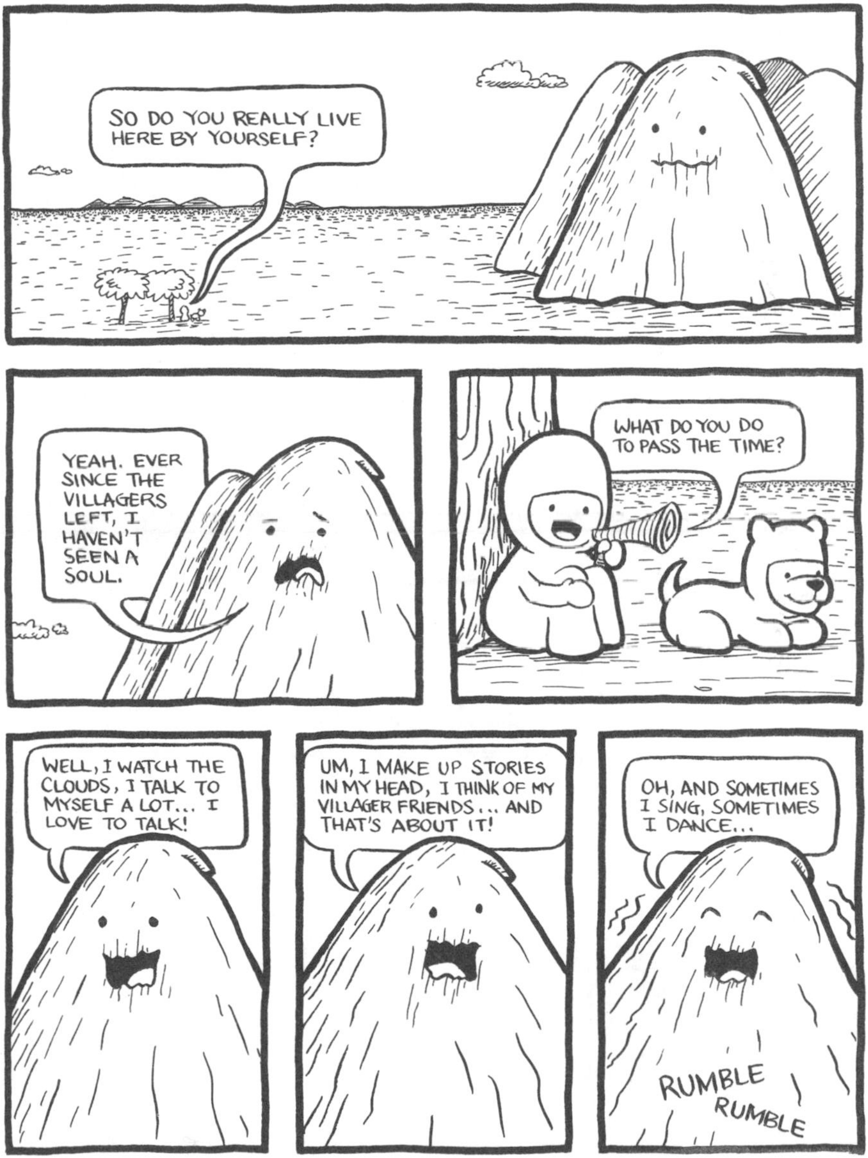
SO DO YOU REALLY LIVE HERE BY YOURSELF?
YEAH. EVER SINCE THE VILLAGERS LEFT, I HAVEN'T SEEN A SOUL.
WHAT DO YOU DO TO PASS THE TIME?
WELL, I WATCH THE CLOUDS, I TALK TO MYSELF A LOT... I LOVE TO TALK!
UM, I MAKE UP STORIES IN MY HEAD, I THINK OF MY VILLAGER FRIENDS... AND THAT'S ABOUT IT!
OH, AND SOMETIMES I SING, SOMETIMES I DANCE...
RUMBLE
RUMBLE

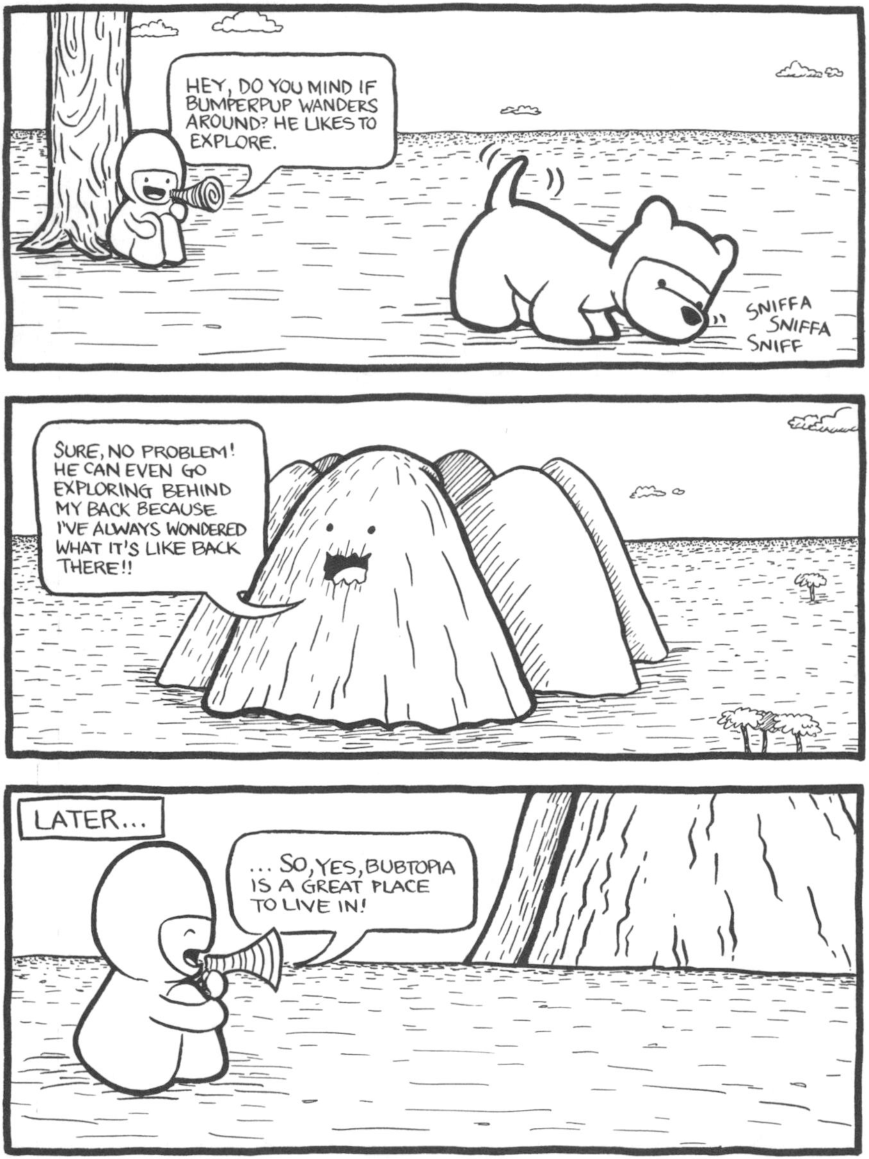
HEY, DO YOU MIND IF BUMPERPUP WANDERS AROUND? HE LIKES TO EXPLORE.
SNIFFA SNIFFA SNIFF
SURE, NO PROBLEM! HE CAN EVEN GO EXPLORING BEHIND MY BACK BECAUSE I'VE ALWAYS WONDERED WHAT IT'S LIKE BACK THERE!!
LATER...
... SO, YES, BUBTOPIA IS A GREAT PLACE TO LIVE IN!

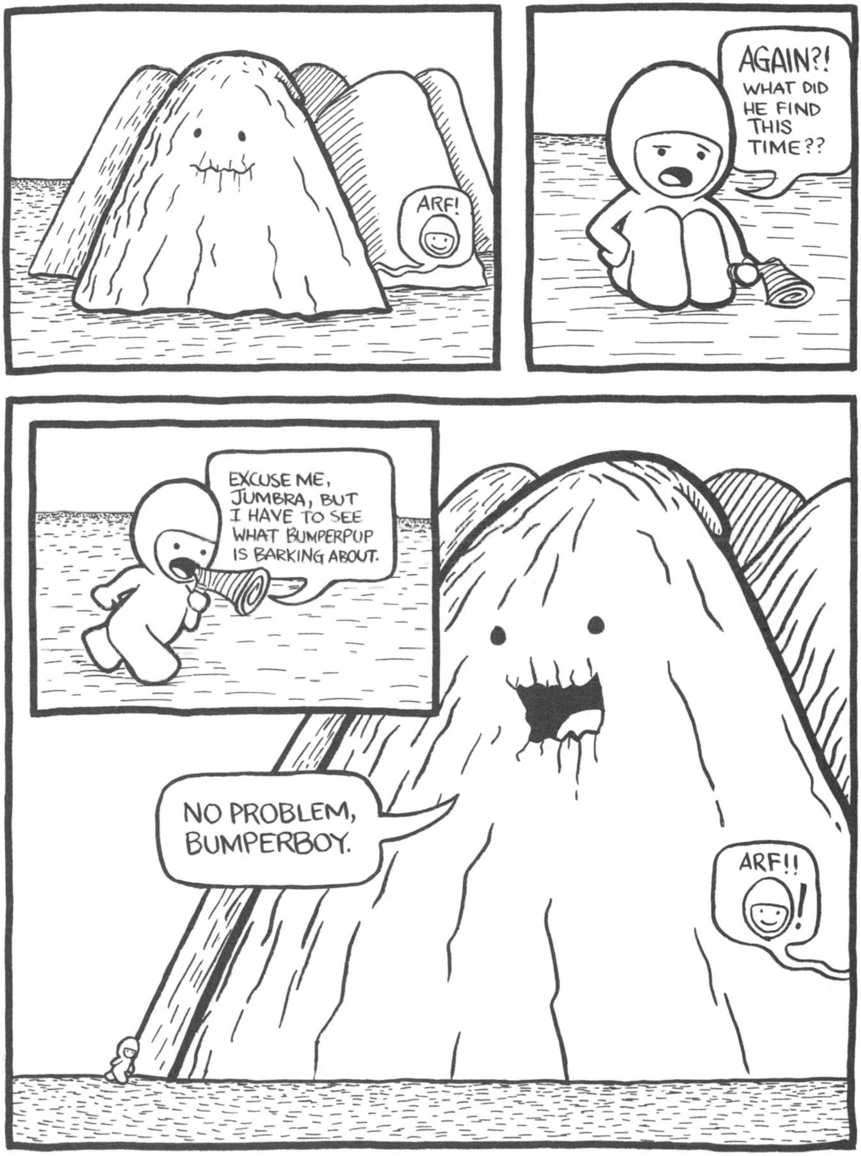
ARF!
AGAIN?! WHAT DID HE FIND THIS TIME??
EXCUSE ME, JUMBRA, BUT I HAVE TO SEE WHAT BUMPERPUP IS BARKING ABOUT.
NO PROBLEM, BUMPERBOY.
ARF!!

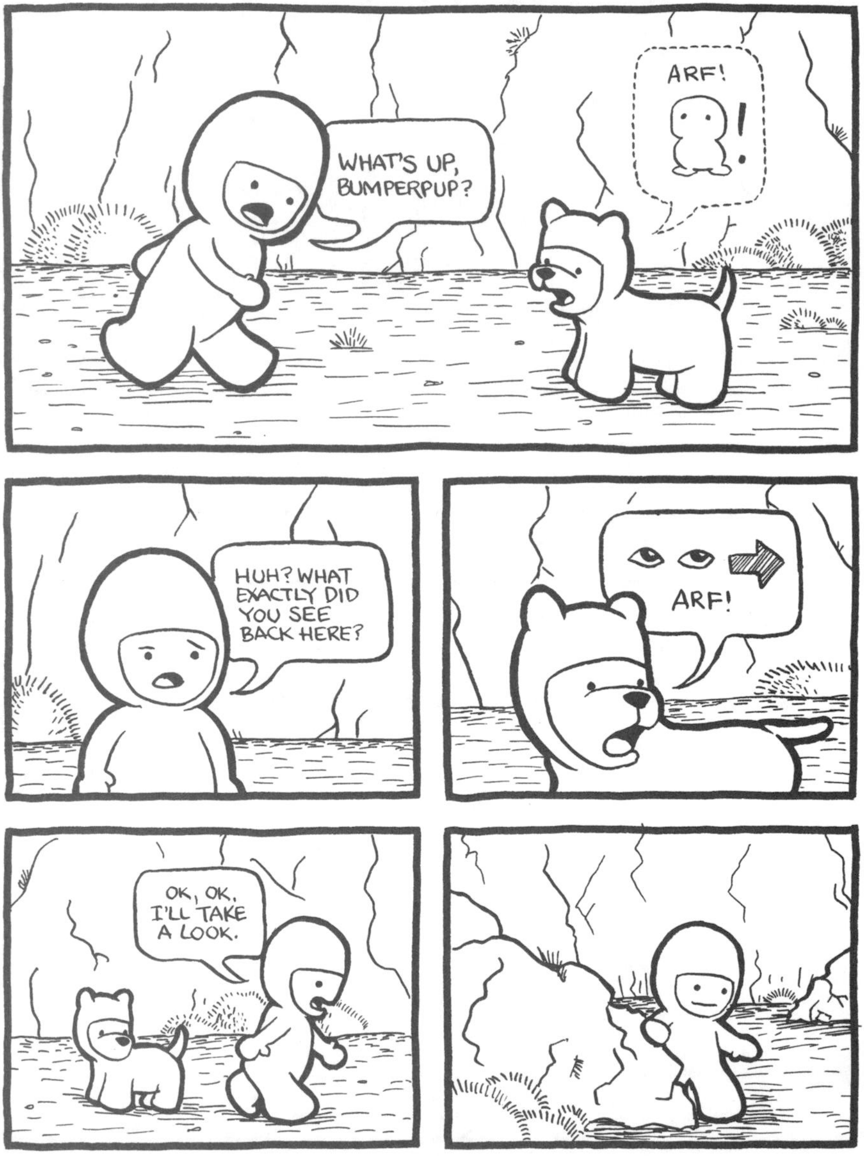
WHAT'S UP, BUMPERPUP?
ARF! !
HUH? WHAT EXACTLY DID YOU SEE BACK HERE?
ARF!
OK, OK. I'LL TAKE A LOOK.

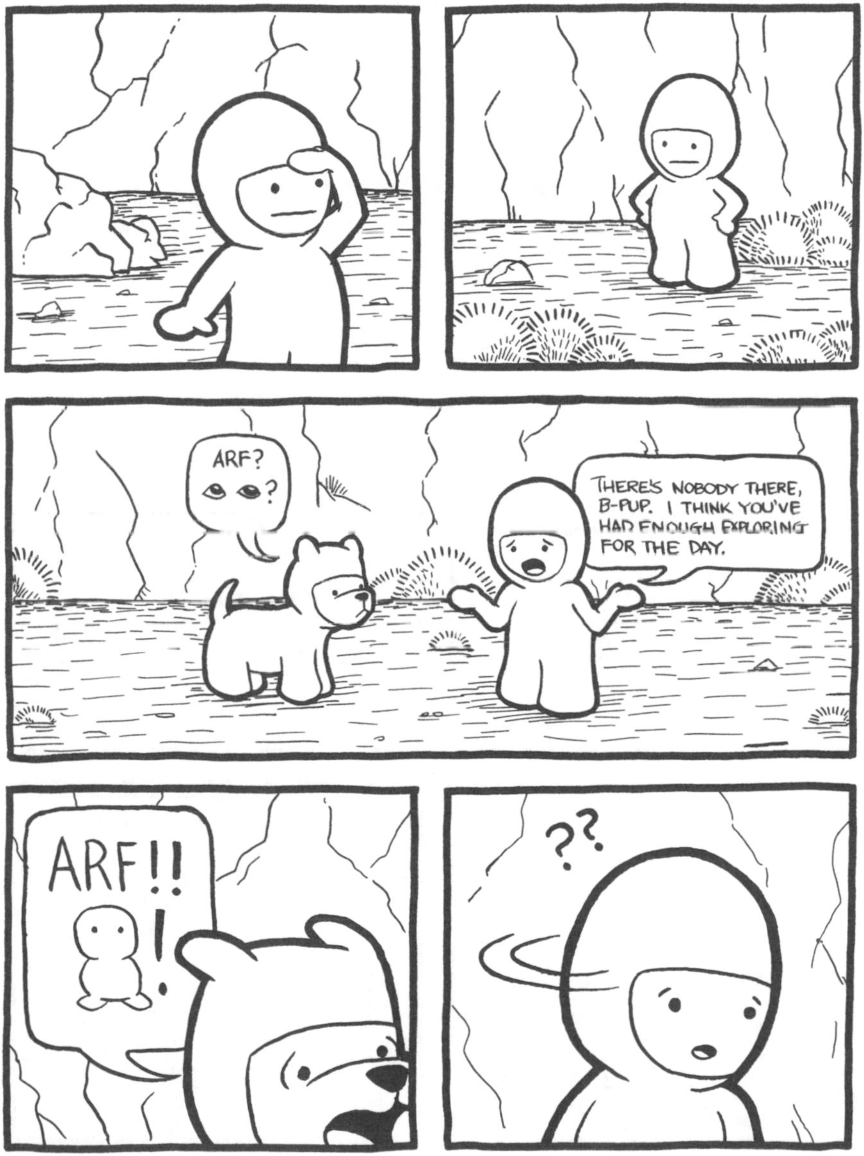
ARF?
?
THERE'S NOBODY THERE, B-PUP. I THINK YOU'VE HAD ENOUGH EXPLORING FOR THE DAY.
ARF!!
!
??

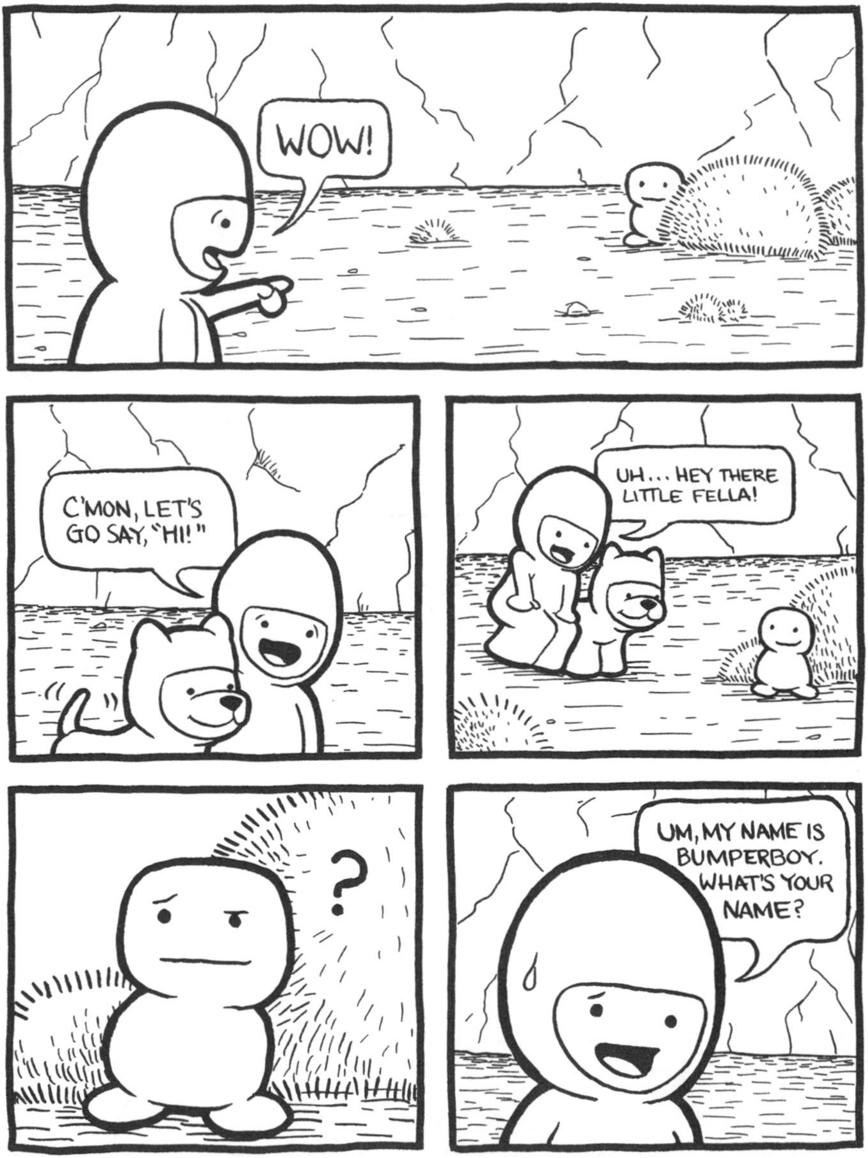
WOW!
C'MON, LET'S GO SAY, "HI!"
UH... HEY THERE LITTLE FELLA!
?
UM, MY NAME IS BUMPERBOY. WHAT'S YOUR NAME?

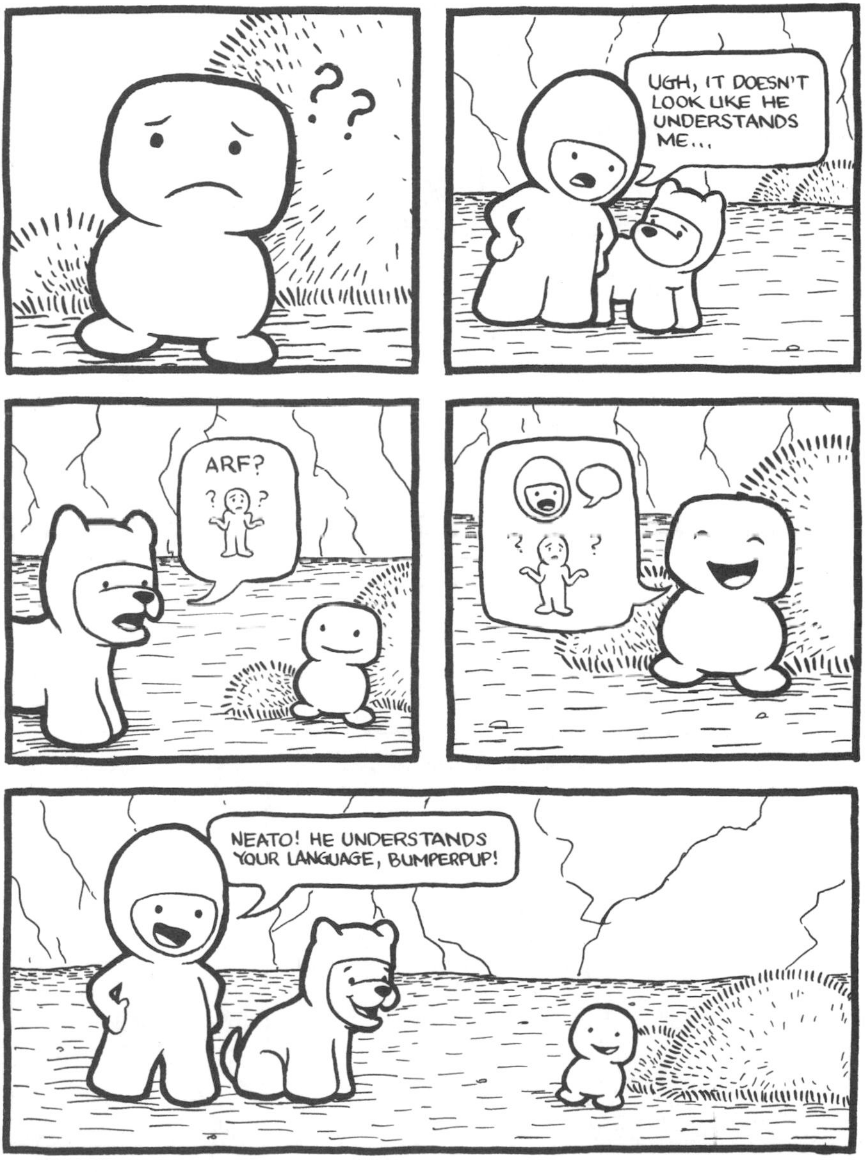
UGH, IT DOESN'T LOOK LIKE HE UNDERSTANDS ME...
ARF?
NEATO! HE UNDERSTANDS YOUR LANGUAGE, BUMPERPUP!

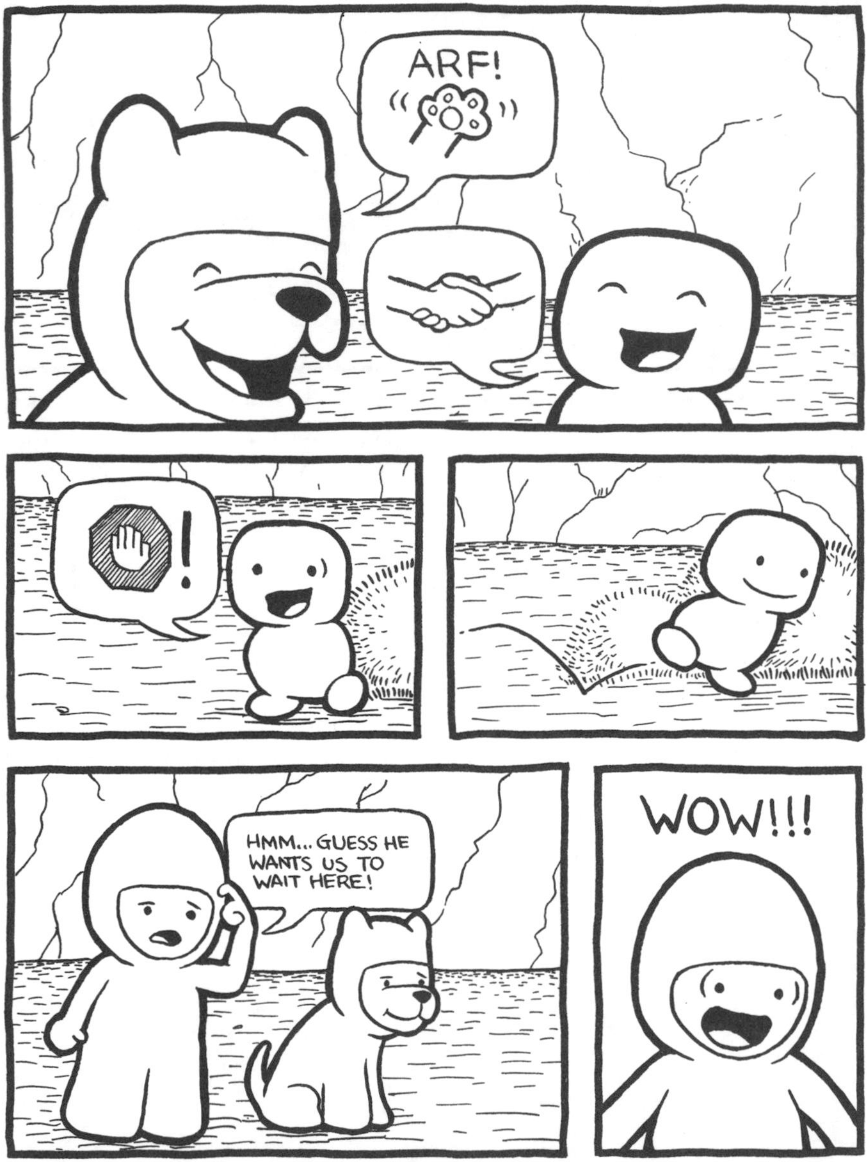
ARF!
HMM... GUESS HE WANTS US TO WAIT HERE!
WOW!!!

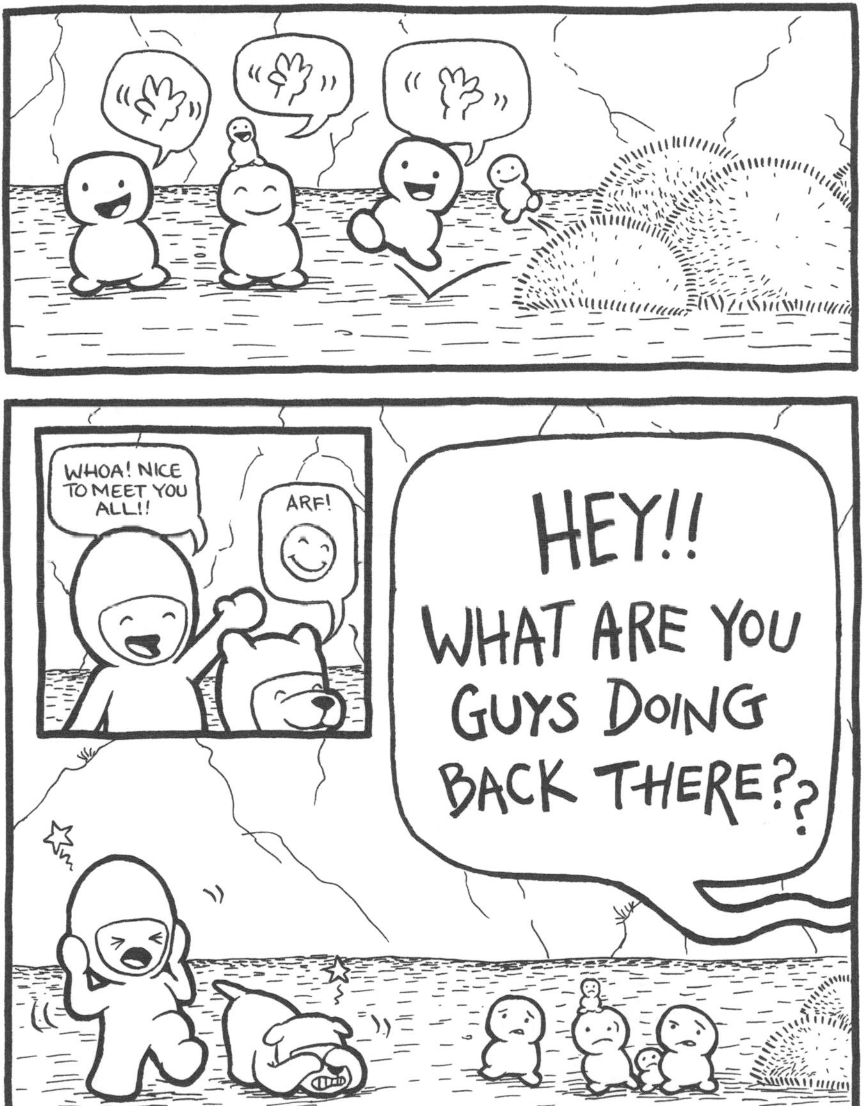
WHOA! NICE TO MEET YOU ALL!!
ARF!
HEY!! WHAT ARE YOU GUYS DOING BACK THERE??

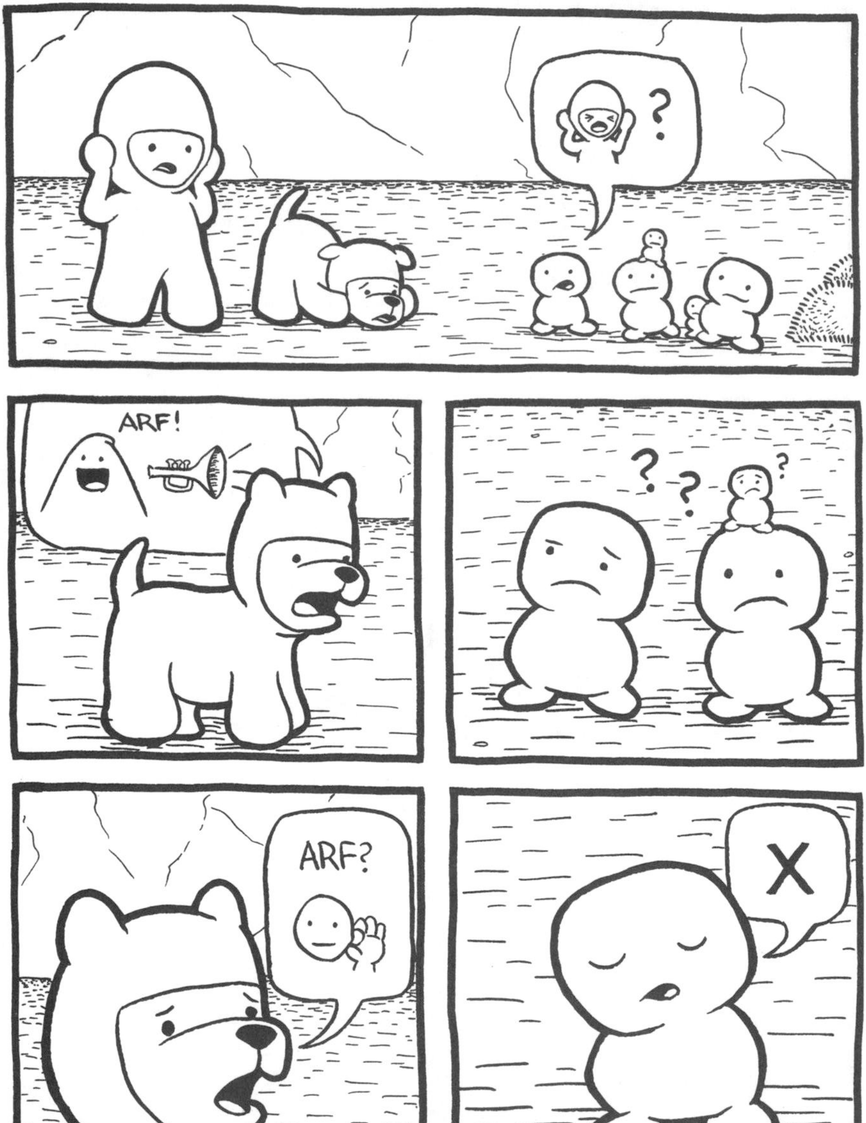
?
ARF!
? ? ?
ARF?
X

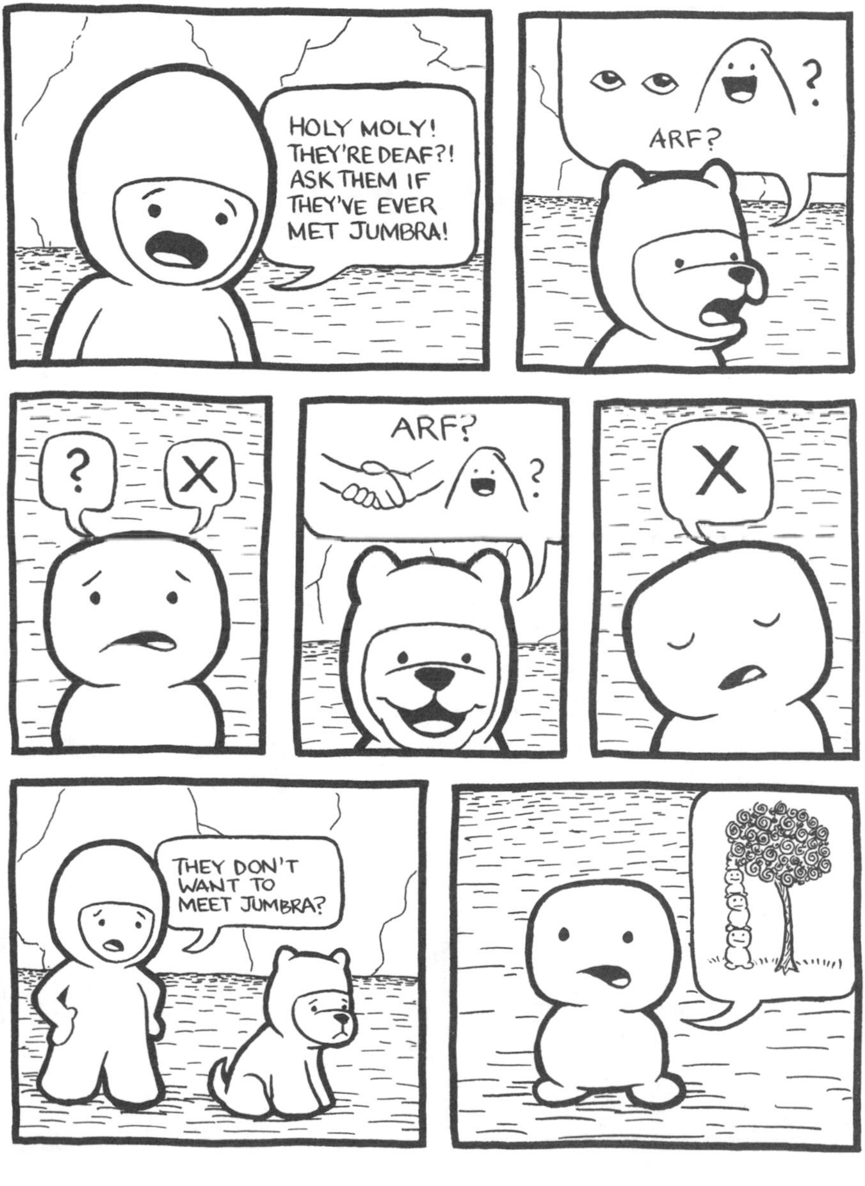
HOLY MOLY! THEY'RE DEAF?! ASK THEM IF THEY'VE EVER MET JUMBRA!
ARF?
?
X
ARF?
?
X
THEY DON'T WANT TO MEET JUMBRA?

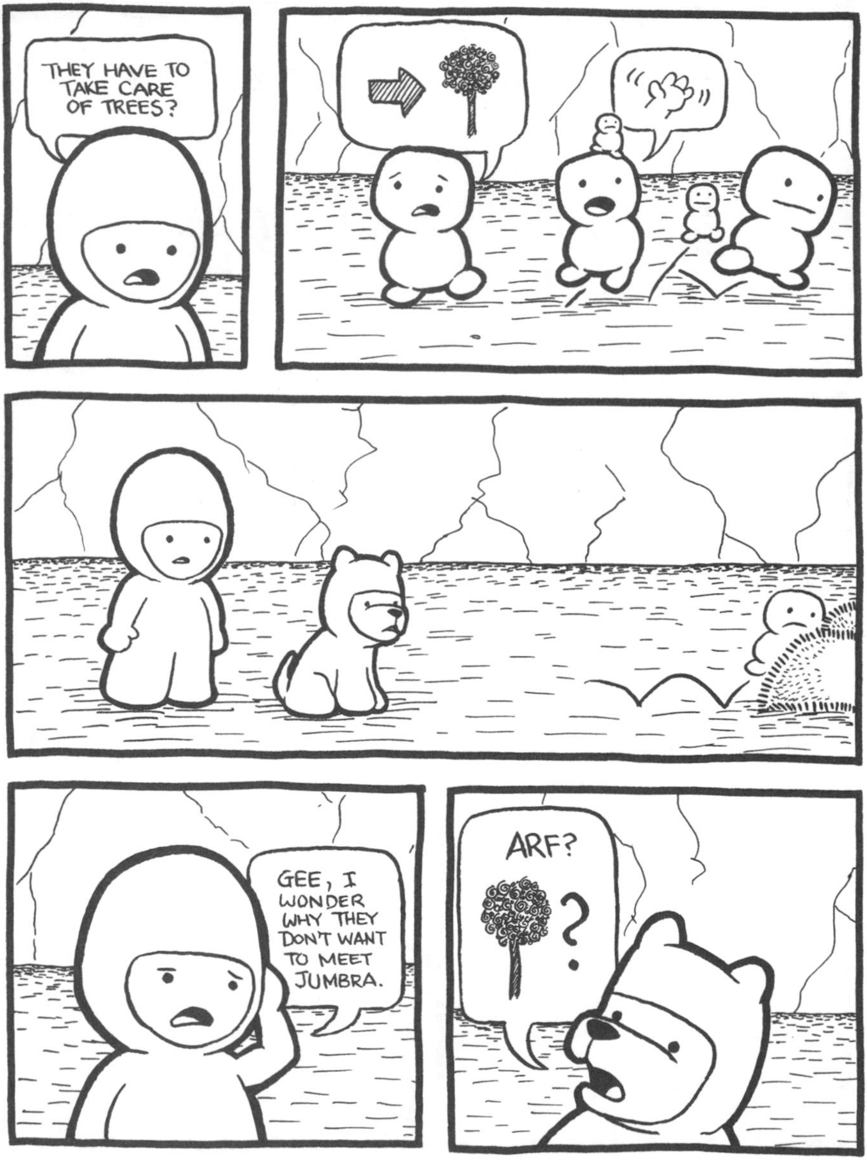
THEY HAVE TO TAKE CARE OF TREES?
GEE, I WONDER WHY THEY DON'T WANT TO MEET JUMBRA.
ARF?
?

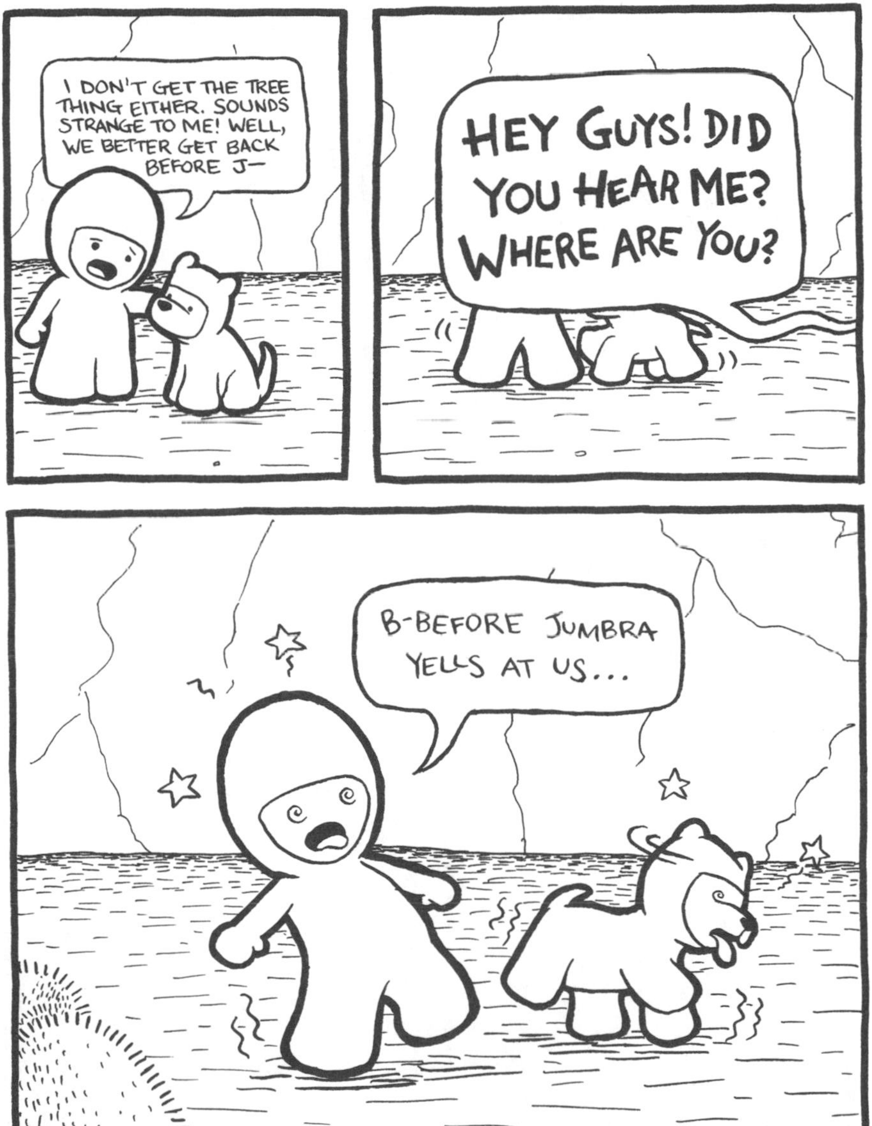
I DON'T GET THE TREE THING EITHER. SOUNDS STRANGE TO ME! WELL, WE BETTER GET BACK BEFORE J—
HEY GUYS! DID YOU HEAR ME? WHERE ARE YOU?
B-BEFORE JUMBRA YELLS AT US...

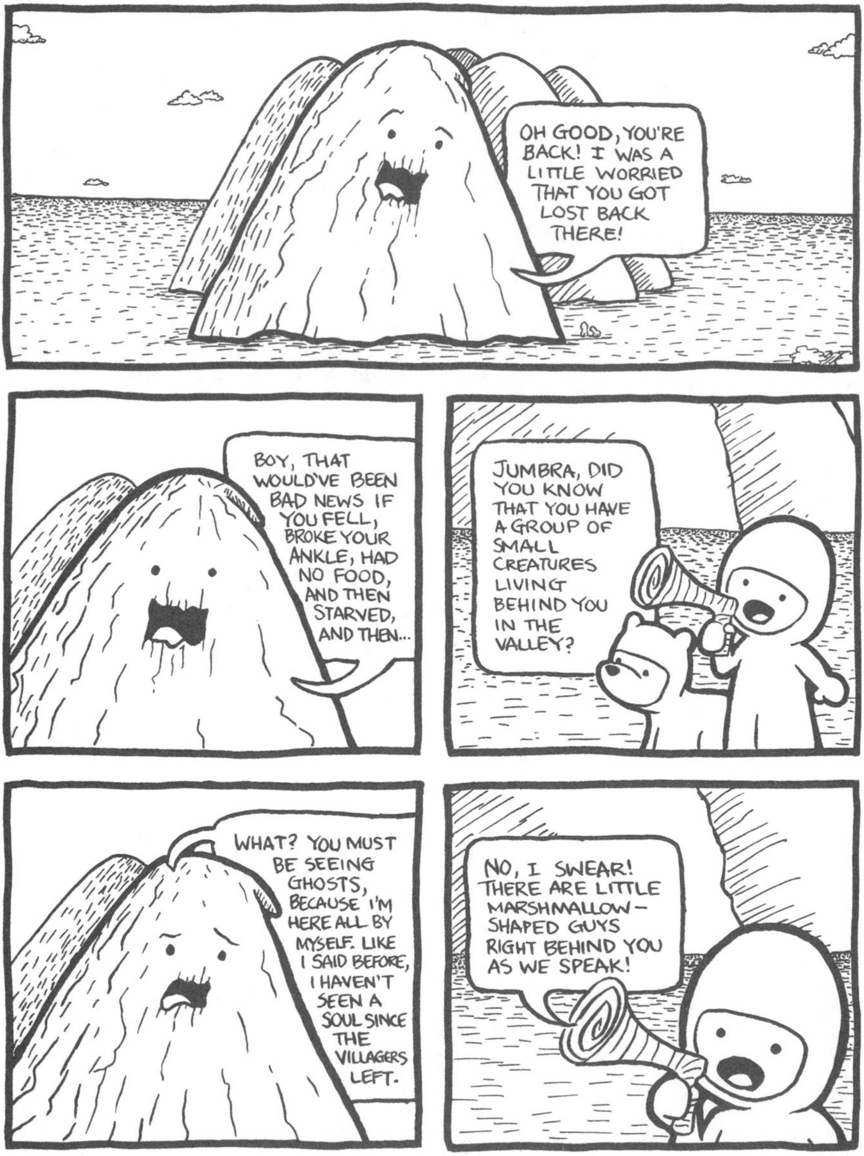
OH GOOD, YOU'RE BACK! I WAS A LITTLE WORRIED THAT YOU GOT LOST BACK THERE!
BOY, THAT WOULD'VE BEEN BAD NEWS IF YOU FELL, BROKE YOUR ANKLE, HAD NO FOOD, AND THEN STARVED, AND THEN...
JUMBRA, DID YOU KNOW THAT YOU HAVE A GROUP OF SMALL CREATURES LIVING BEHIND YOU IN THE VALLEY?
WHAT? YOU MUST BE SEEING GHOSTS, BECAUSE I'M HERE ALL BY MYSELF. LIKE I SAID BEFORE, I HAVEN'T SEEN A SOUL SINCE THE VILLAGERS LEFT.
NO, I SWEAR! THERE ARE LITTLE MARSHMALLOW-SHAPED GUYS RIGHT BEHIND YOU AS WE SPEAK!

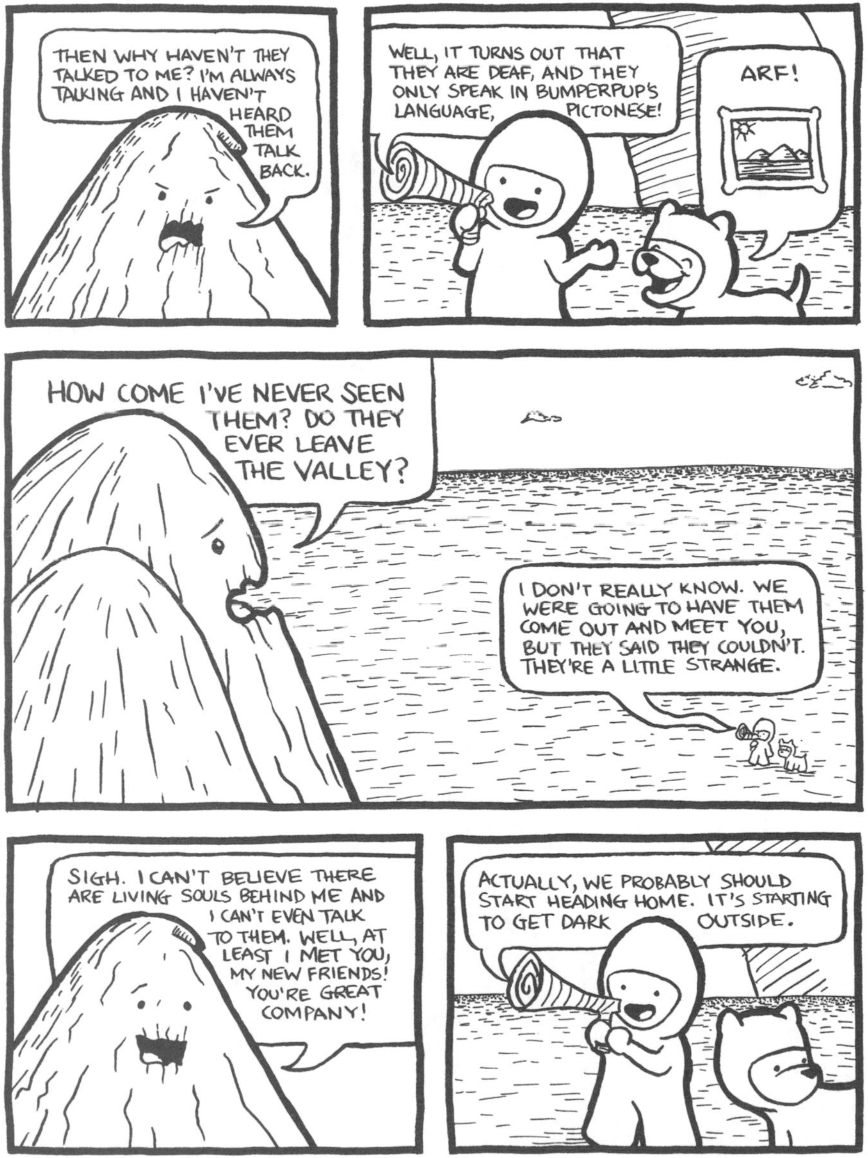
THEN WHY HAVEN'T THEY TALKED TO ME? I'M ALWAYS TALKING AND I HAVEN'T HEARD THEM TALK BACK.
WELL, IT TURNS OUT THAT THEY ARE DEAF, AND THEY ONLY SPEAK IN BUMPERPUP'S LANGUAGE, PICTONESE!
ARF!
HOW COME I'VE NEVER SEEN THEM? DO THEY EVER LEAVE THE VALLEY?
I DON'T REALLY KNOW. WE WERE GOING TO HAVE THEM COME OUT AND MEET YOU, BUT THEY SAID THEY COULDN'T. THEY'RE A LITTLE STRANGE.
SIGH. I CAN'T BELIEVE THERE ARE LIVING SOULS BEHIND ME AND I CAN'T EVEN TALK TO THEM. WELL, AT LEAST I MET YOU, MY NEW FRIENDS! YOU'RE GREAT COMPANY!
ACTUALLY, WE PROBABLY SHOULD START HEADING HOME. IT'S STARTING TO GET DARK OUTSIDE.

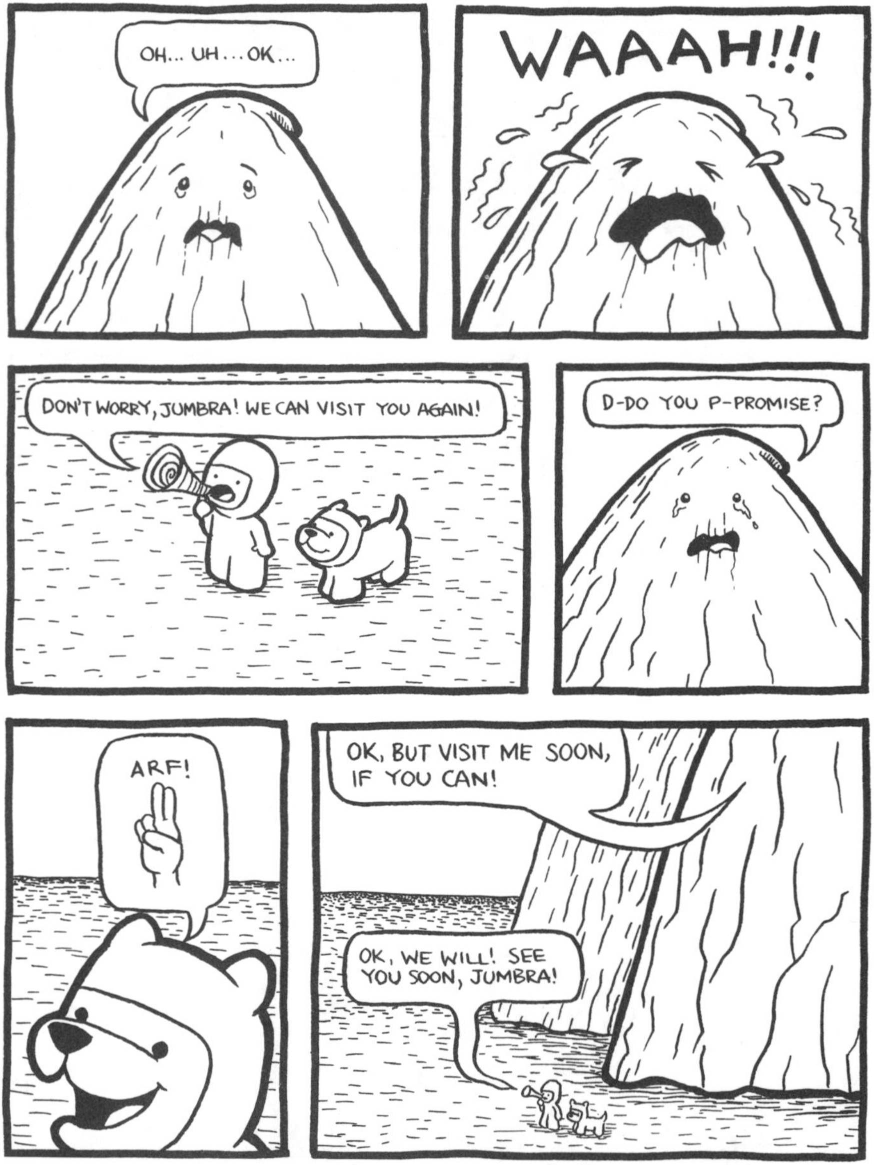
OH... UH... OK...
WAAAH!!!
DON'T WORRY, JUMBRA! WE CAN VISIT YOU AGAIN!
D-DO YOU P-PROMISE?
ARF!
OK, BUT VISIT ME SOON, IF YOU CAN!
OK, WE WILL! SEE YOU SOON, JUMBRA!

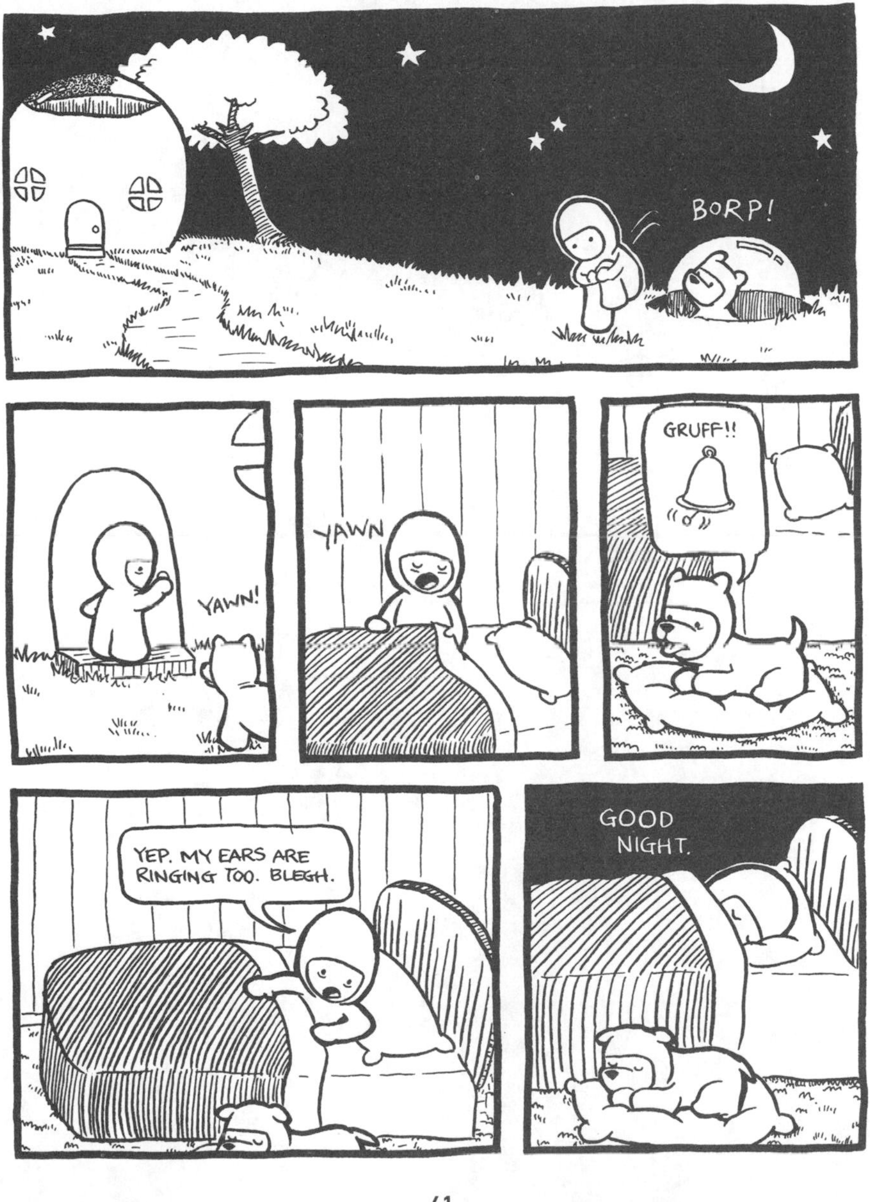
BORP!
YAWN!
YAWN
GRUFF!!
YEP. MY EARS ARE RINGING TOO. BLEGH.
GOOD NIGHT.

PART THREE

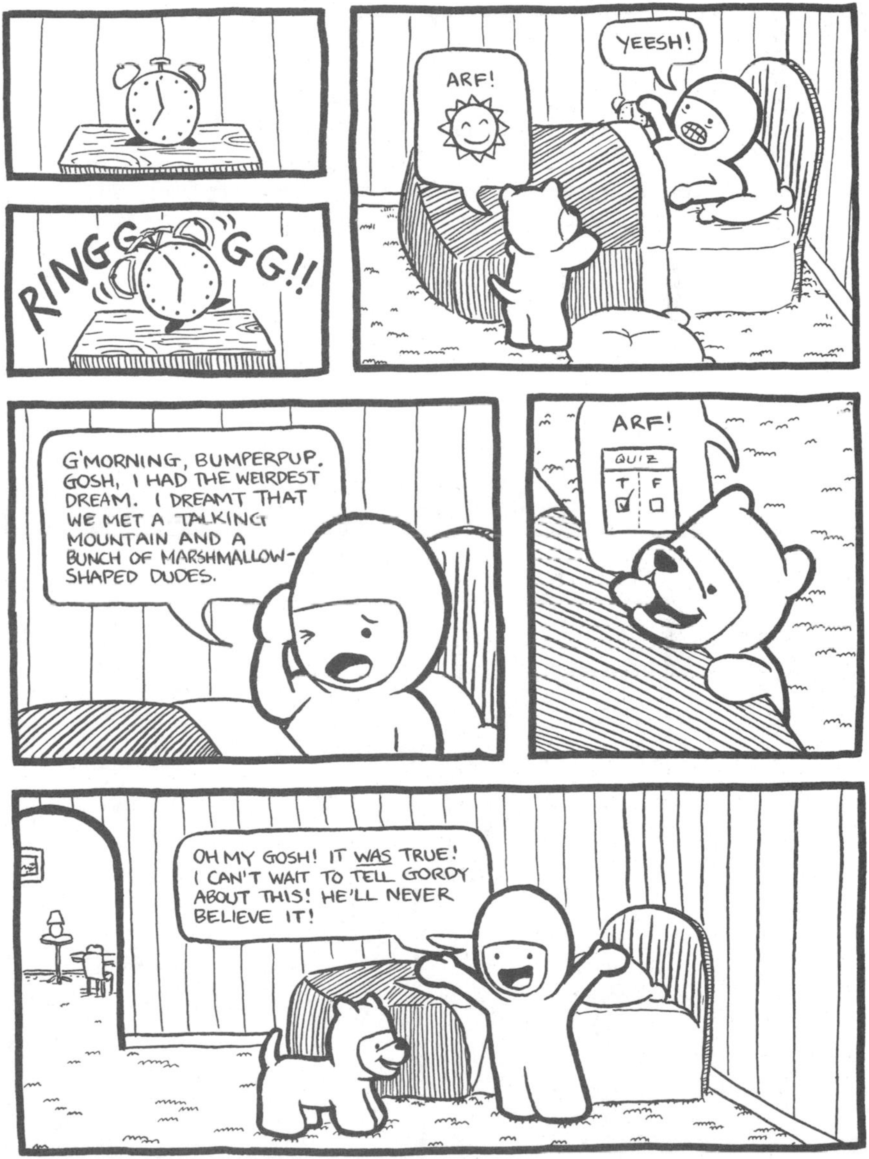
RINGGGGG!!
YEESH!
ARF!
G'MORNING, BUMPERPUP. GOSH, I HAD THE WEIRDEST DREAM. I DREAMT THAT WE MET A TALKING MOUNTAIN AND A BUNCH OF MARSHMALLOW-SHAPED DUDES.
ARF!
QUIZ
T F
OH MY GOSH! IT WAS TRUE! I CAN'T WAIT TO TELL GORDY ABOUT THIS! HE'LL NEVER BELIEVE IT!

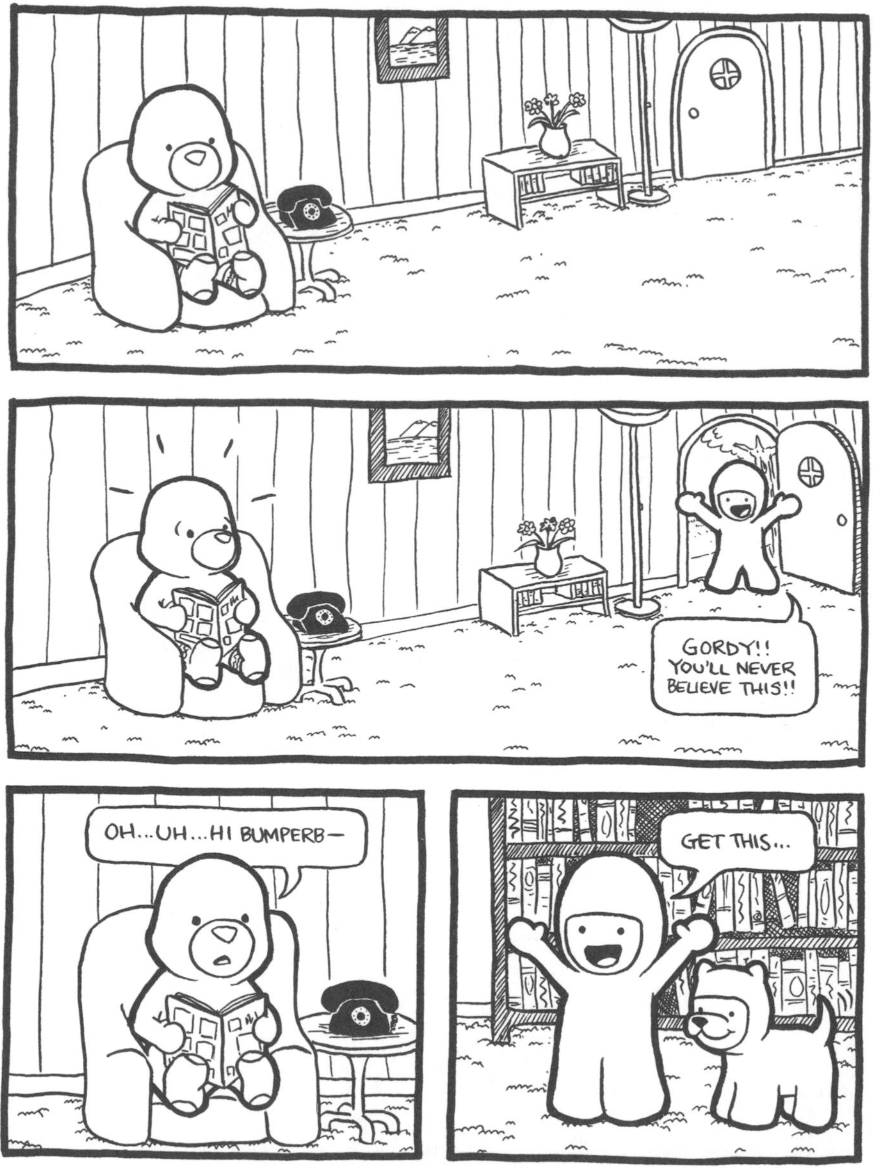
GORDY!! YOU'LL NEVER BELIEVE THIS!!
OH...UH...HI BUMPERB—
GET THIS...

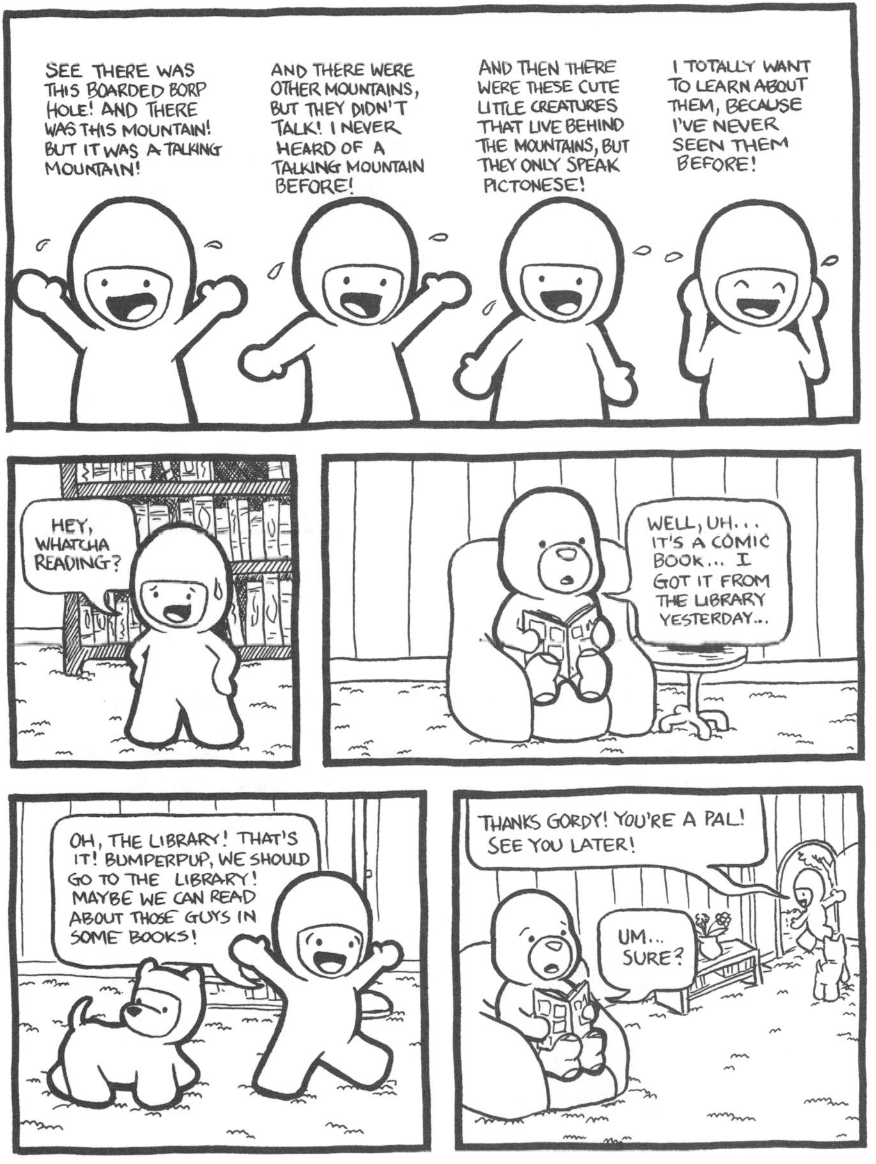
SEE THERE WAS THIS BOARDED BORP HOLE! AND THERE WAS THIS MOUNTAIN! BUT IT WAS A TALKING MOUNTAIN!
AND THERE WERE OTHER MOUNTAINS, BUT THEY DIDN'T TALK! I NEVER HEARD OF A TALKING MOUNTAIN BEFORE!
AND THEN THERE WERE THESE CUTE LITTLE CREATURES THAT LIVE BEHIND THE MOUNTAINS, BUT THEY ONLY SPEAK PICTONESE!
I TOTALLY WANT TO LEARN ABOUT THEM, BECAUSE I'VE NEVER SEEN THEM BEFORE!
HEY, WHATCHA READING?
WELL, UH... IT'S A COMIC BOOK... I GOT IT FROM THE LIBRARY YESTERDAY...
OH, THE LIBRARY! THAT'S IT! BUMPERPUP, WE SHOULD GO TO THE LIBRARY! MAYBE WE CAN READ ABOUT THOSE GUYS IN SOME BOOKS!
THANKS GORDY! YOU'RE A PAL! SEE YOU LATER!
UM... SURE?

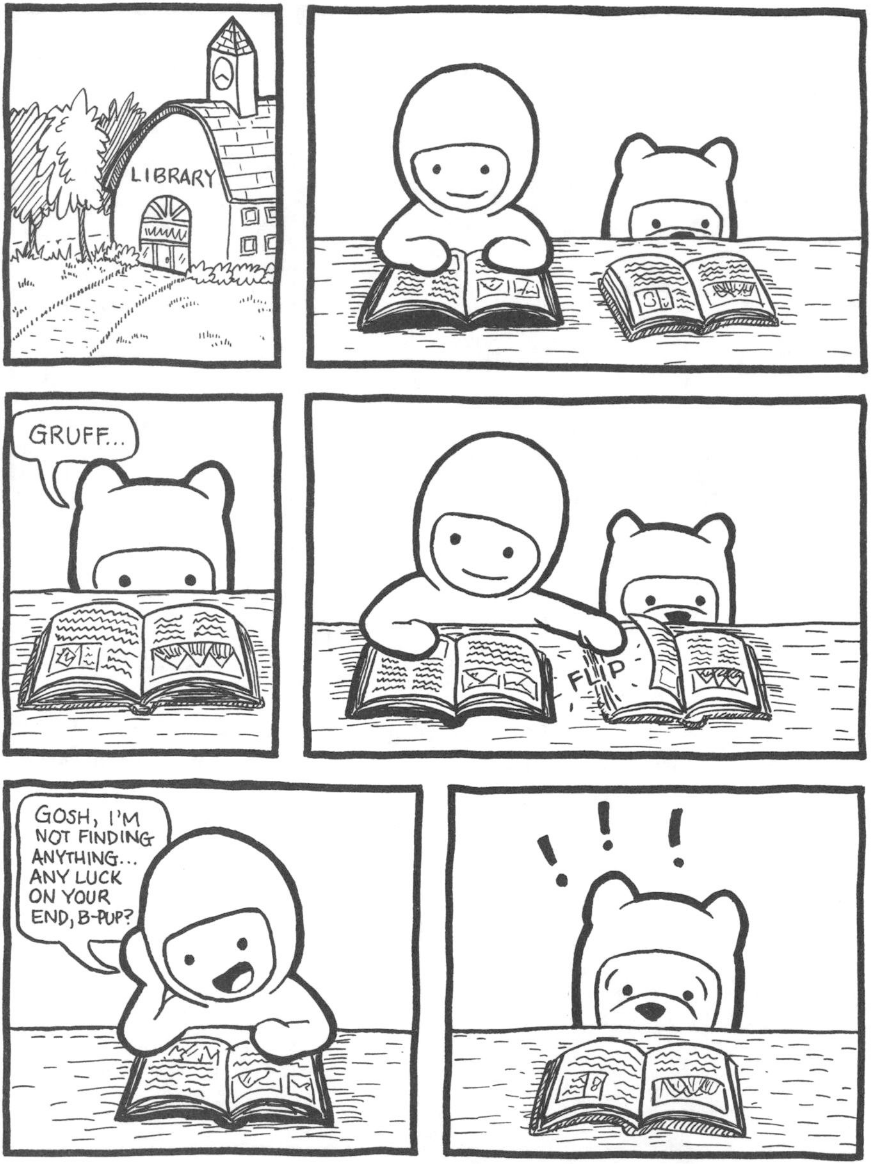
LIBRARY
GRUFF...
FLIP
GOSH, I'M NOT FINDING ANYTHING... ANY LUCK ON YOUR END, B-PUP?
! ! !

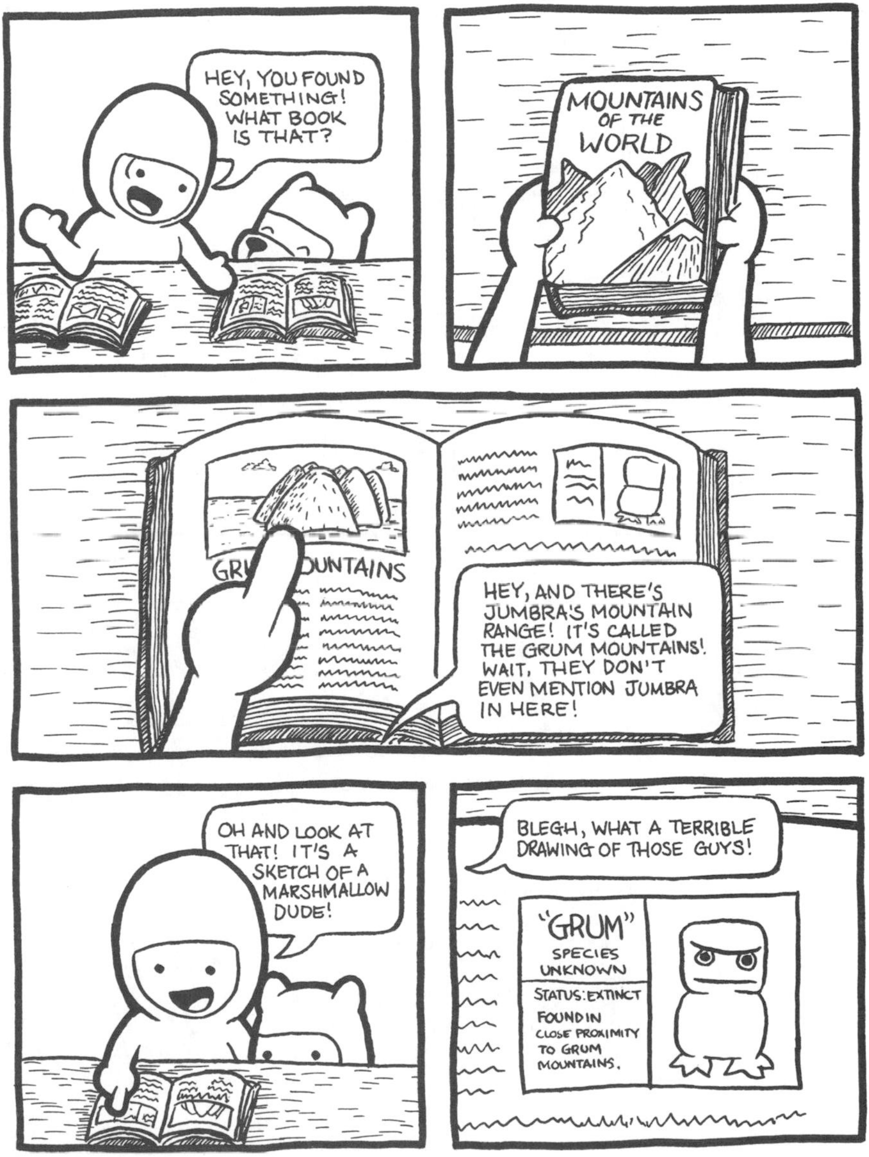
HEY, YOU FOUND SOMETHING! WHAT BOOK IS THAT?
MOUNTAINS OF THE WORLD
GRU OUNTAINS
HEY, AND THERE'S JUMBRA'S MOUNTAIN RANGE! IT'S CALLED THE GRUM MOUNTAINS! WAIT, THEY DON'T EVEN MENTION JUMBRA IN HERE!
OH AND LOOK AT THAT! IT'S A SKETCH OF A MARSHMALLOW DUDE!
BLEGH, WHAT A TERRIBLE DRAWING OF THOSE GUYS!
"GRUM" SPECIES UNKNOWN
STATUS: EXTINCT
FOUND IN CLOSE PROXIMITY TO GRUM MOUNTAINS.

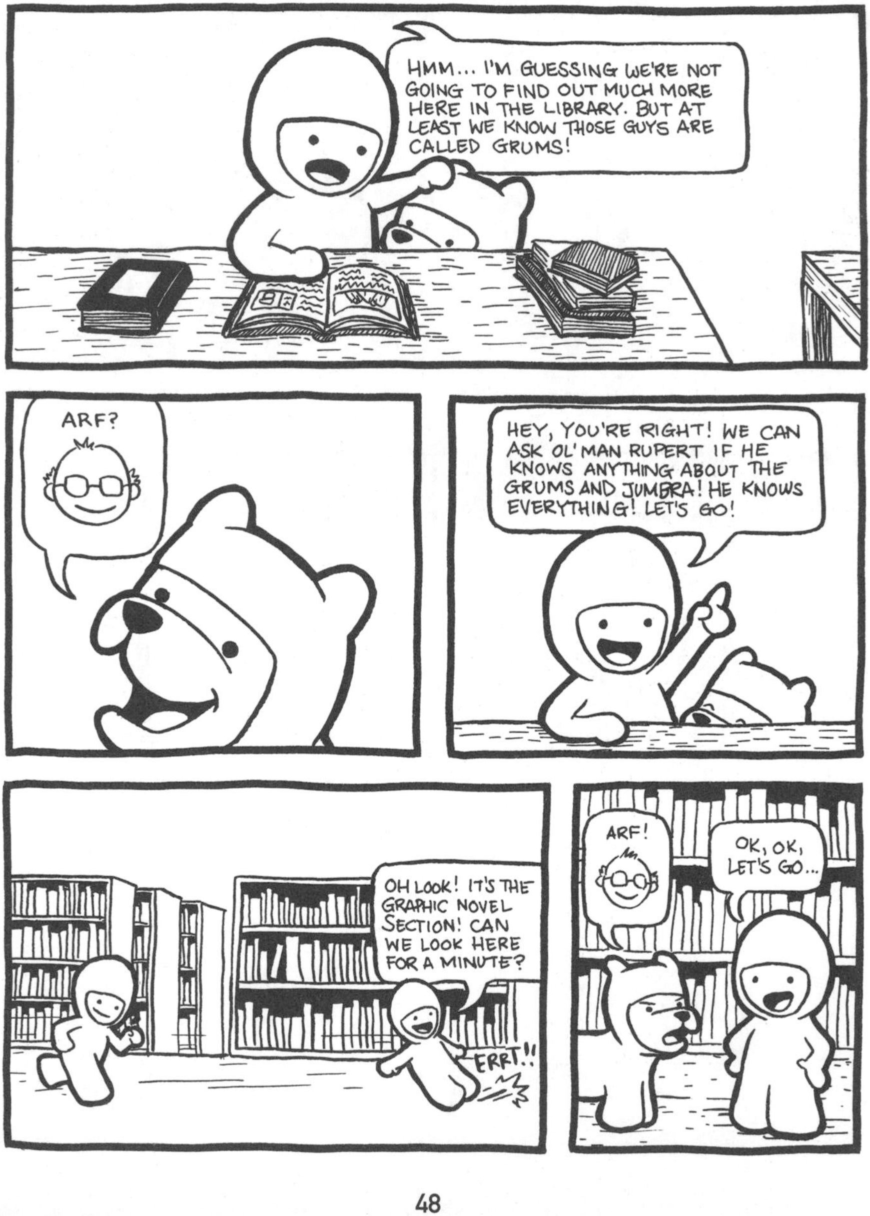
HMM... I'M GUESSING WE'RE NOT GOING TO FIND OUT MUCH MORE HERE IN THE LIBRARY. BUT AT LEAST WE KNOW THOSE GUYS ARE CALLED GRUMS!
ARF?
HEY, YOU'RE RIGHT! WE CAN ASK OL' MAN RUPERT IF HE KNOWS ANYTHING ABOUT THE GRUMS AND JUMBRA! HE KNOWS EVERYTHING! LET'S GO!
OH LOOK! IT'S THE GRAPHIC NOVEL SECTION! CAN WE LOOK HERE FOR A MINUTE?
ERRT!!
ARF!
OK, OK, LET'S GO...

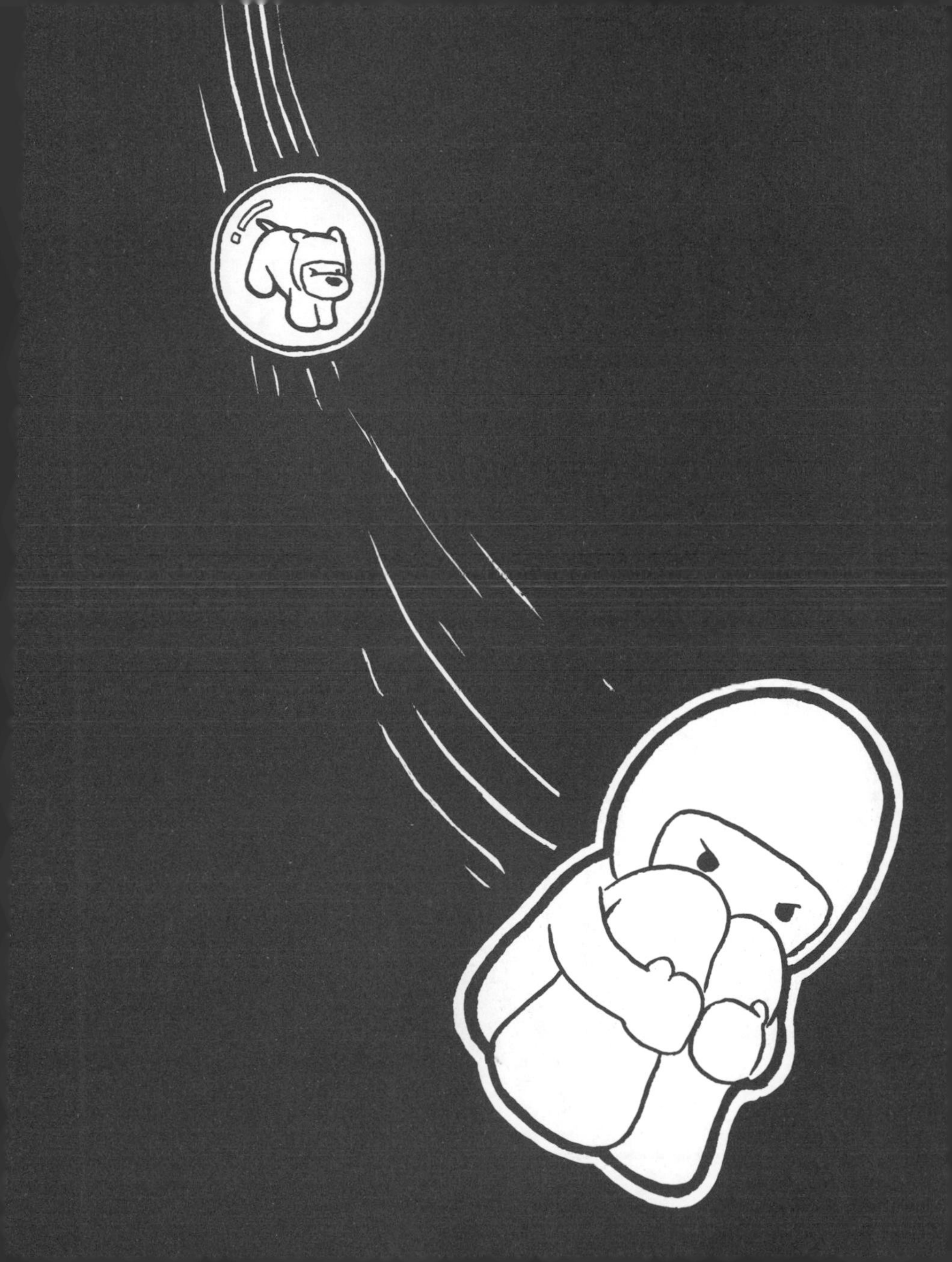

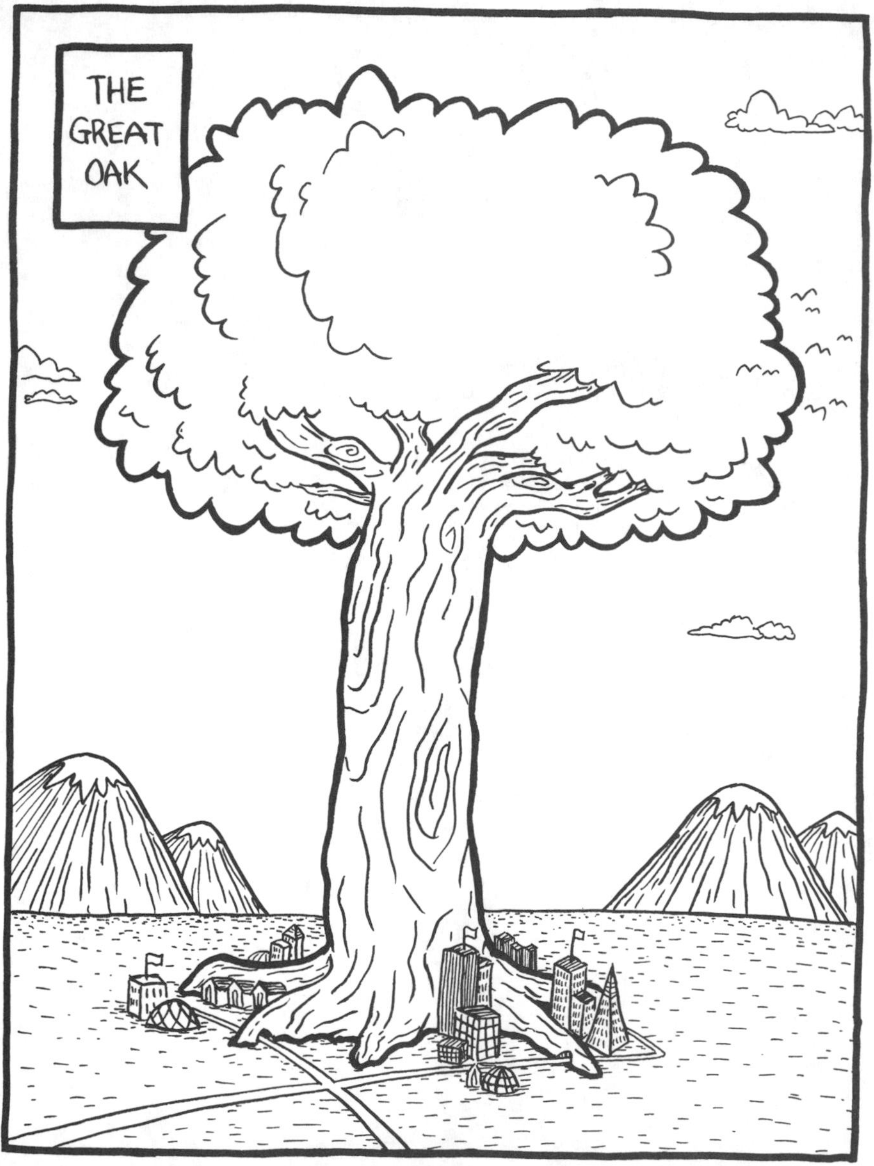
THE GREAT OAK

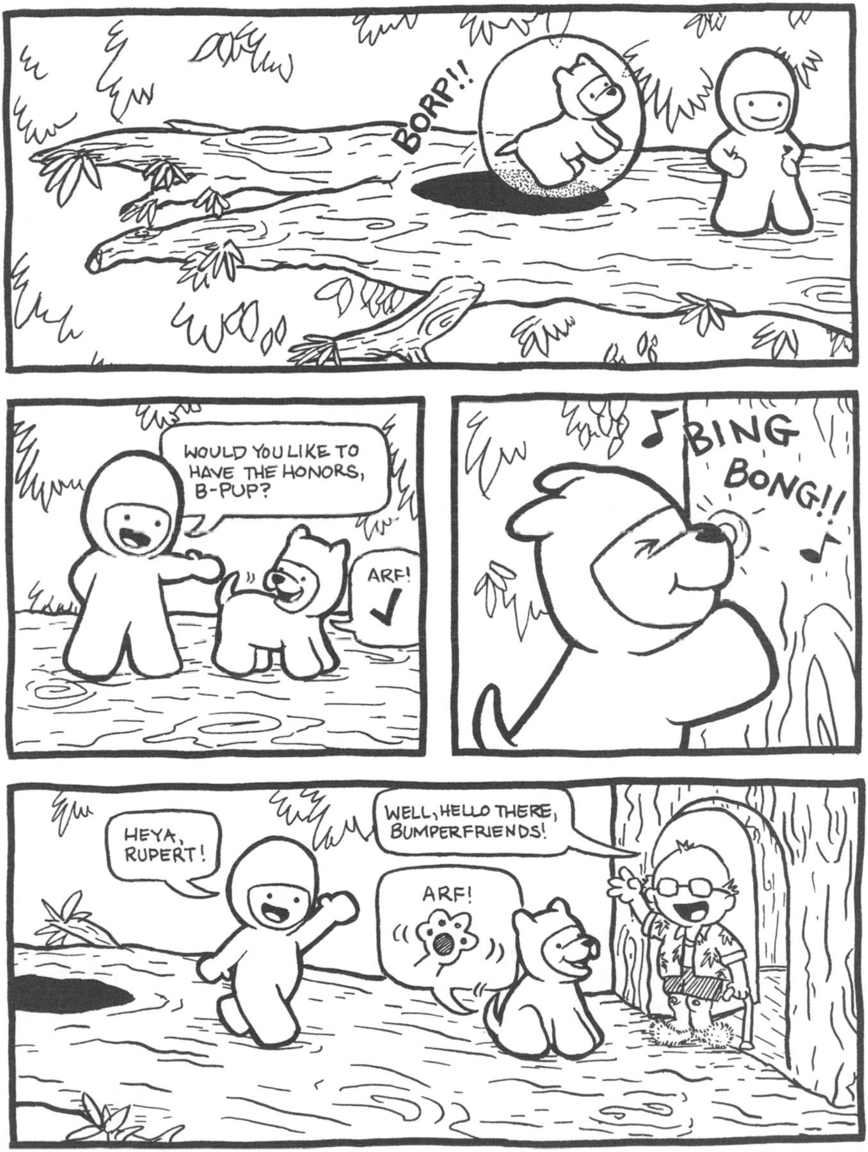

BORP!!
WOULD YOU LIKE TO HAVE THE HONORS, B-PUP?
ARF! ✓
BING BONG!!
HEYA, RUPERT!
WELL, HELLO THERE, BUMPERFRIENDS!
ARF!

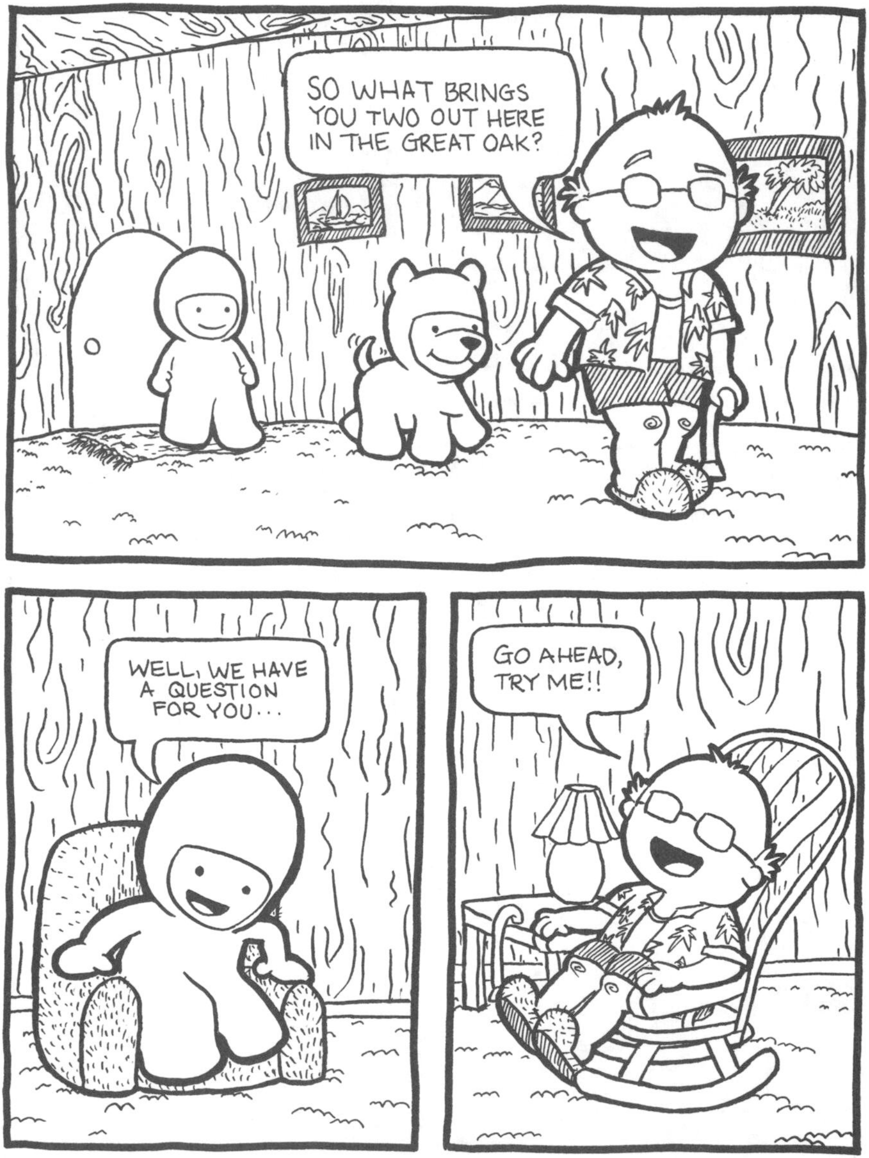
SO WHAT BRINGS YOU TWO OUT HERE IN THE GREAT OAK?
WELL, WE HAVE A QUESTION FOR YOU...
GO AHEAD, TRY ME!!

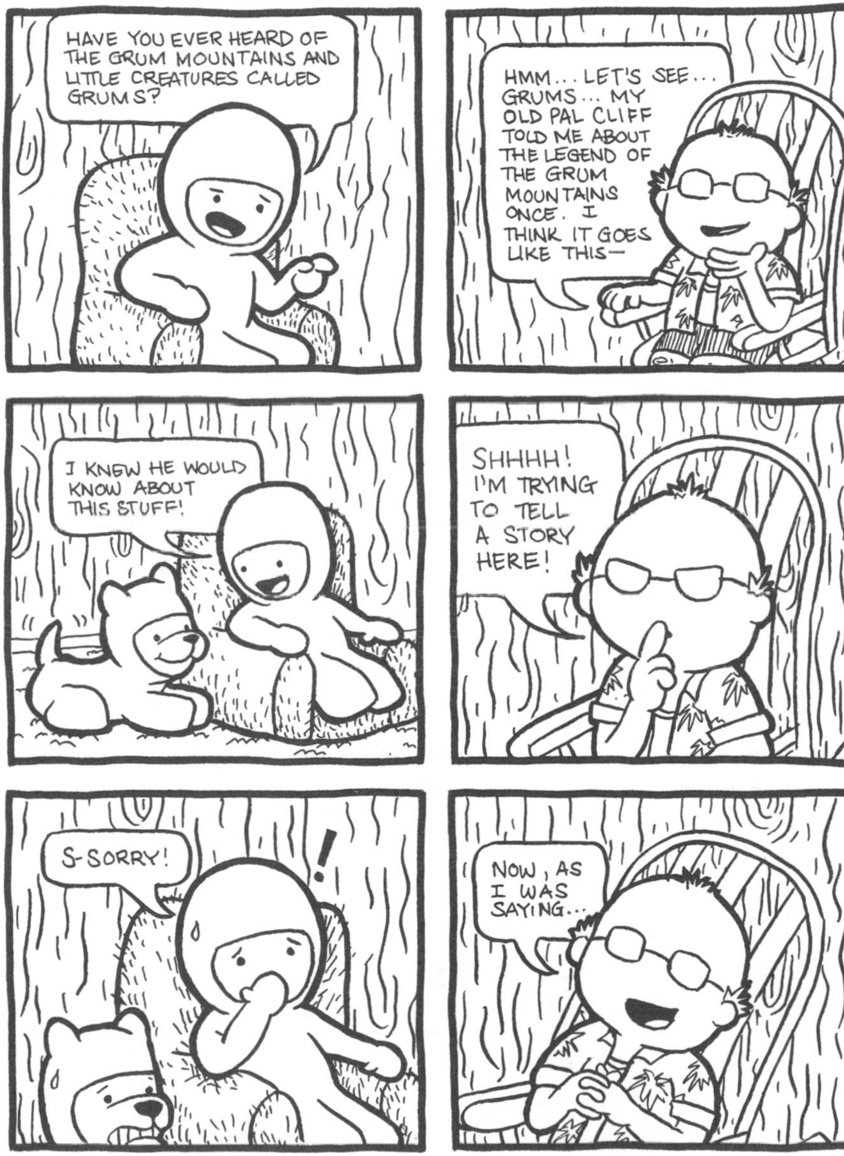

HAVE YOU EVER HEARD OF THE GRUM MOUNTAINS AND LITTLE CREATURES CALLED GRUMS?
HMM... LET'S SEE... GRUMS... MY OLD PAL CLIFF TOLD ME ABOUT THE LEGEND OF THE GRUM MOUNTAINS ONCE. I THINK IT GOES LIKE THIS—
I KNEW HE WOULD KNOW ABOUT THIS STUFF!
SHHHH! I'M TRYING TO TELL A STORY HERE!
S-SORRY!
!
NOW, AS I WAS SAYING...

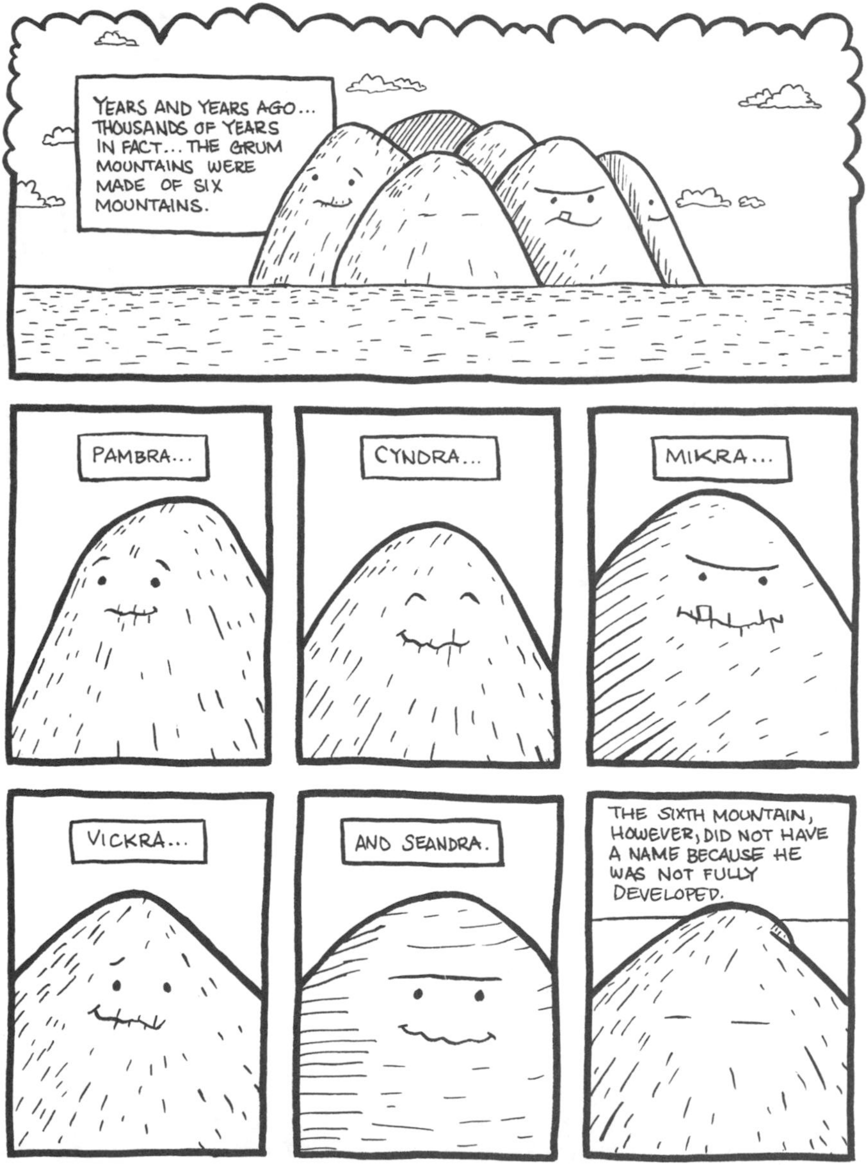
YEARS AND YEARS AGO... THOUSANDS OF YEARS IN FACT... THE GRUM MOUNTAINS WERE MADE OF SIX MOUNTAINS.
PAMBRA...
CYNDRA...
MIKRA...
VICKRA...
AND SEANDRA.
THE SIXTH MOUNTAIN, HOWEVER, DID NOT HAVE A NAME BECAUSE HE WAS NOT FULLY DEVELOPED.

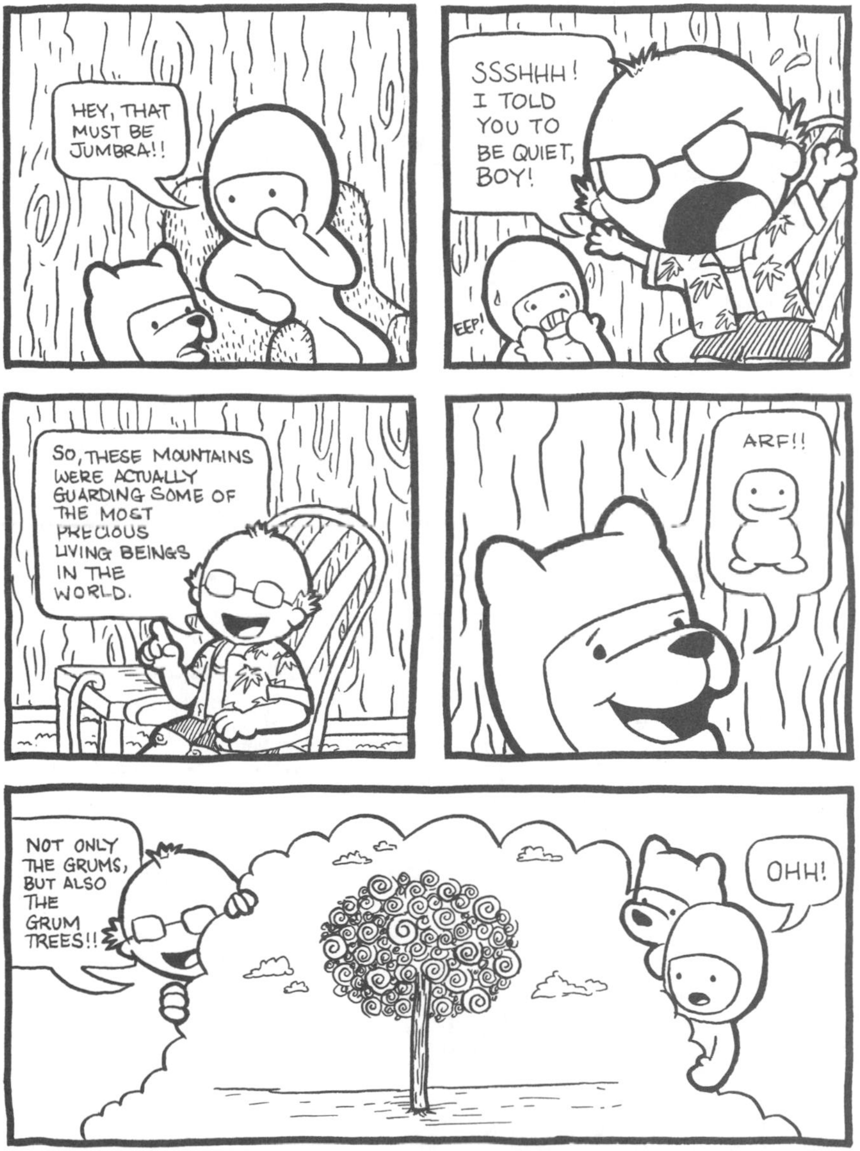
HEY, THAT MUST BE JUMBRA!!
SSSHHH! I TOLD YOU TO BE QUIET, BOY!
EEP!
SO, THESE MOUNTAINS WERE ACTUALLY GUARDING SOME OF THE MOST PRECIOUS LIVING BEINGS IN THE WORLD.
ARF!!
NOT ONLY THE GRUMS, BUT ALSO THE GRUM TREES!!
OHH!

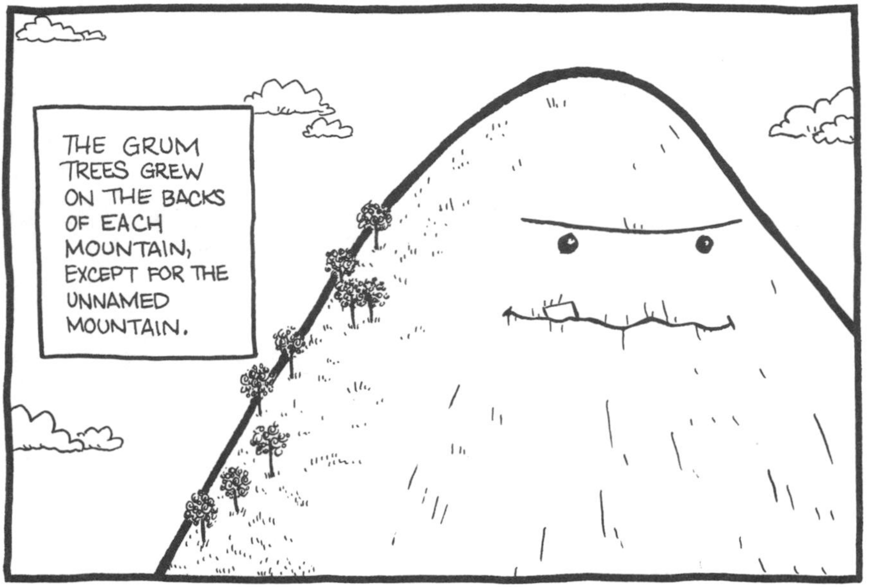
THE GRUM TREES GREW ON THE BACKS OF EACH MOUNTAIN, EXCEPT FOR THE UNNAMED MOUNTAIN.

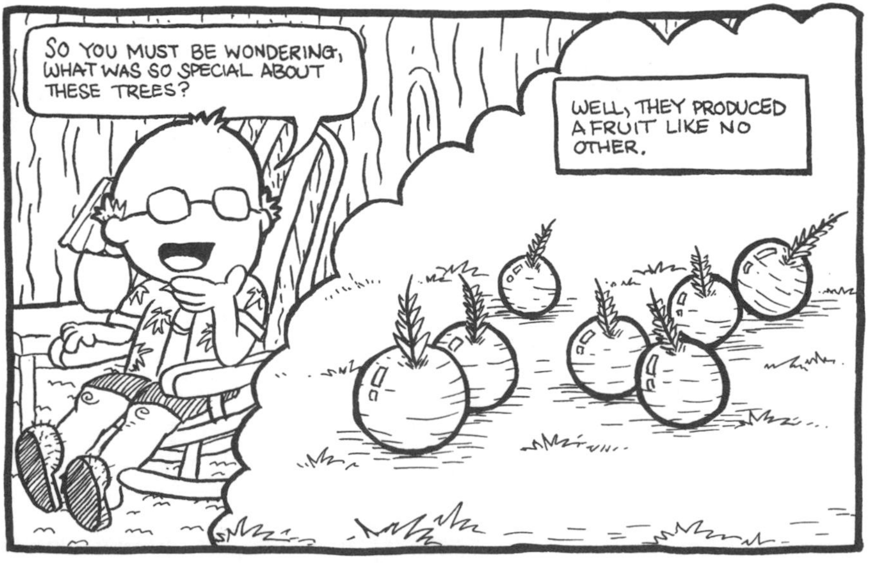
SO YOU MUST BE WONDERING, WHAT WAS SO SPECIAL ABOUT THESE TREES?
WELL, THEY PRODUCED A FRUIT LIKE NO OTHER.

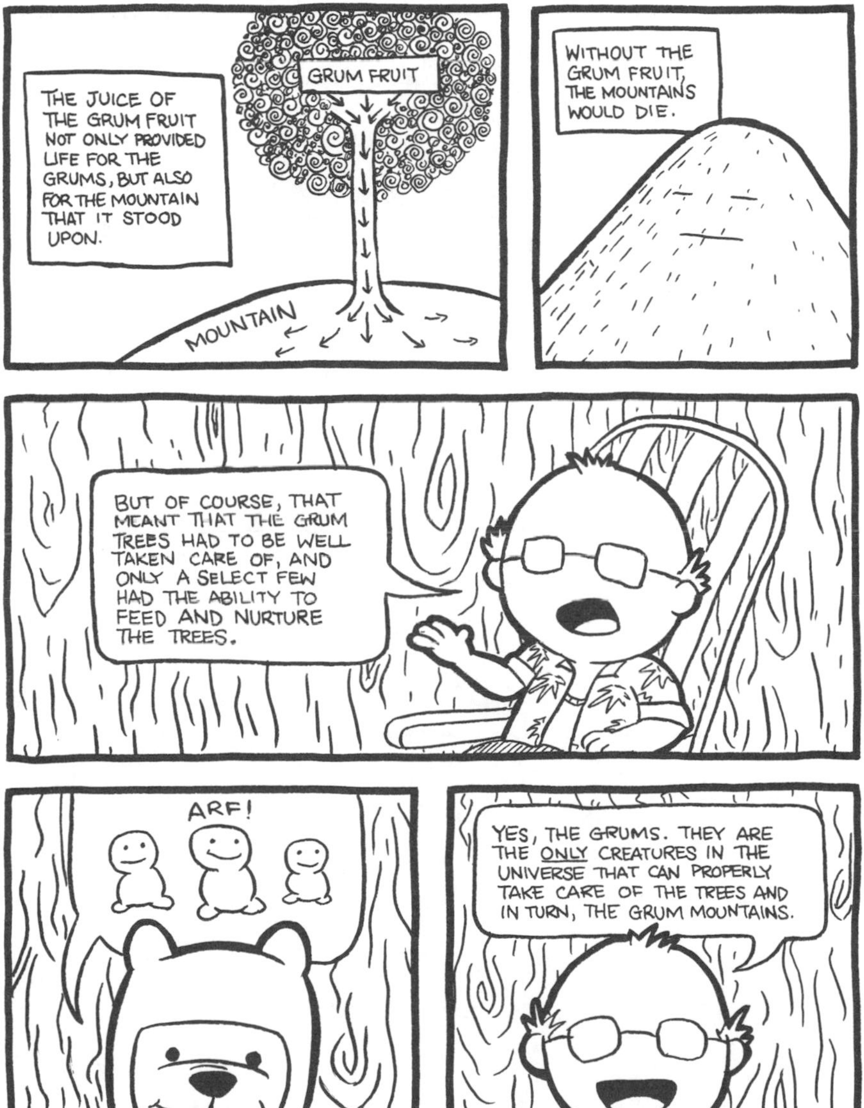
THE JUICE OF THE GRUM FRUIT NOT ONLY PROVIDED LIFE FOR THE GRUMS, BUT ALSO FOR THE MOUNTAIN THAT IT STOOD UPON.
GRUM FRUIT
MOUNTAIN
WITHOUT THE GRUM FRUIT, THE MOUNTAINS WOULD DIE.
BUT OF COURSE, THAT MEANT THAT THE GRUM TREES HAD TO BE WELL TAKEN CARE OF, AND ONLY A SELECT FEW HAD THE ABILITY TO FEED AND NURTURE THE TREES.
ARF!
YES, THE GRUMS. THEY ARE THE ONLY CREATURES IN THE UNIVERSE THAT CAN PROPERLY TAKE CARE OF THE TREES AND IN TURN, THE GRUM MOUNTAINS.

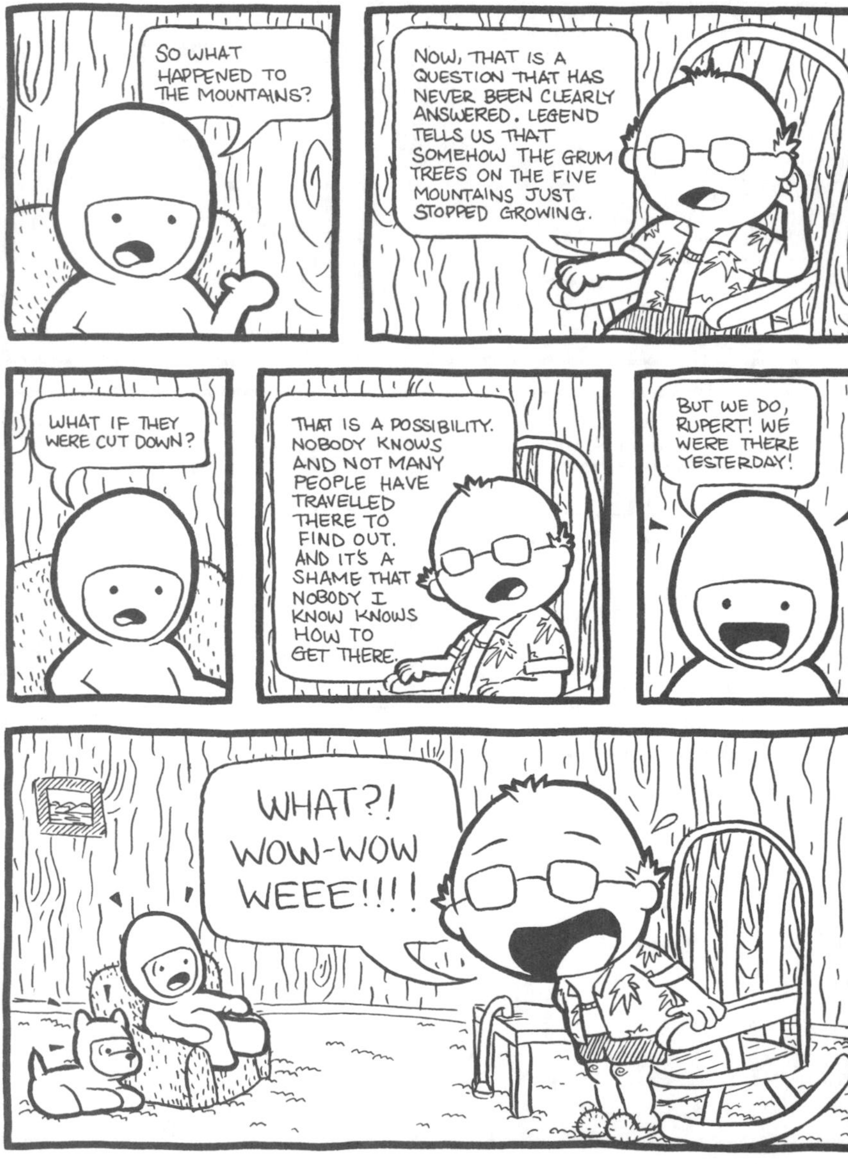
SO WHAT HAPPENED TO THE MOUNTAINS?
NOW, THAT IS A QUESTION THAT HAS NEVER BEEN CLEARLY ANSWERED. LEGEND TELLS US THAT SOMEHOW THE GRUM TREES ON THE FIVE MOUNTAINS JUST STOPPED GROWING.
WHAT IF THEY WERE CUT DOWN?
THAT IS A POSSIBILITY. NOBODY KNOWS AND NOT MANY PEOPLE HAVE TRAVELLED THERE TO FIND OUT. AND IT'S A SHAME THAT NOBODY I KNOW KNOWS HOW TO GET THERE.
BUT WE DO, RUPERT! WE WERE THERE YESTERDAY!
WHAT?! WOW-WOW WEEE!!!!

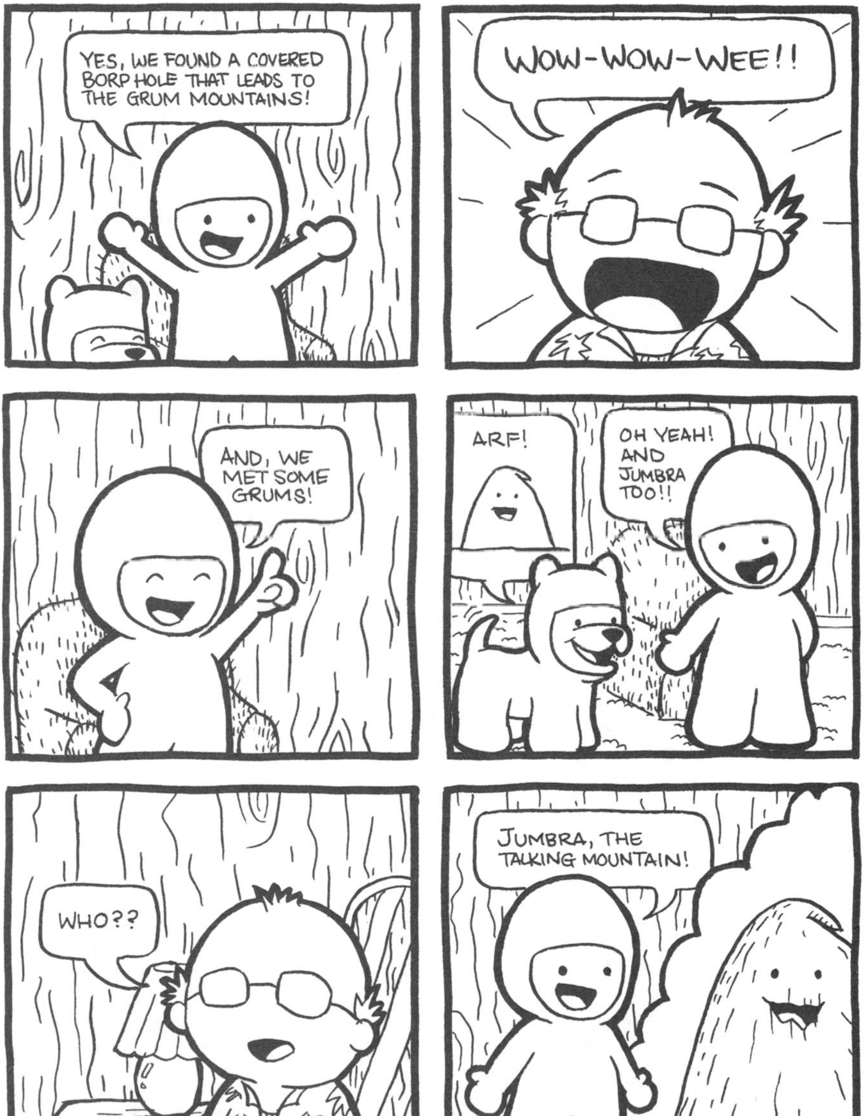
YES, WE FOUND A COVERED BORP HOLE THAT LEADS TO THE GRUM MOUNTAINS!
WOW-WOW-WEE!!
AND, WE MET SOME GRUMS!
ARF!
OH YEAH! AND JUMBRA TOO!!
WHO??
JUMBRA, THE TALKING MOUNTAIN!

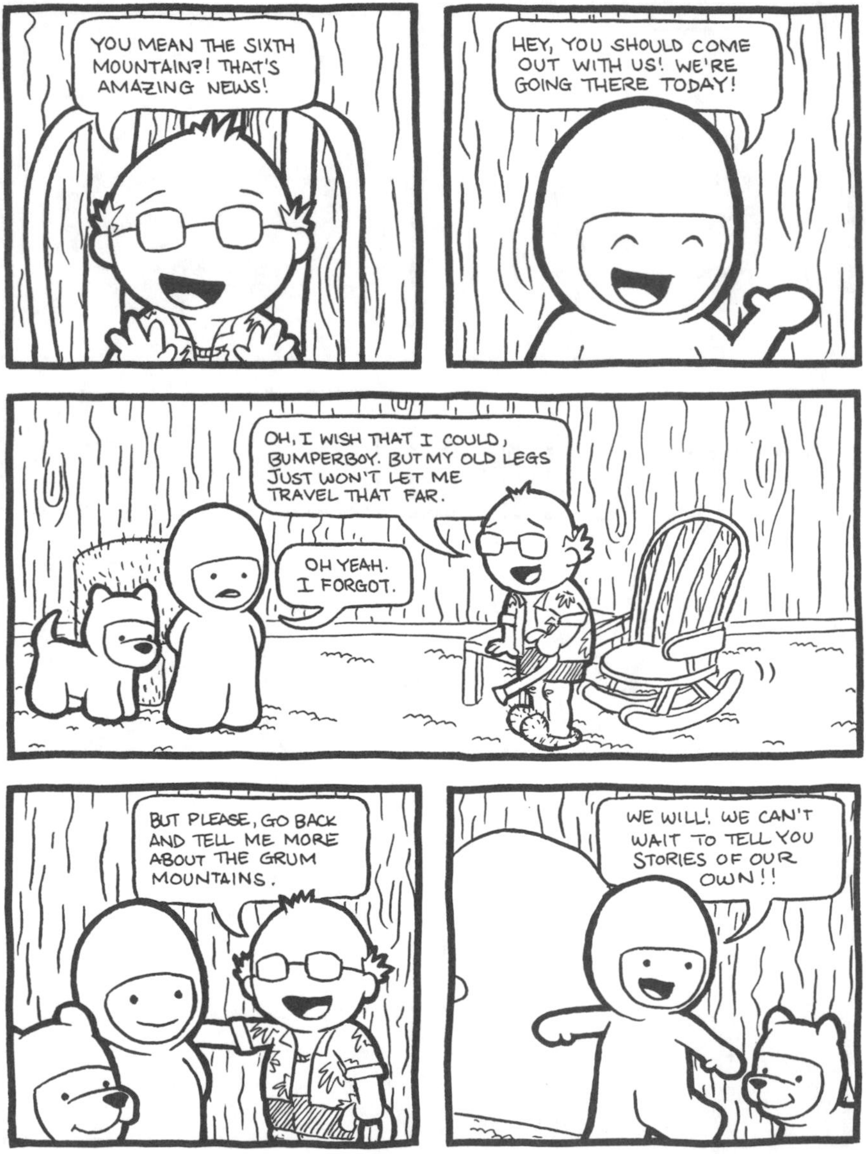
YOU MEAN THE SIXTH MOUNTAIN?! THAT'S AMAZING NEWS!
HEY, YOU SHOULD COME OUT WITH US! WE'RE GOING THERE TODAY!
OH, I WISH THAT I COULD, BUMPERBOY. BUT MY OLD LEGS JUST WON'T LET ME TRAVEL THAT FAR.
OH YEAH. I FORGOT.
BUT PLEASE, GO BACK AND TELL ME MORE ABOUT THE GRUM MOUNTAINS.
WE WILL! WE CAN'T WAIT TO TELL YOU STORIES OF OUR OWN!!

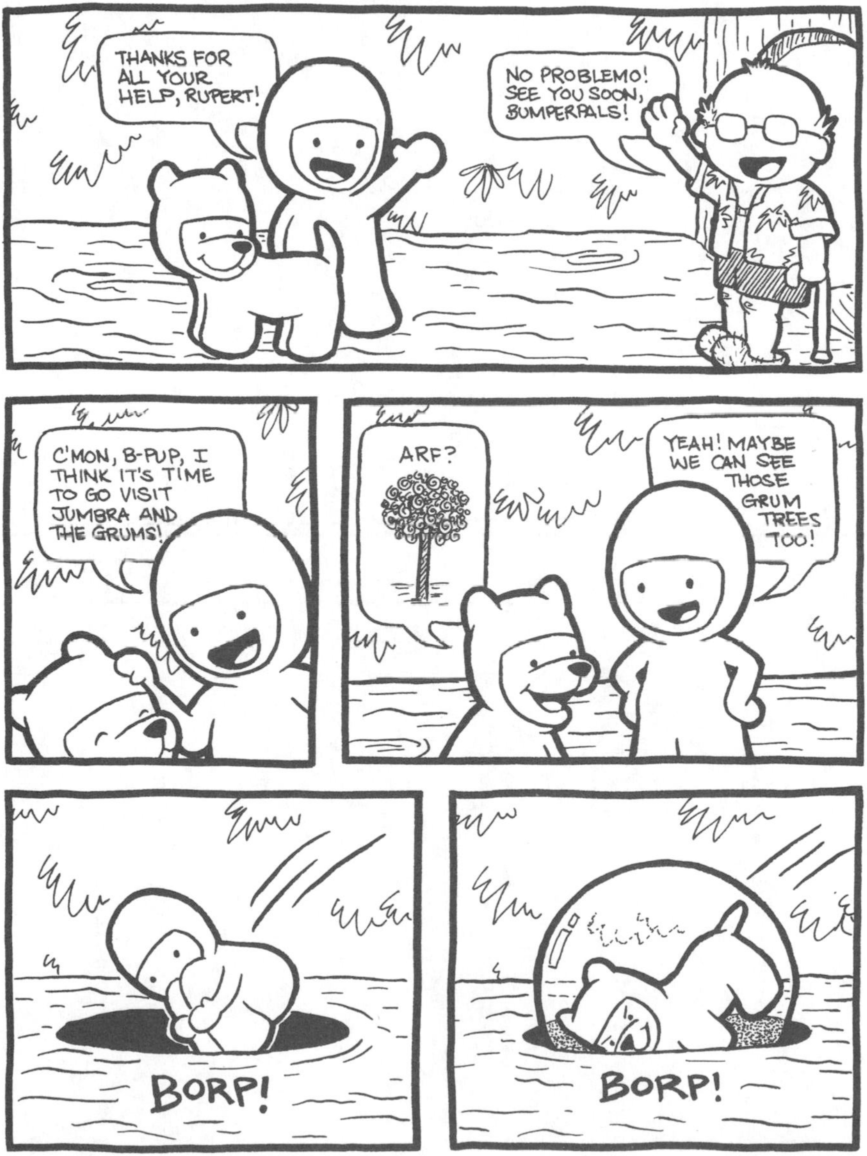

THANKS FOR ALL YOUR HELP, RUPERT!
NO PROBLEMO! SEE YOU SOON, BUMPERPALS!
C'MON, B-PUP, I THINK IT'S TIME TO GO VISIT JUMBRA AND THE GRUMS!
ARF?
YEAH! MAYBE WE CAN SEE THOSE GRUM TREES TOO!
BORP!
BORP!

PART FOUR

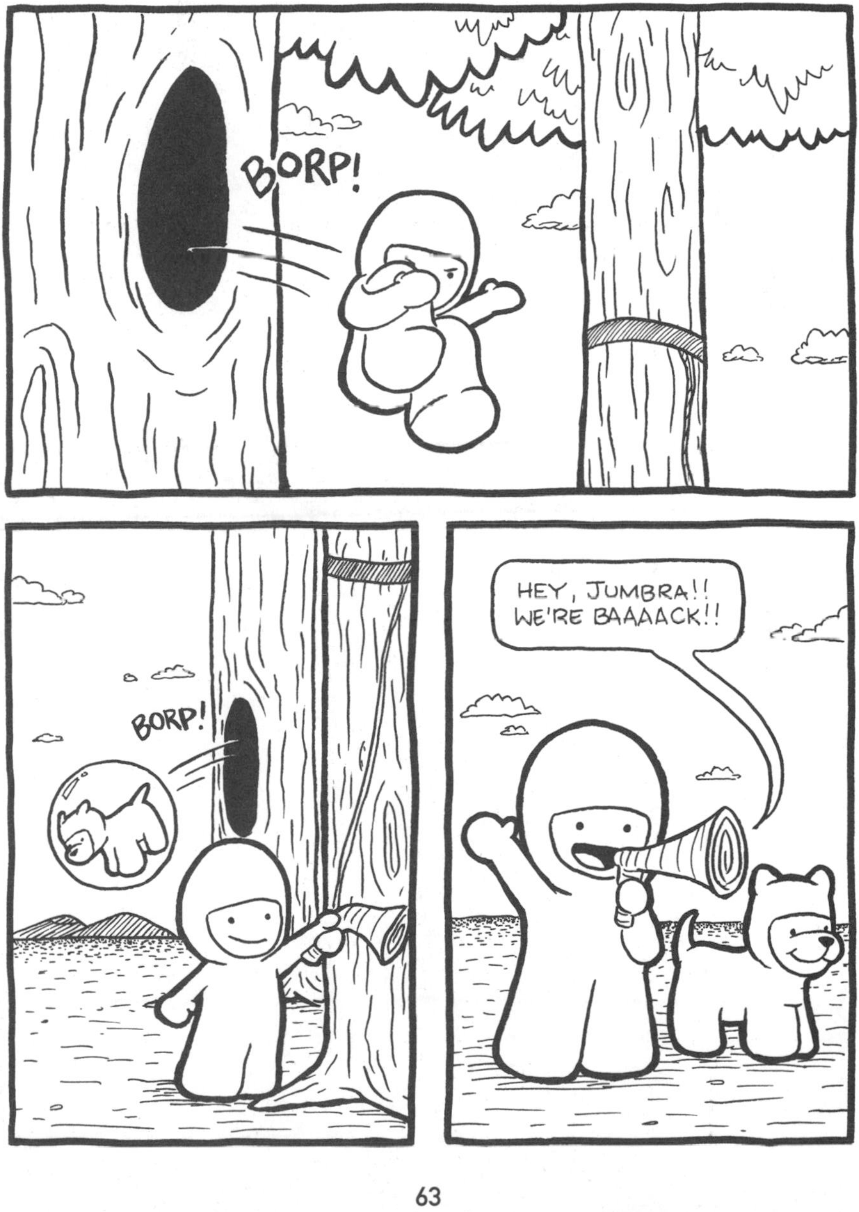
BORP!
BORP!
HEY, JUMBRA!! WE'RE BAAAACK!!

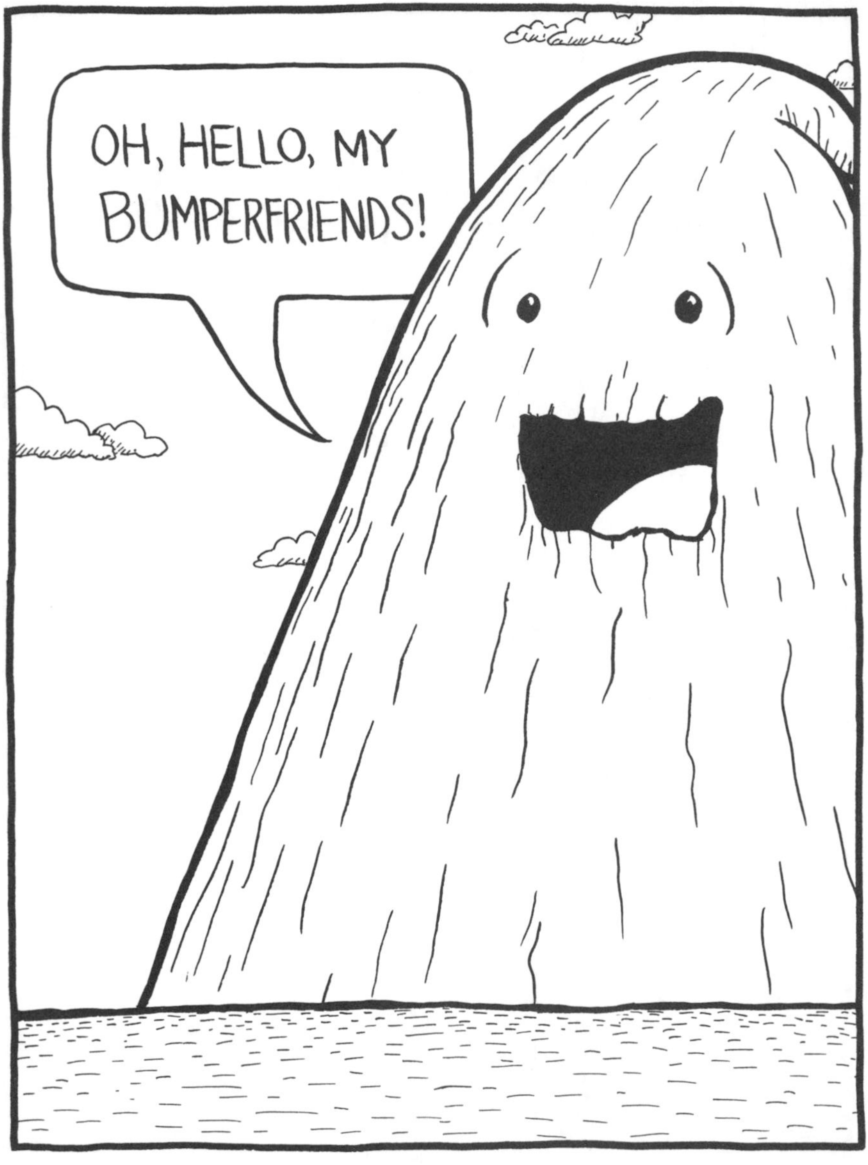
OH, HELLO, MY BUMPERFRIENDS!

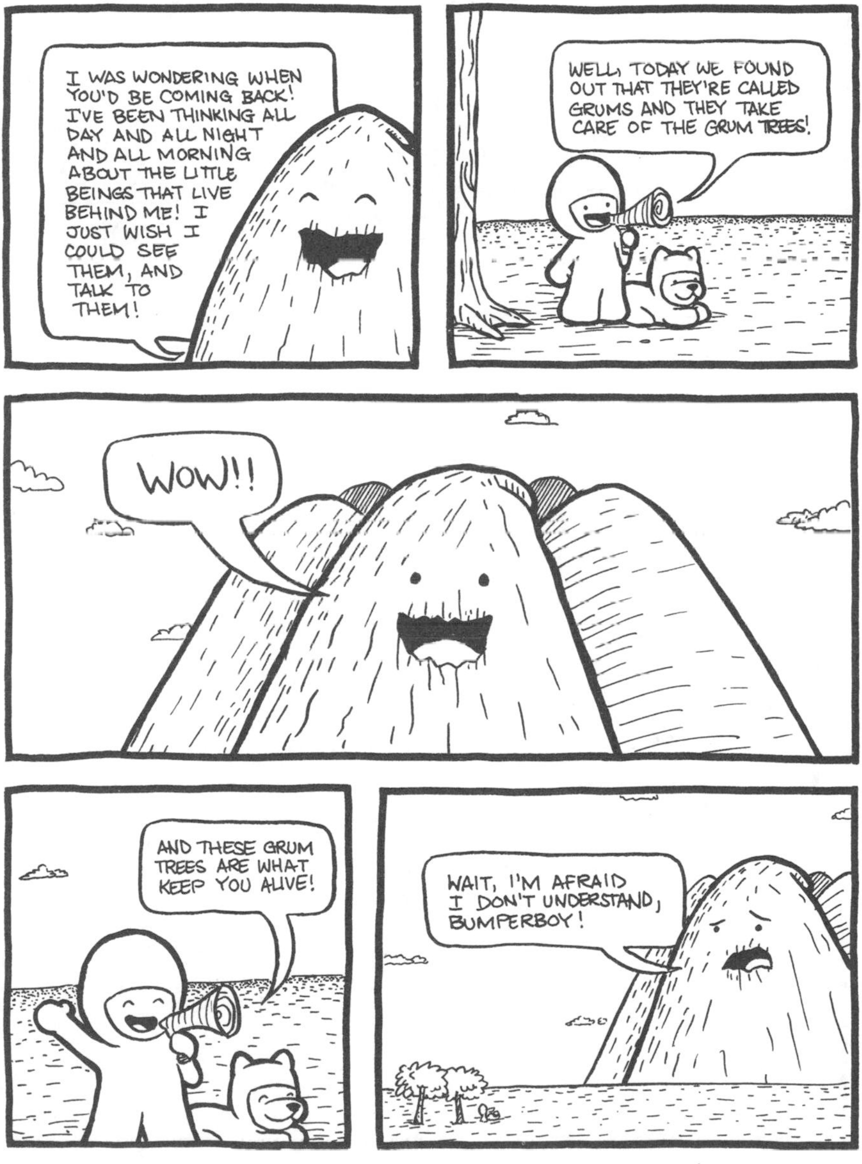
I WAS WONDERING WHEN YOU'D BE COMING BACK! I'VE BEEN THINKING ALL DAY AND ALL NIGHT AND ALL MORNING ABOUT THE LITTLE BEINGS THAT LIVE BEHIND ME! I JUST WISH I COULD SEE THEM, AND TALK TO THEM!
WELL, TODAY WE FOUND OUT THAT THEY'RE CALLED GRUMS AND THEY TAKE CARE OF THE GRUM TREES!
WOW!!
AND THESE GRUM TREES ARE WHAT KEEP YOU ALIVE!
WAIT, I'M AFRAID I DON'T UNDERSTAND, BUMPERBOY!

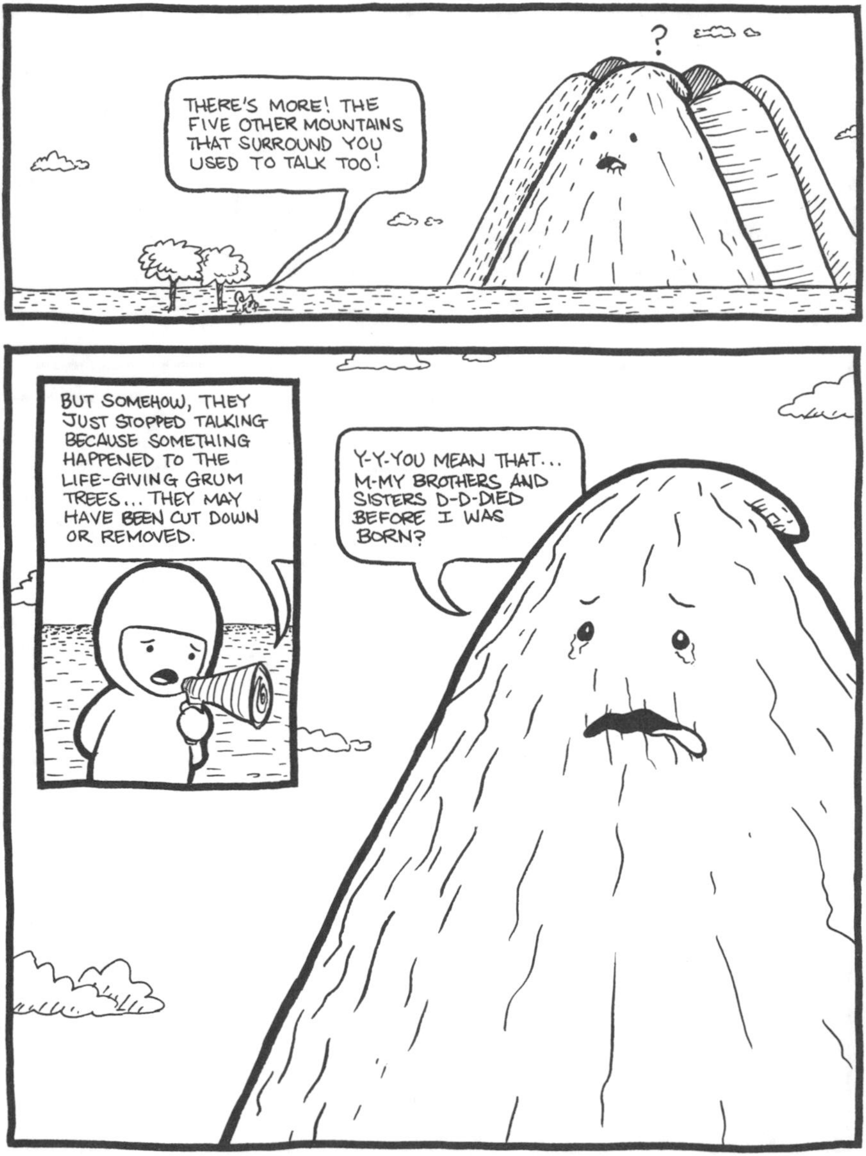

?
THERE'S MORE! THE FIVE OTHER MOUNTAINS THAT SURROUND YOU USED TO TALK TOO!
BUT SOMEHOW, THEY JUST STOPPED TALKING BECAUSE SOMETHING HAPPENED TO THE LIFE-GIVING GRUM TREES... THEY MAY HAVE BEEN CUT DOWN OR REMOVED.
Y-Y-YOU MEAN THAT... M-MY BROTHERS AND SISTERS D-D-DIED BEFORE I WAS BORN?

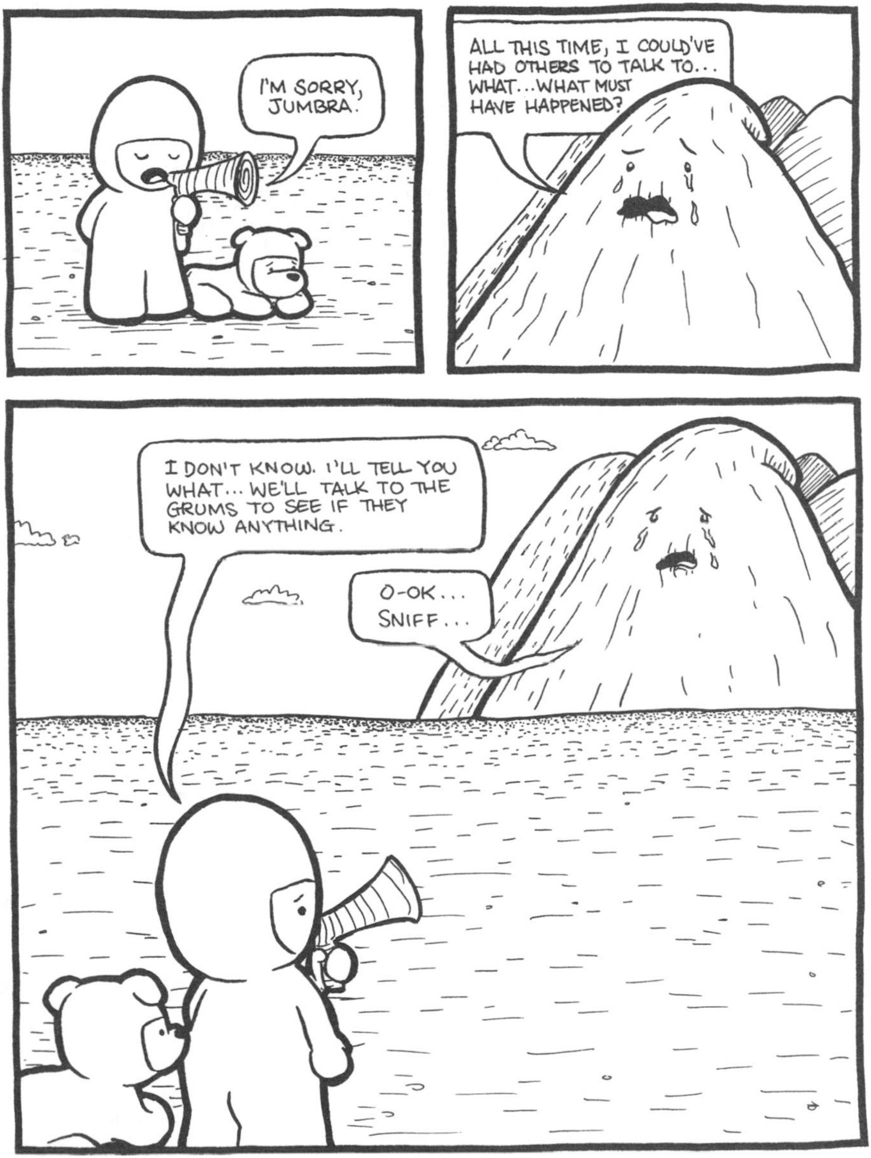
I'M SORRY, JUMBRA.
ALL THIS TIME, I COULD'VE HAD OTHERS TO TALK TO... WHAT...WHAT MUST HAVE HAPPENED?
I DON'T KNOW. I'LL TELL YOU WHAT... WE'LL TALK TO THE GRUMS TO SEE IF THEY KNOW ANYTHING.
O-OK... SNIFF...

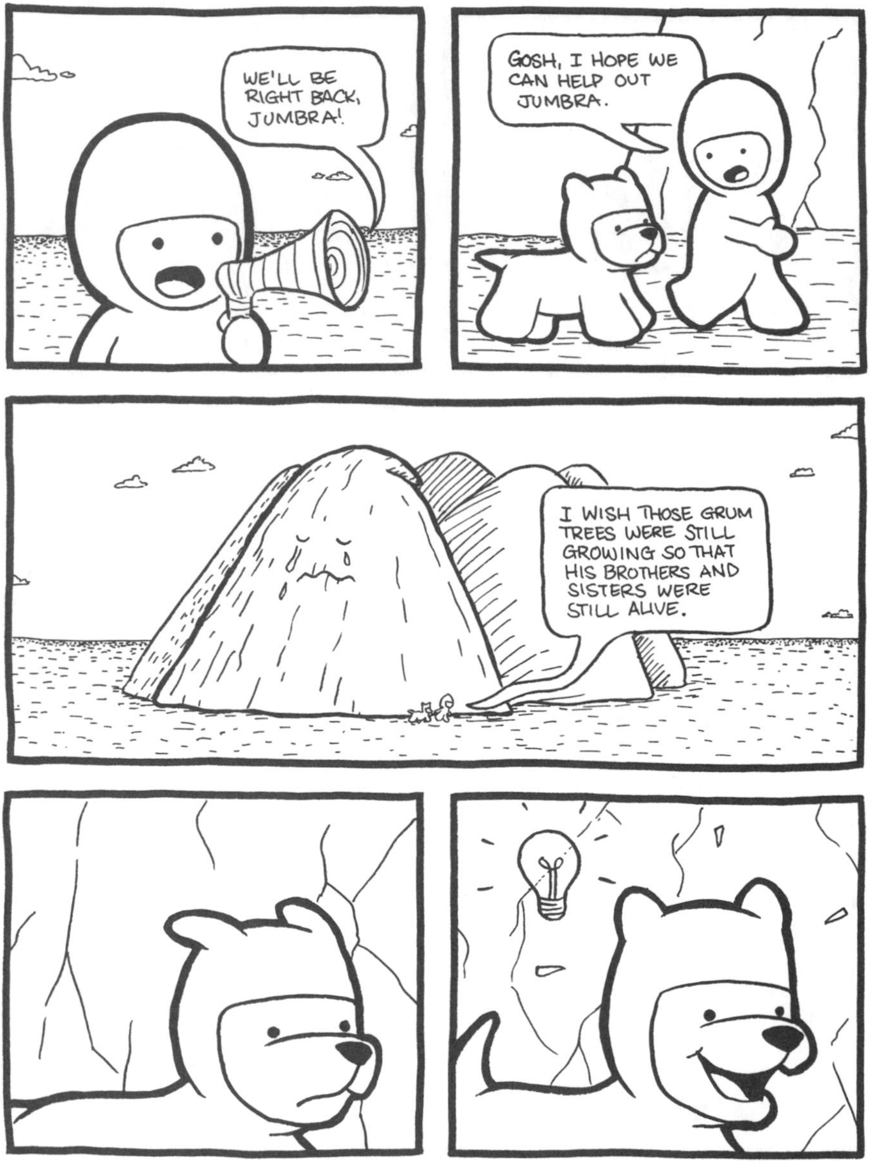
WE'LL BE RIGHT BACK, JUMBRA!
GOSH, I HOPE WE CAN HELP OUT JUMBRA.
I WISH THOSE GRUM TREES WERE STILL GROWING SO THAT HIS BROTHERS AND SISTERS WERE STILL ALIVE.

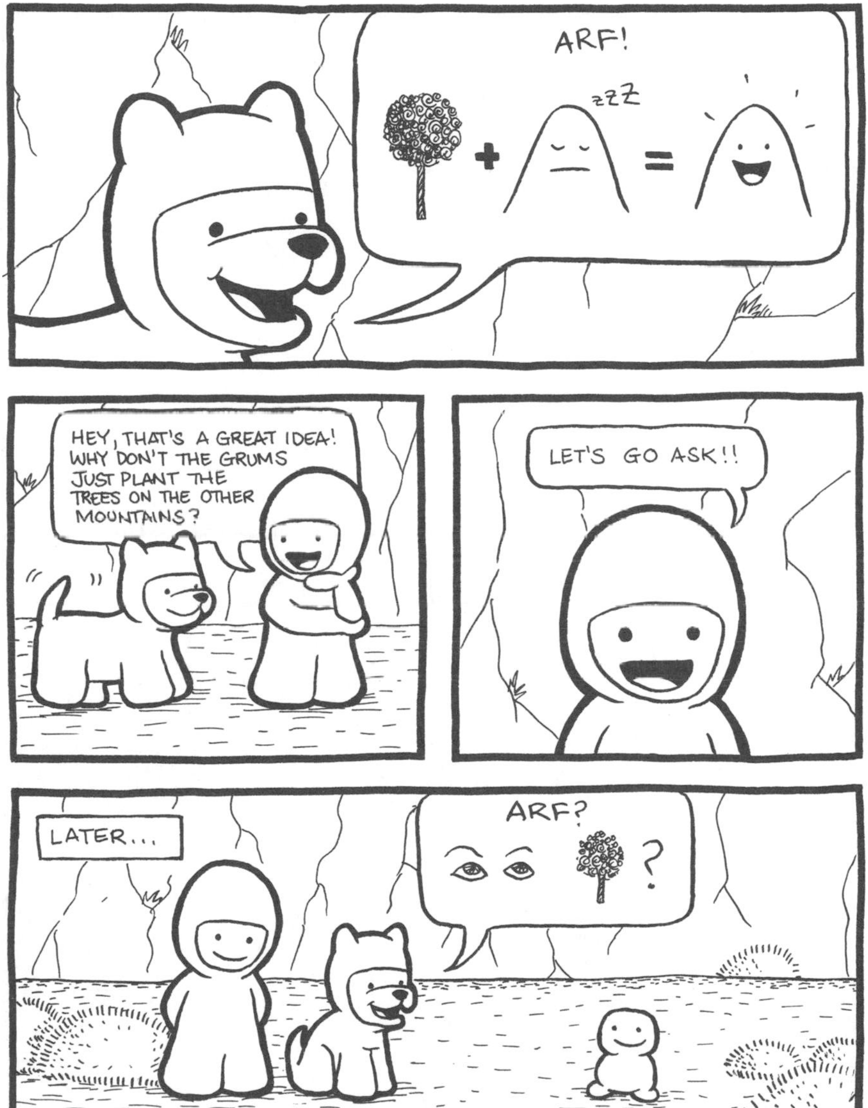
ARF!
zzZ
+
=
HEY, THAT'S A GREAT IDEA! WHY DON'T THE GRUMS JUST PLANT THE TREES ON THE OTHER MOUNTAINS?
LET'S GO ASK!!
LATER...
ARF?
?

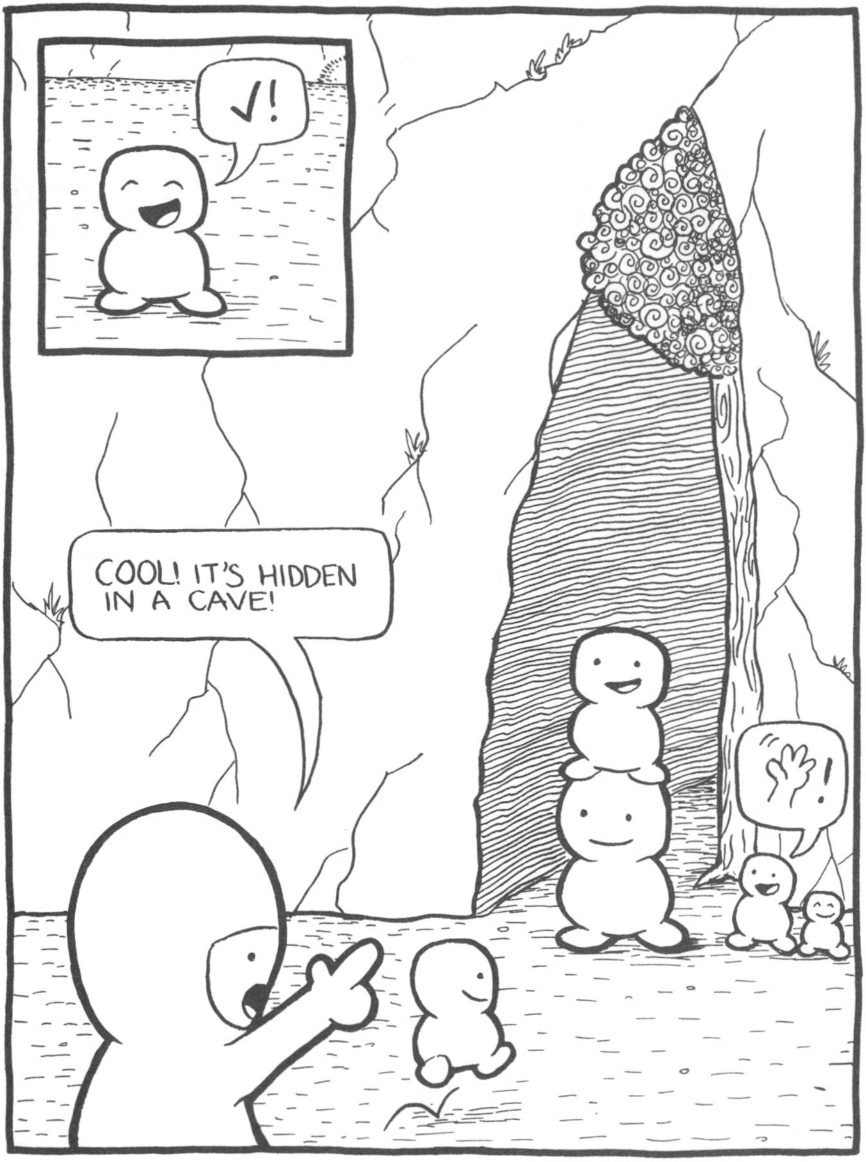
√!
COOL! IT'S HIDDEN IN A CAVE!
!

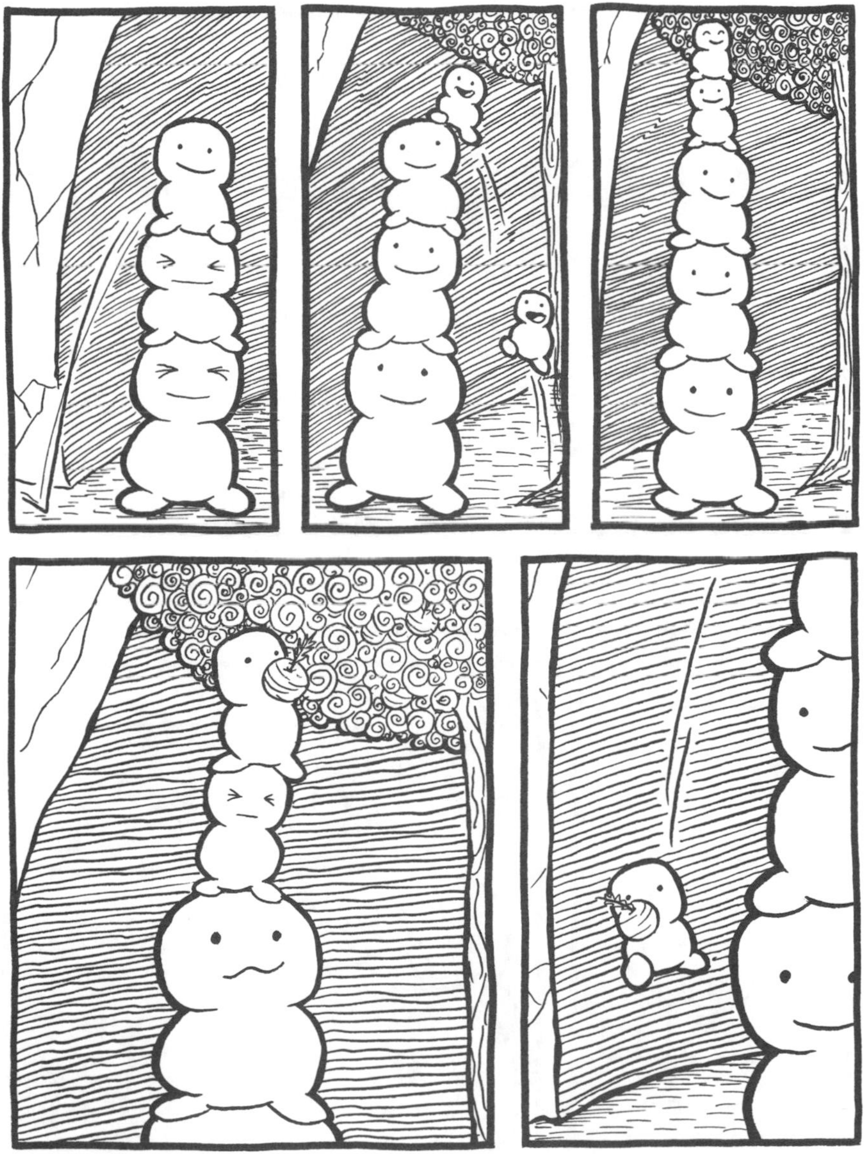

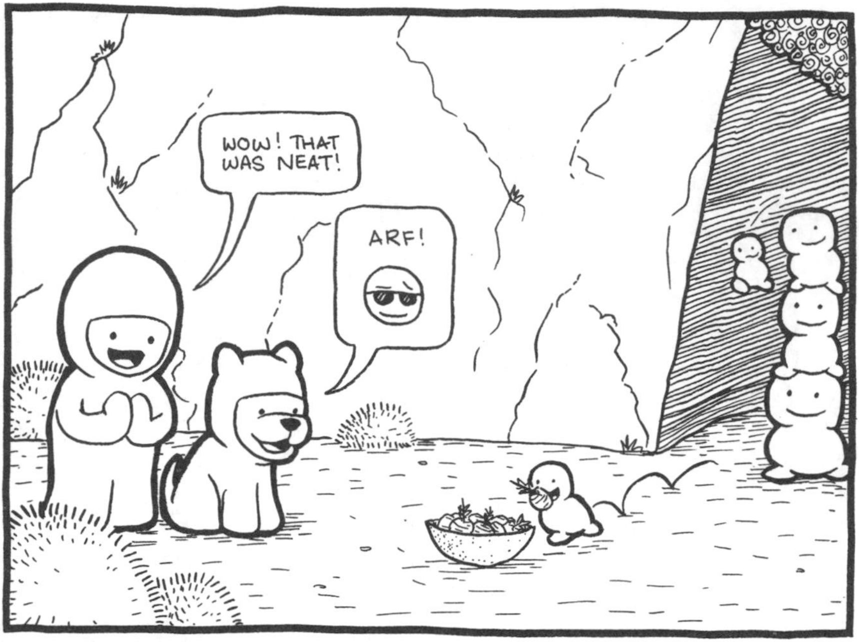
WOW! THAT WAS NEAT!
ARF!

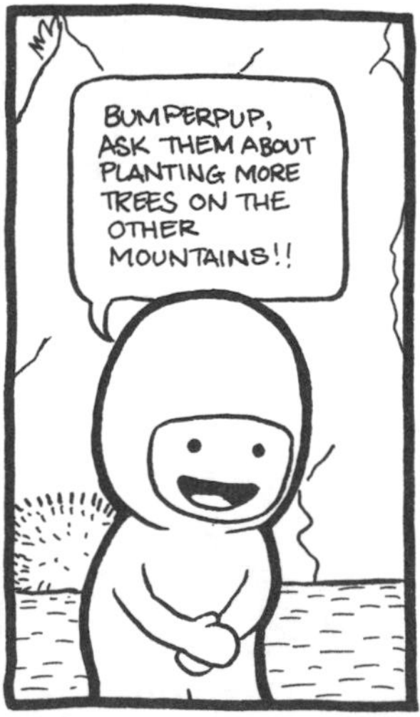
BUMPERPUP, ASK THEM ABOUT PLANTING MORE TREES ON THE OTHER MOUNTAINS!!

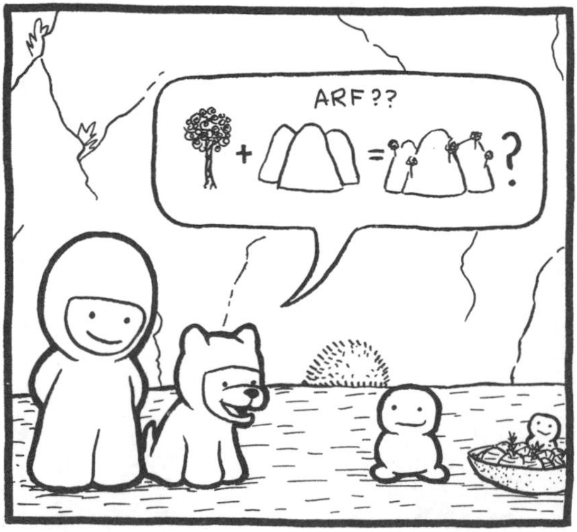
ARF??

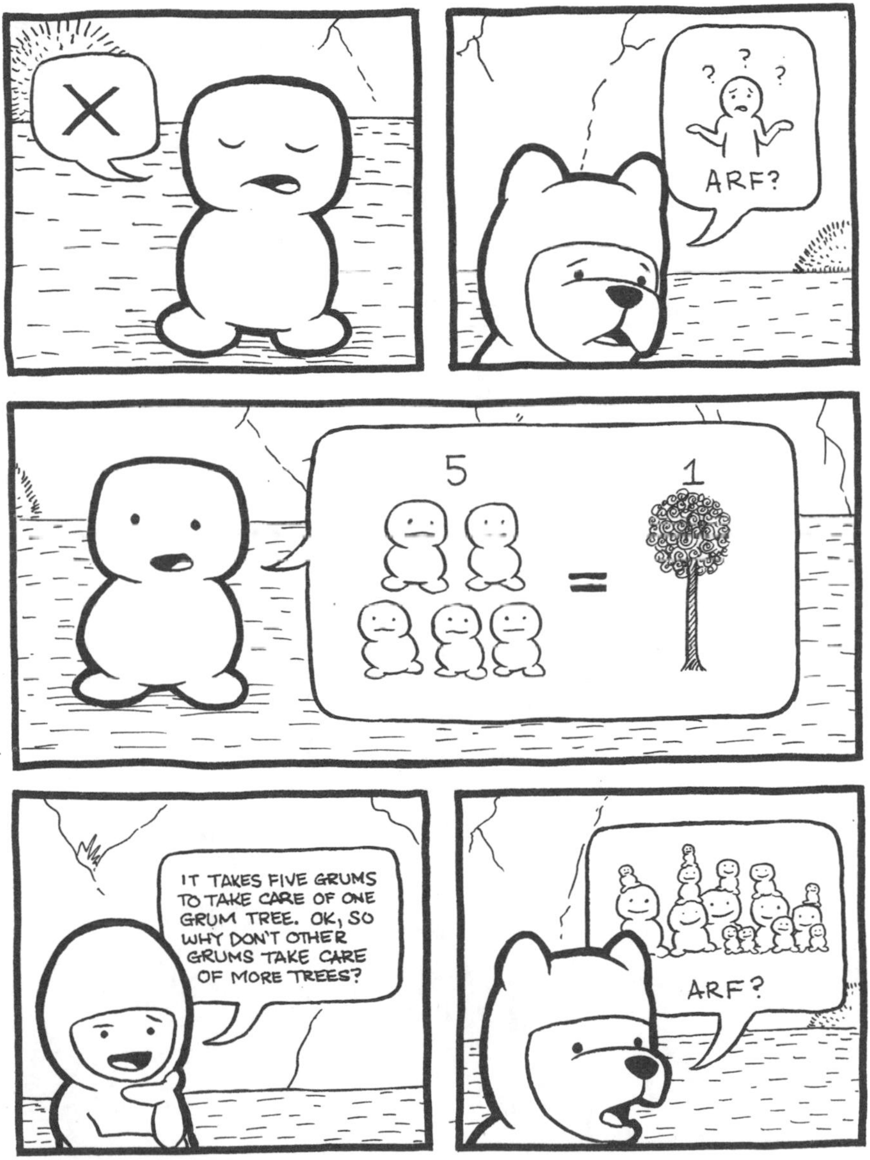
X
ARF?
5
1
IT TAKES FIVE GRUMS TO TAKE CARE OF ONE GRUM TREE. OK, SO WHY DON'T OTHER GRUMS TAKE CARE OF MORE TREES?
ARF?

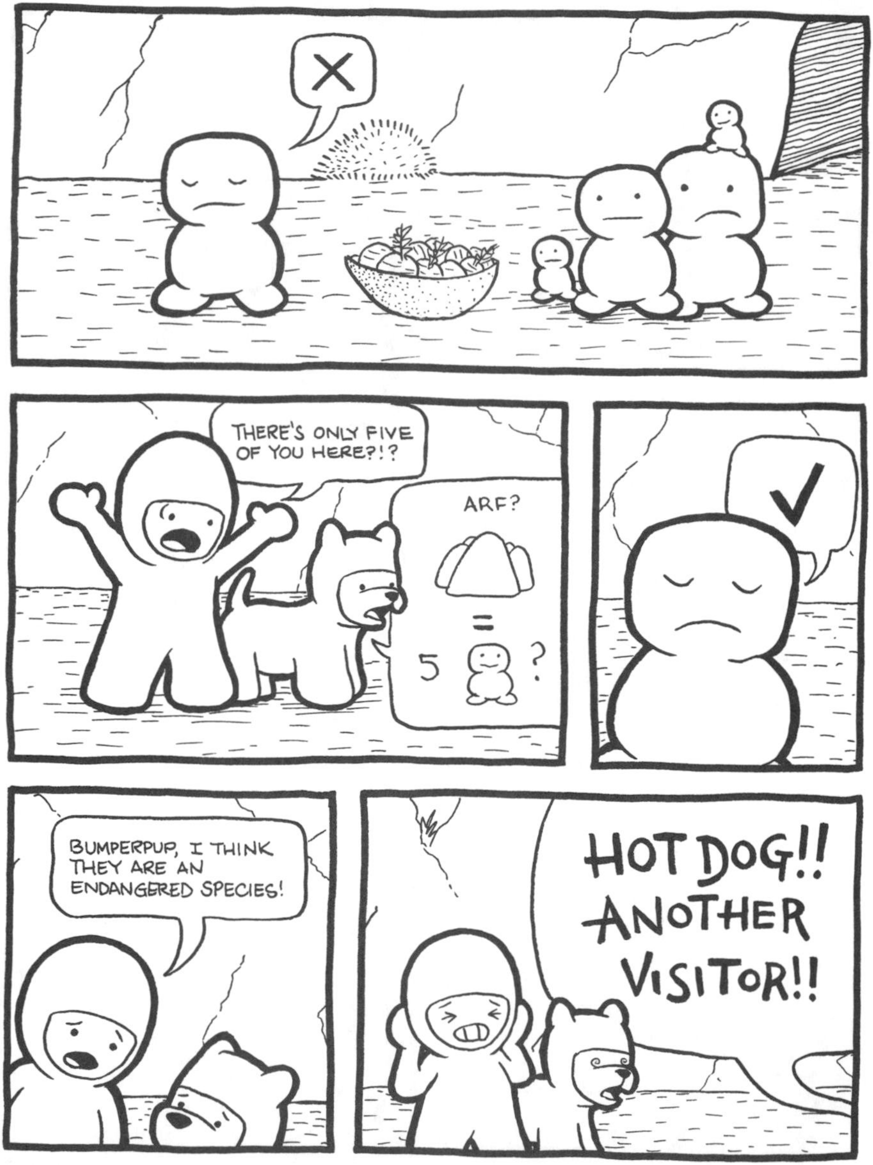
THERE'S ONLY FIVE OF YOU HERE?!?
ARF?
5 ?
BUMPERPUP, I THINK THEY ARE AN ENDANGERED SPECIES!
HOT DOG!! ANOTHER VISITOR!!

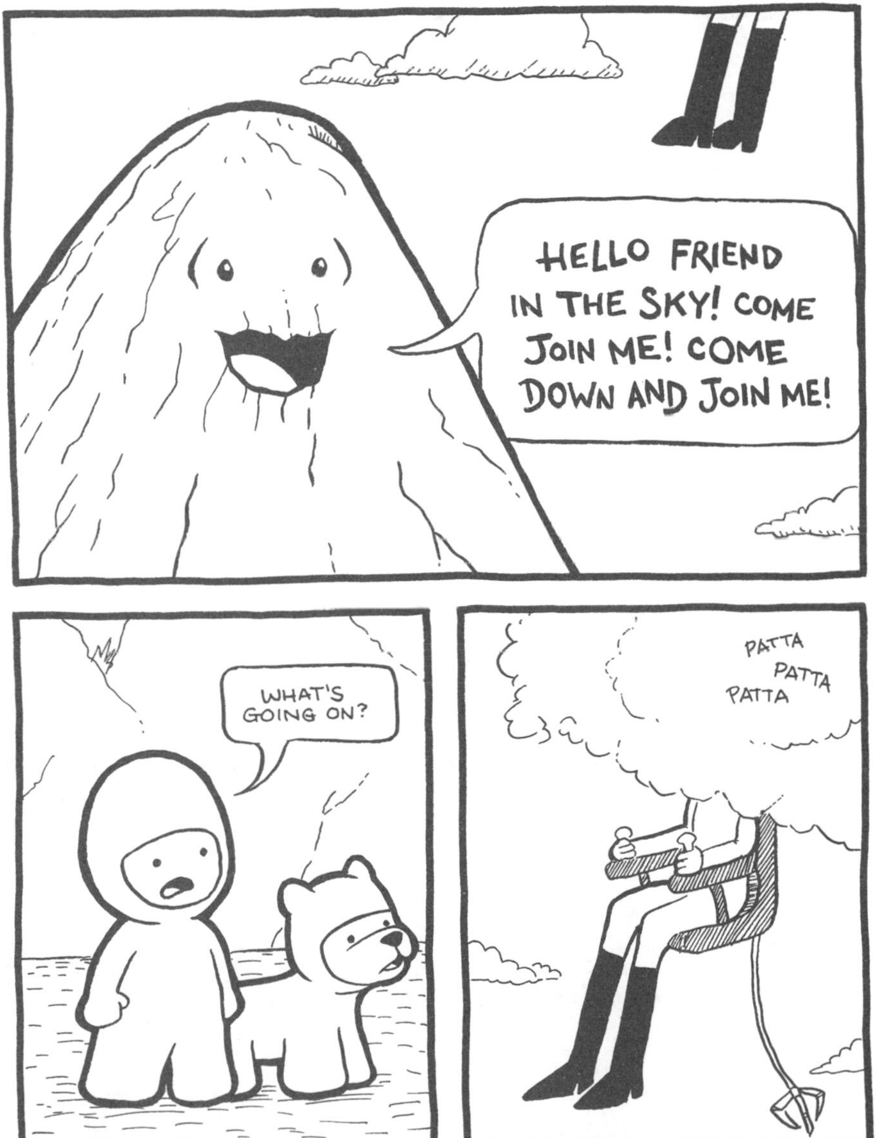
HELLO FRIEND IN THE SKY! COME JOIN ME! COME DOWN AND JOIN ME!
WHAT'S GOING ON?
PATTA PATTA PATTA

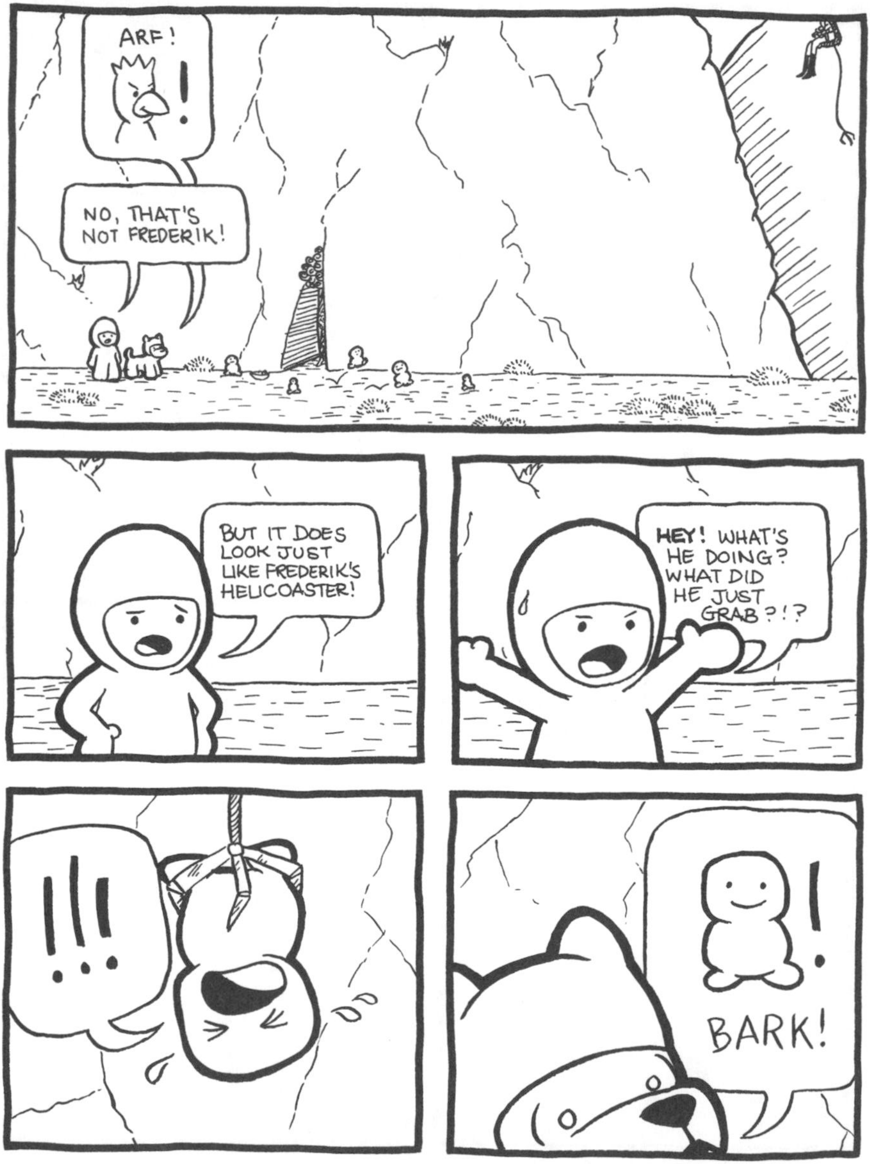
ARF! !
NO, THAT'S NOT FREDERIK!
BUT IT DOES LOOK JUST LIKE FREDERIK'S HELICOASTER!
HEY! WHAT'S HE DOING? WHAT DID HE JUST GRAB?!?
!!!...
! BARK!

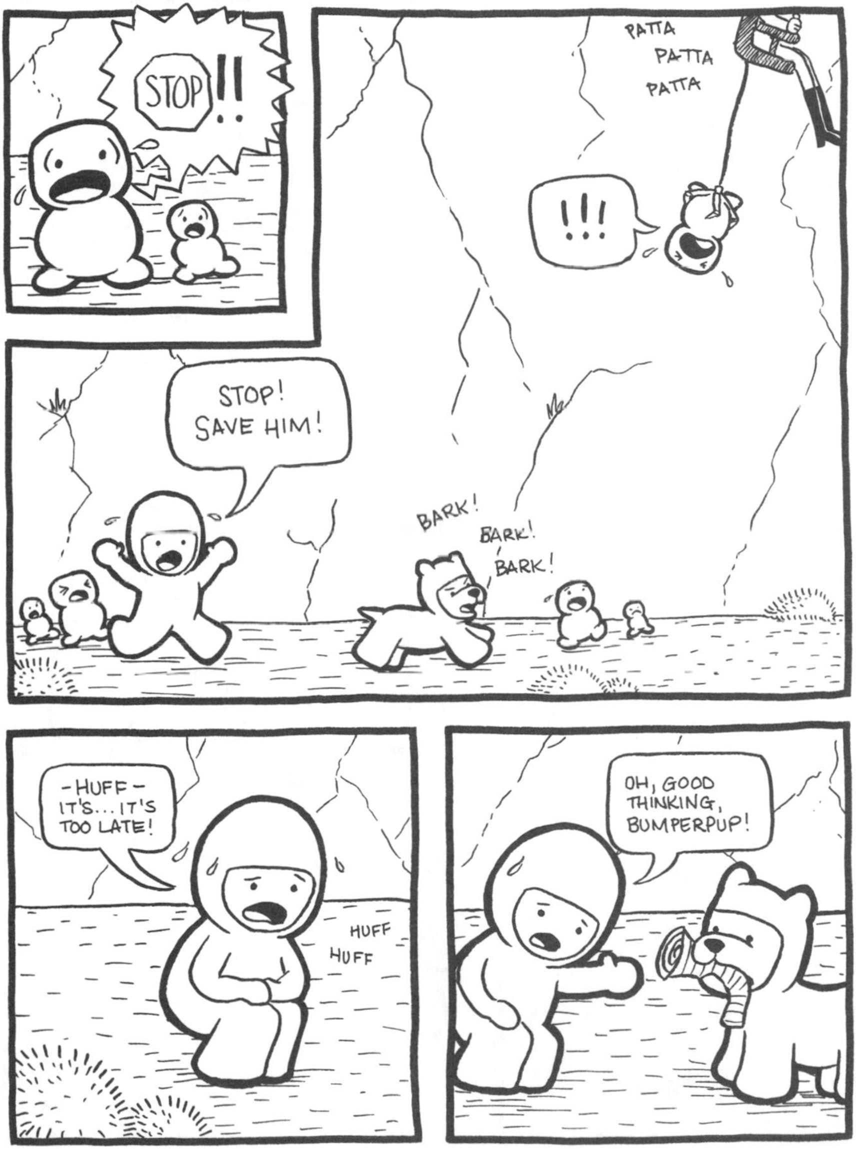
STOP!!
PATTA PATTA PATTA
!!!
STOP! SAVE HIM!
BARK! BARK! BARK!
-HUFF- IT'S... IT'S TOO LATE!
HUFF HUFF
OH, GOOD THINKING, BUMPERPUP!

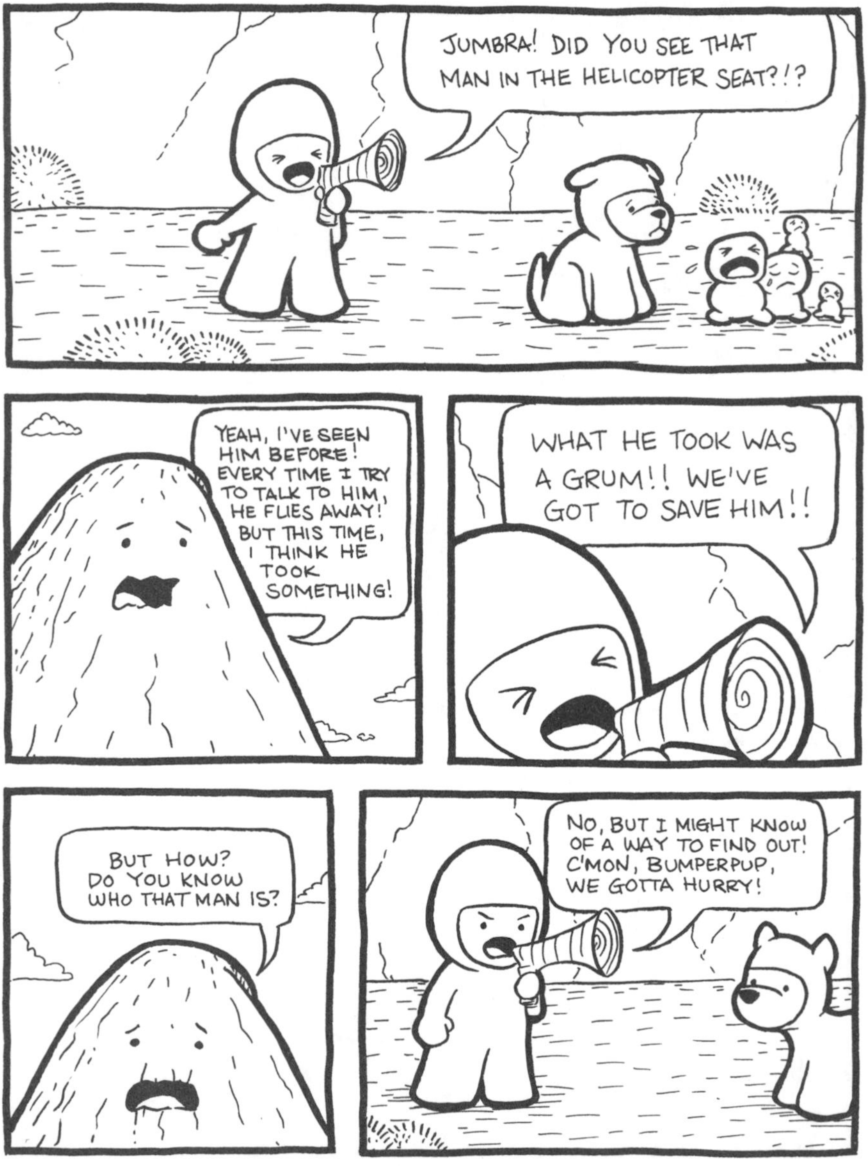
JUMBRA! DID YOU SEE THAT MAN IN THE HELICOPTER SEAT?!?
YEAH, I'VE SEEN HIM BEFORE! EVERY TIME I TRY TO TALK TO HIM, HE FLIES AWAY! BUT THIS TIME, I THINK HE TOOK SOMETHING!
WHAT HE TOOK WAS A GRUM!! WE'VE GOT TO SAVE HIM!!
BUT HOW? DO YOU KNOW WHO THAT MAN IS?
NO, BUT I MIGHT KNOW OF A WAY TO FIND OUT! C'MON, BUMPERPUP, WE GOTTA HURRY!

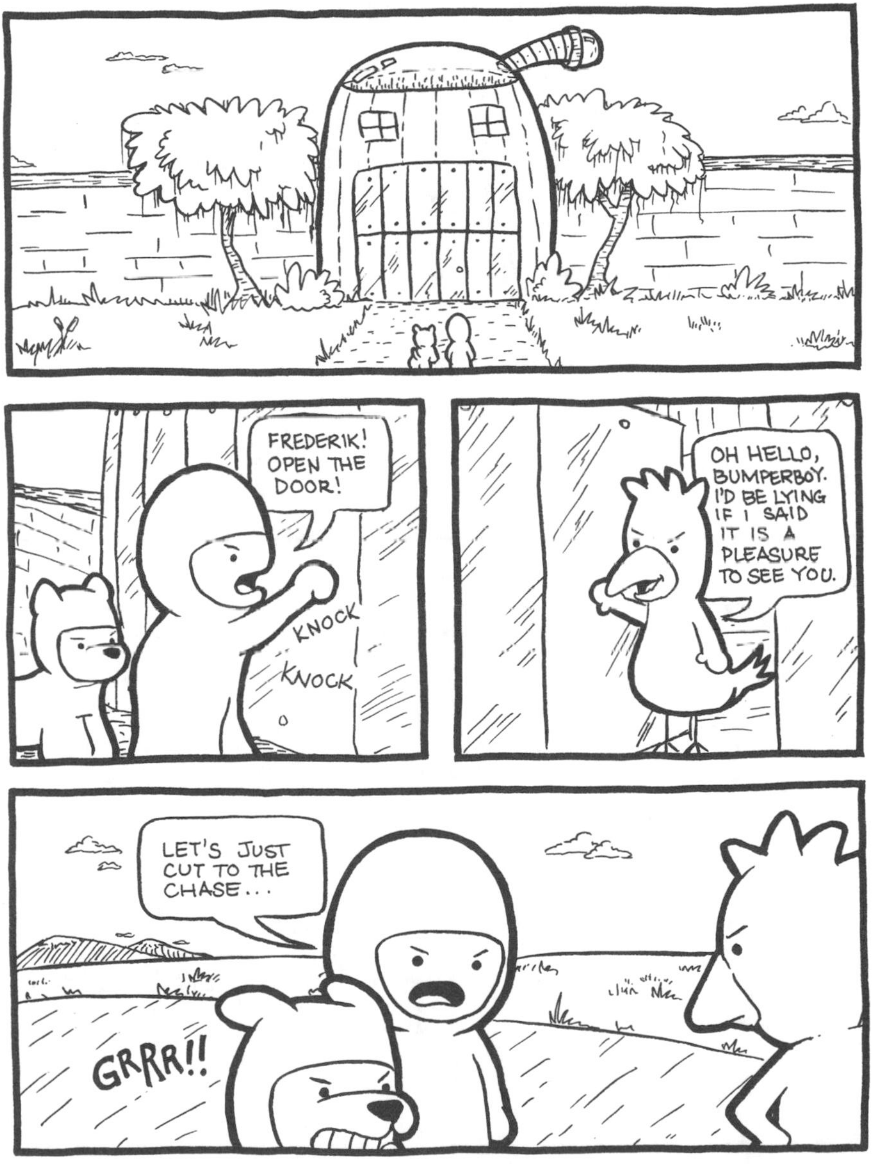
FREDERIK! OPEN THE DOOR!
KNOCK
KNOCK
OH HELLO, BUMPERBOY. I'D BE LYING IF I SAID IT IS A PLEASURE TO SEE YOU.
LET'S JUST CUT TO THE CHASE...
GRRR!!

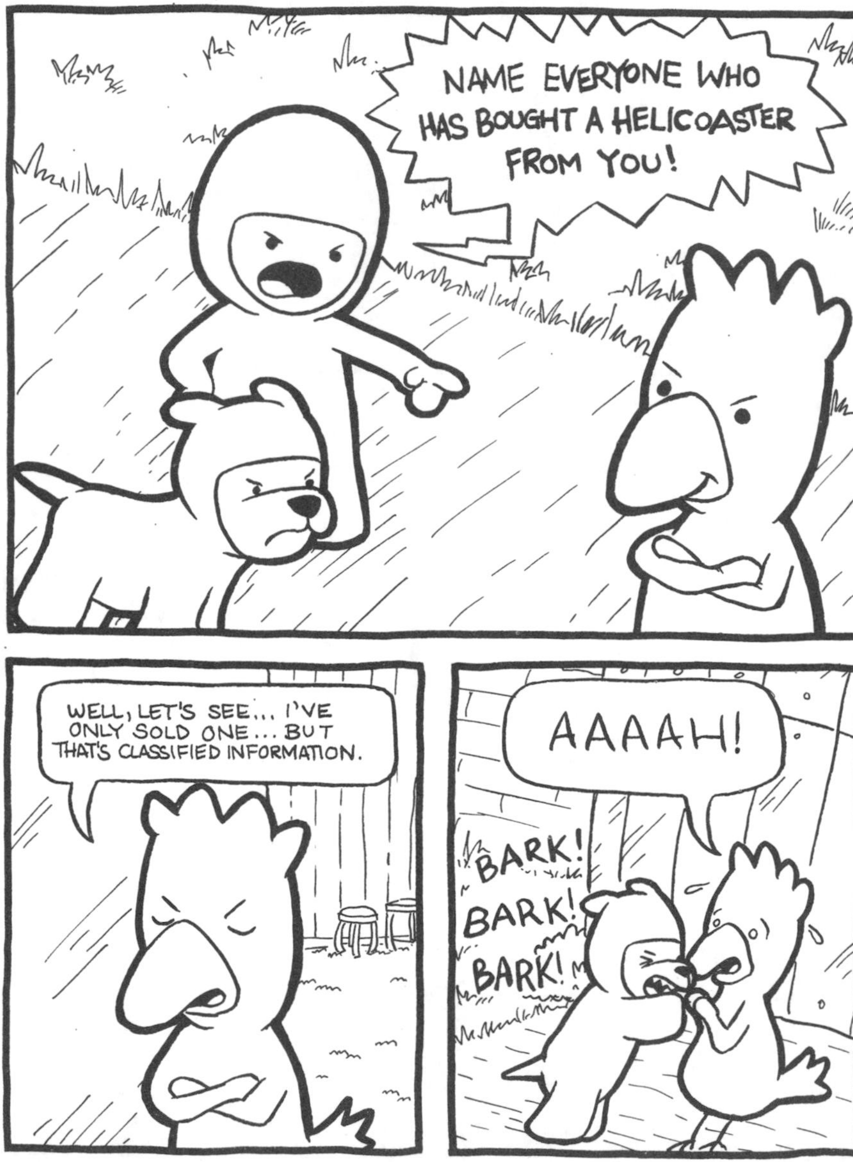
NAME EVERYONE WHO HAS BOUGHT A HELICOASTER FROM YOU!
WELL, LET'S SEE... I'VE ONLY SOLD ONE... BUT THAT'S CLASSIFIED INFORMATION.
AAAAH!
BARK!
BARK!
BARK!

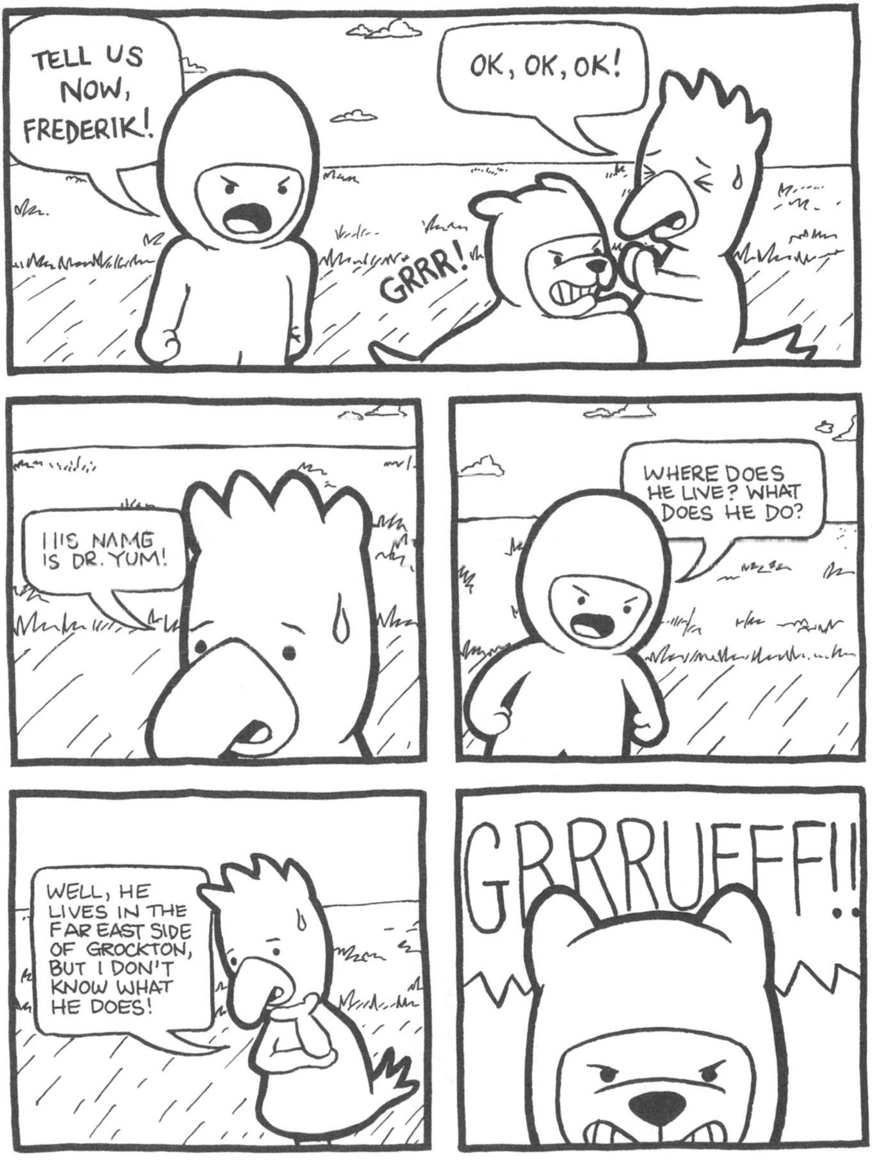
TELL US NOW, FREDERIK!
OK, OK, OK!
GRRR!
HIS NAME IS DR. YUM!
WHERE DOES HE LIVE? WHAT DOES HE DO?
WELL, HE LIVES IN THE FAR EAST SIDE OF GROCKTON, BUT I DON'T KNOW WHAT HE DOES!
GRRRUFFF!!

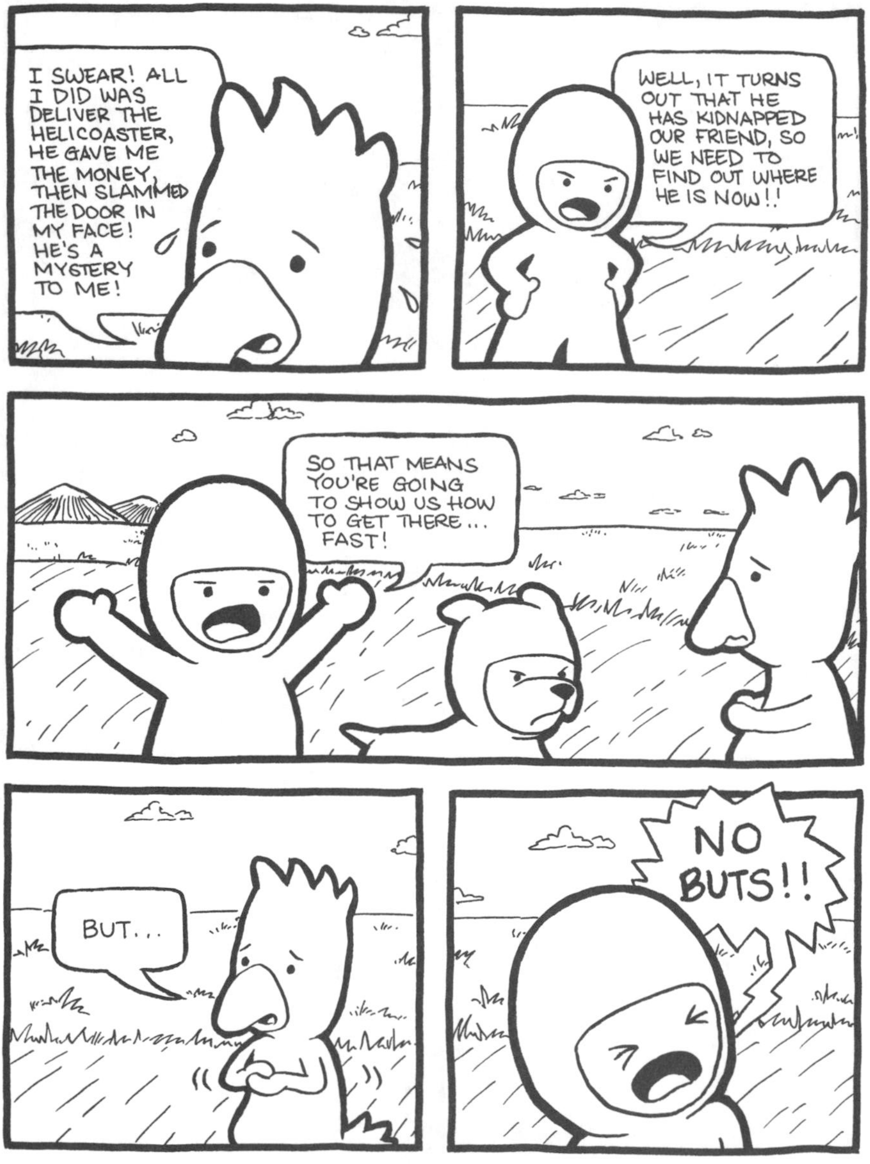
I SWEAR! ALL I DID WAS DELIVER THE HELICOASTER, HE GAVE ME THE MONEY, THEN SLAMMED THE DOOR IN MY FACE! HE'S A MYSTERY TO ME!
WELL, IT TURNS OUT THAT HE HAS KIDNAPPED OUR FRIEND, SO WE NEED TO FIND OUT WHERE HE IS NOW!!
SO THAT MEANS YOU'RE GOING TO SHOW US HOW TO GET THERE... FAST!
BUT...
NO BUTS!!

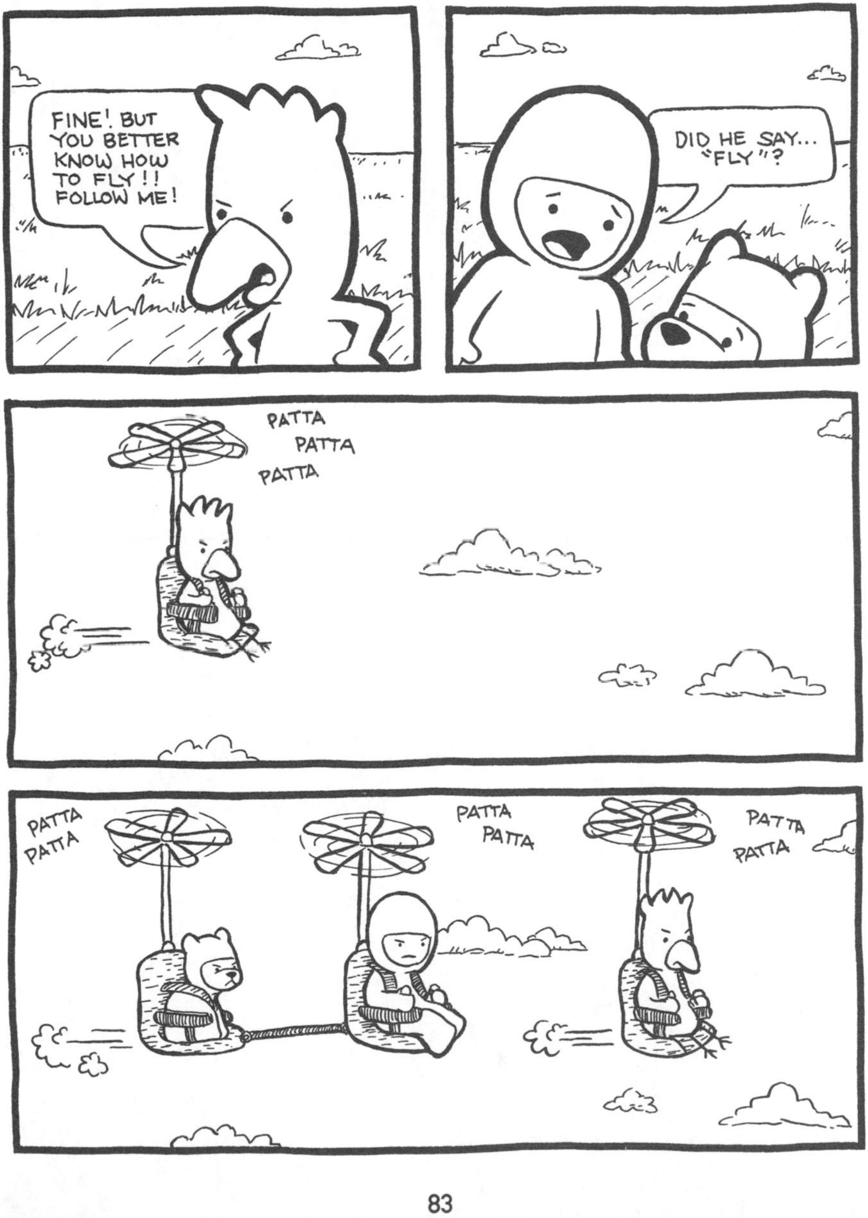
FINE! BUT YOU BETTER KNOW HOW TO FLY!! FOLLOW ME!
DID HE SAY... "FLY"?
PATTA
PATTA
PATTA
PATTA
PATTA
PATTA
PATTA
PATTA
PATTA

PART FIVE

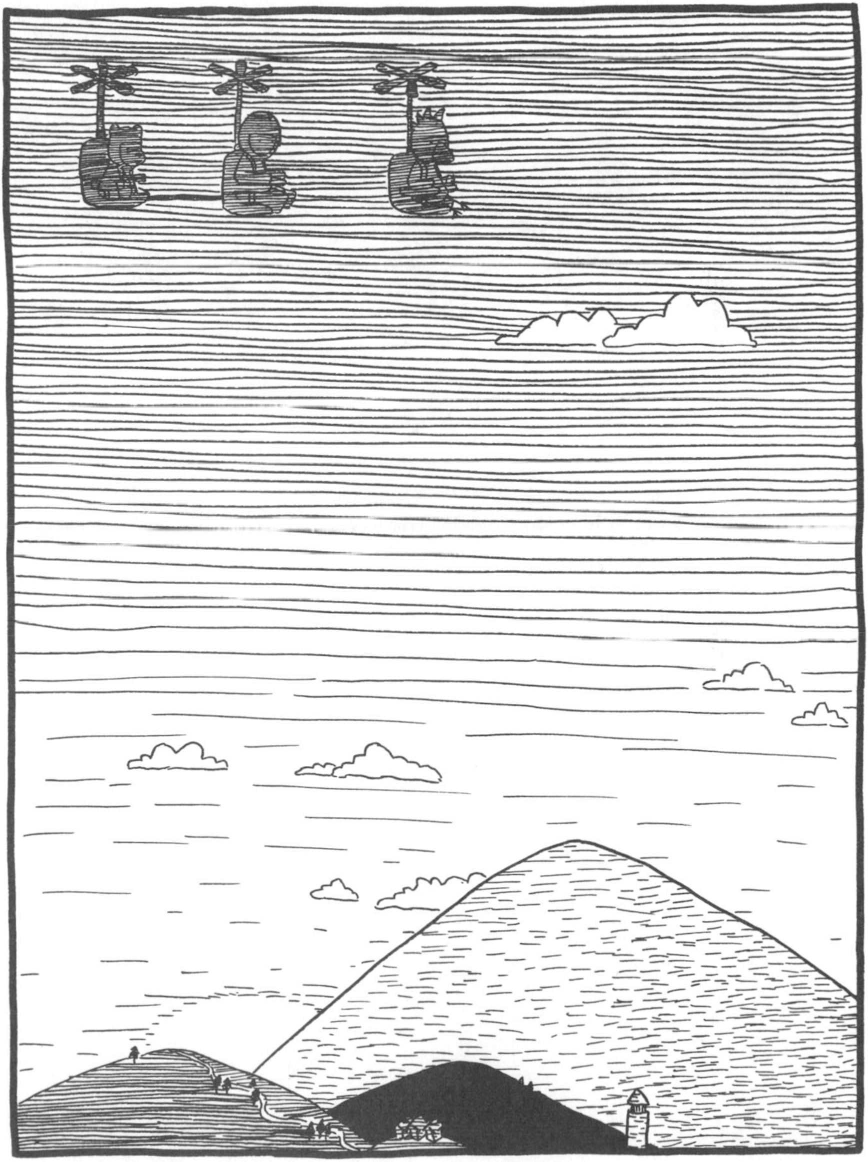

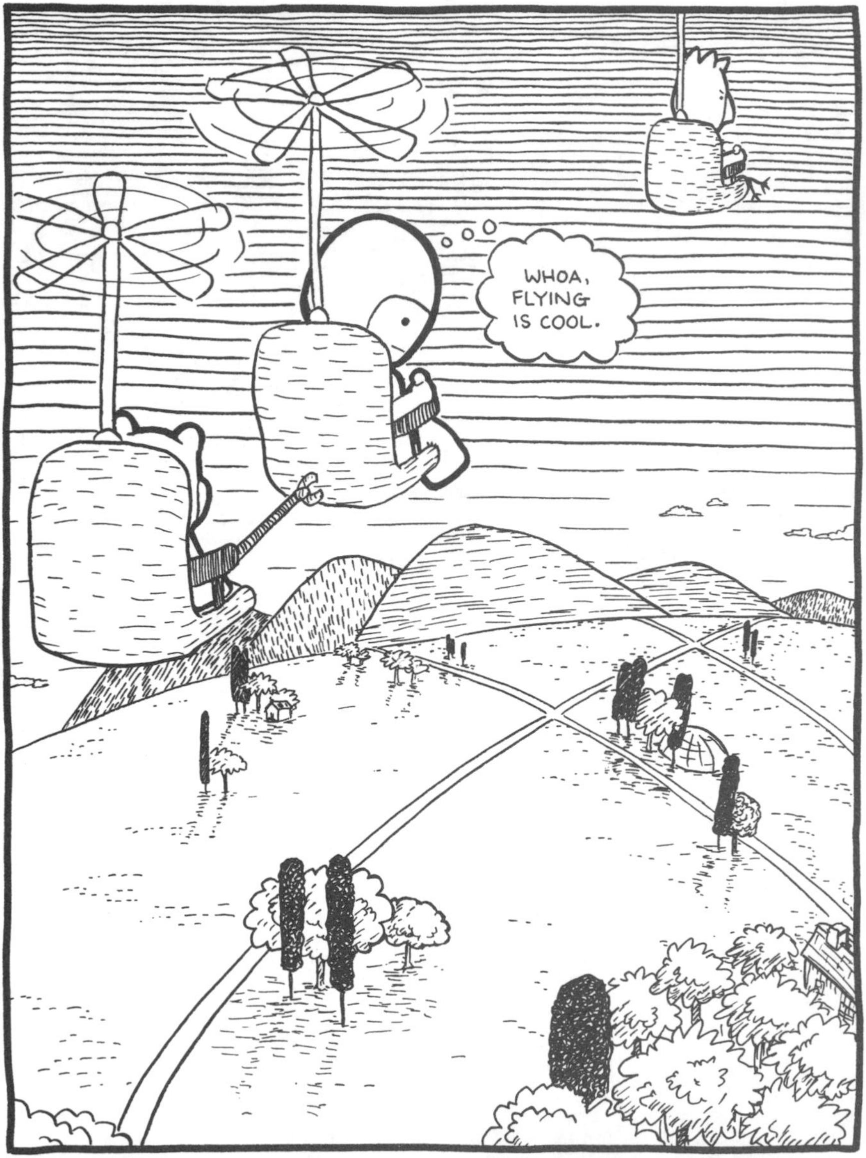
WHOA, FLYING IS COOL.

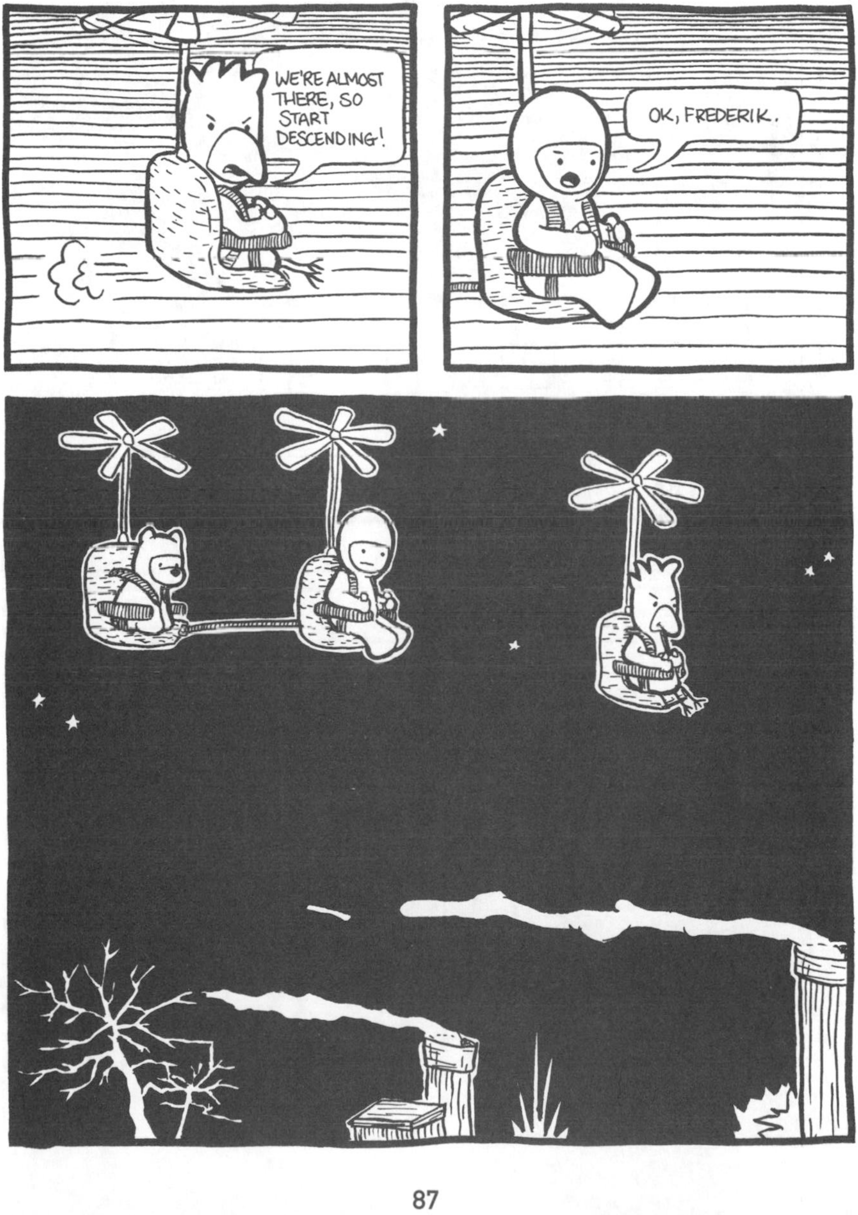
WE'RE ALMOST THERE, SO START DESCENDING!
OK, FREDERIK.

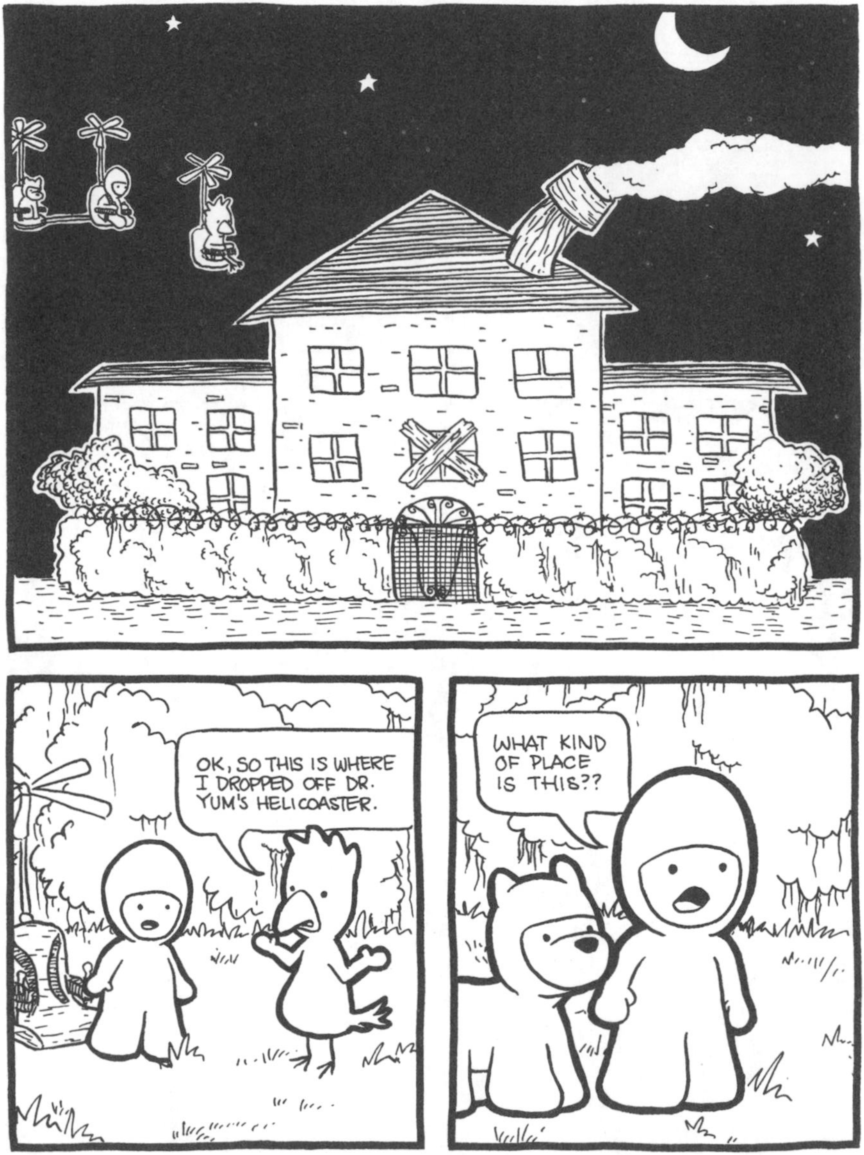
OK, SO THIS IS WHERE I DROPPED OFF DR. YUM'S HELICOASTER.
WHAT KIND OF PLACE IS THIS??

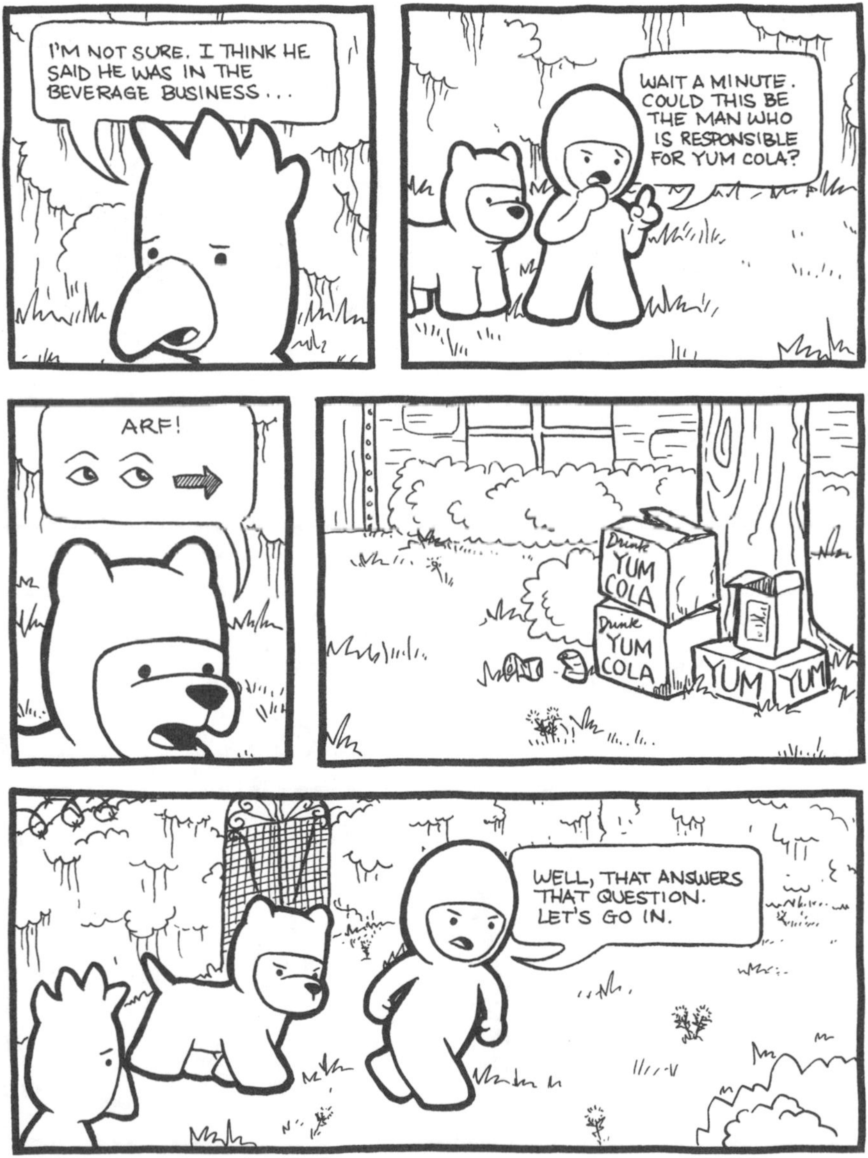
I'M NOT SURE. I THINK HE SAID HE WAS IN THE BEVERAGE BUSINESS...
WAIT A MINUTE. COULD THIS BE THE MAN WHO IS RESPONSIBLE FOR YUM COLA?
ARF!
Drink YUM COLA
Drink YUM COLA
YUM
YUM
WELL, THAT ANSWERS THAT QUESTION. LET'S GO IN.

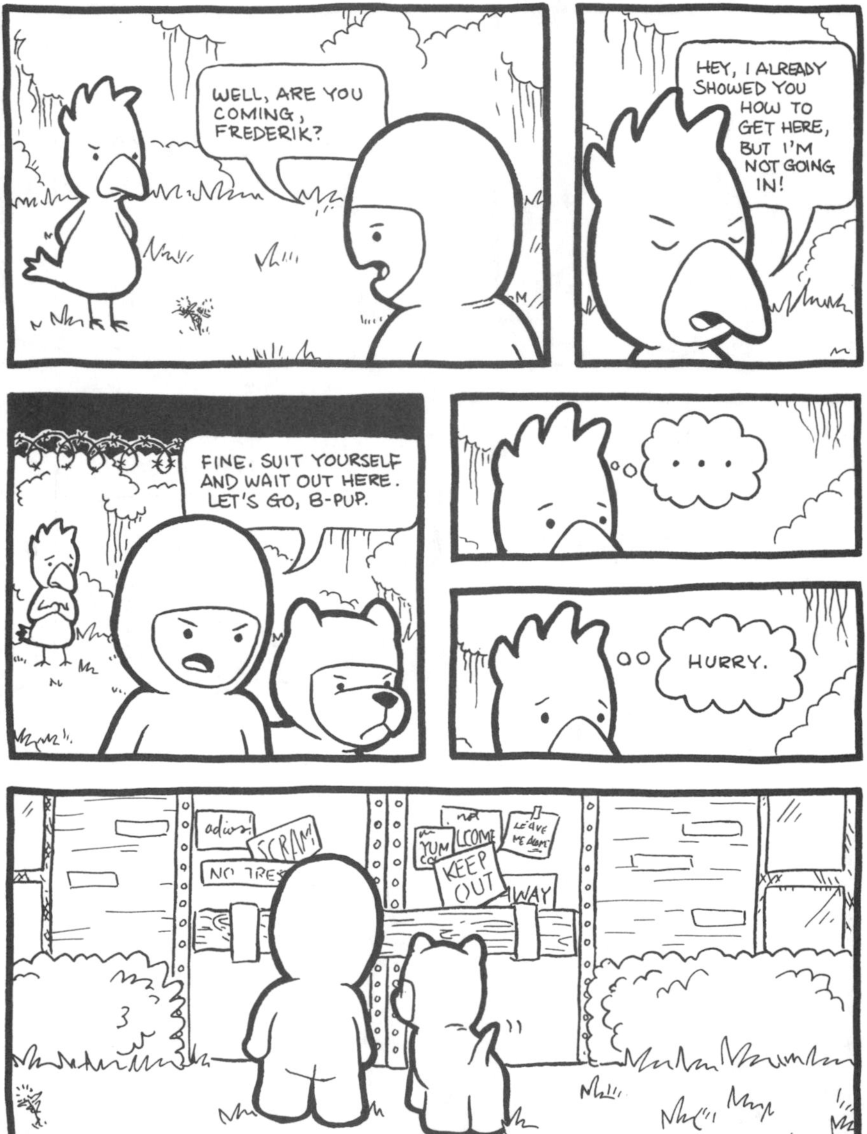
WELL, ARE YOU COMING, FREDERIK?
HEY, I ALREADY SHOWED YOU HOW TO GET HERE, BUT I'M NOT GOING IN!
FINE. SUIT YOURSELF AND WAIT OUT HERE. LET'S GO, B-PUP.
. . .
HURRY.
adios.
SCRAM!
KEEP OUT
LEAVE ME ALONE

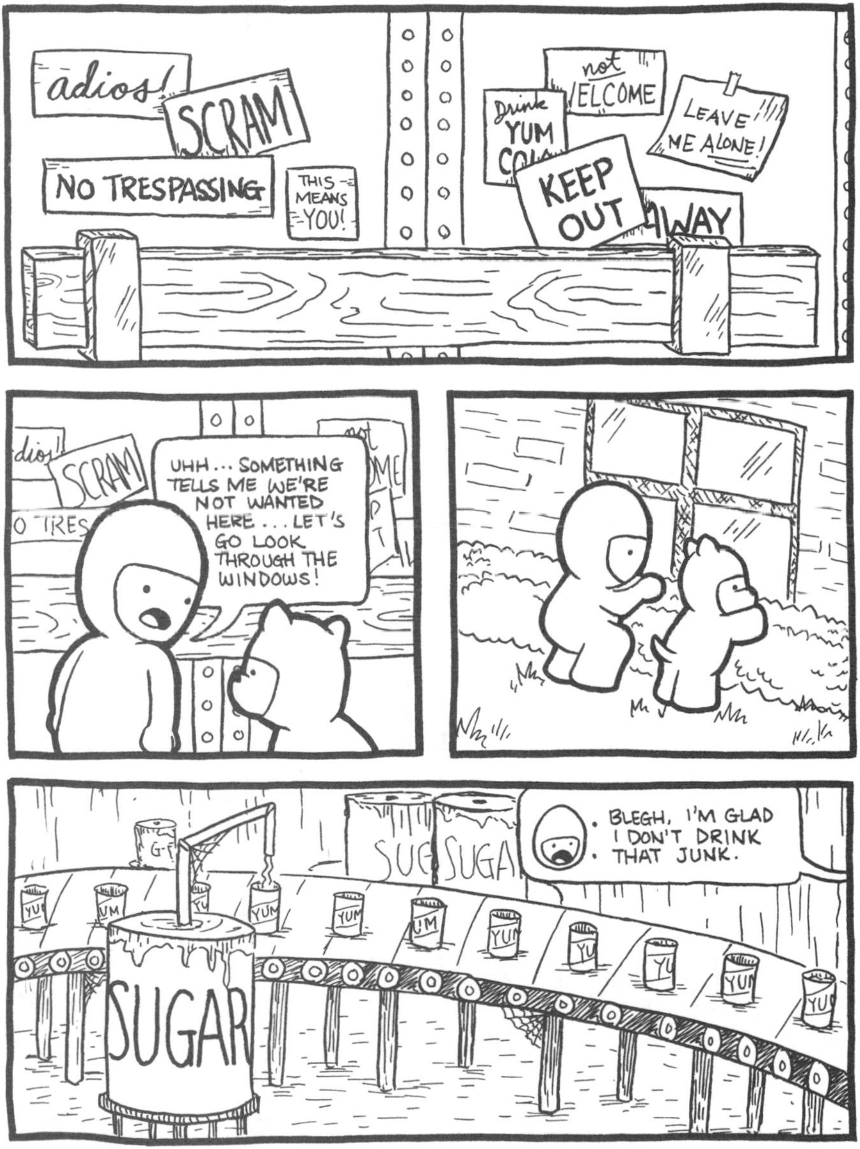
adios!
SCRAM
NO TRESPASSING
THIS MEANS YOU!
not WELCOME
Drink YUM
LEAVE ME ALONE!
KEEP OUT
UHH... SOMETHING TELLS ME WE'RE NOT WANTED HERE... LET'S GO LOOK THROUGH THE WINDOWS!
SUGAR
BLEGH, I'M GLAD I DON'T DRINK THAT JUNK.

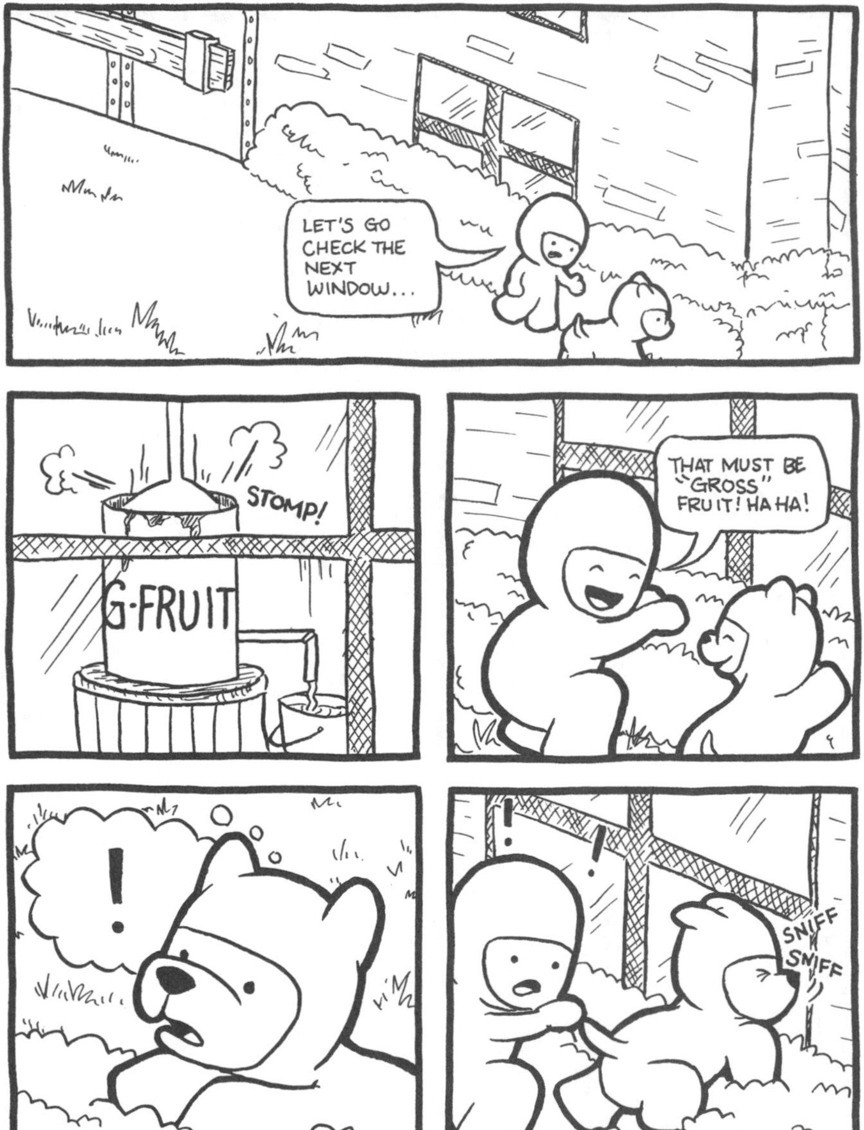
LET'S GO CHECK THE NEXT WINDOW...
G-FRUIT
STOMP!
THAT MUST BE "GROSS" FRUIT! HA HA!
!
!
!
SNIFF SNIFF

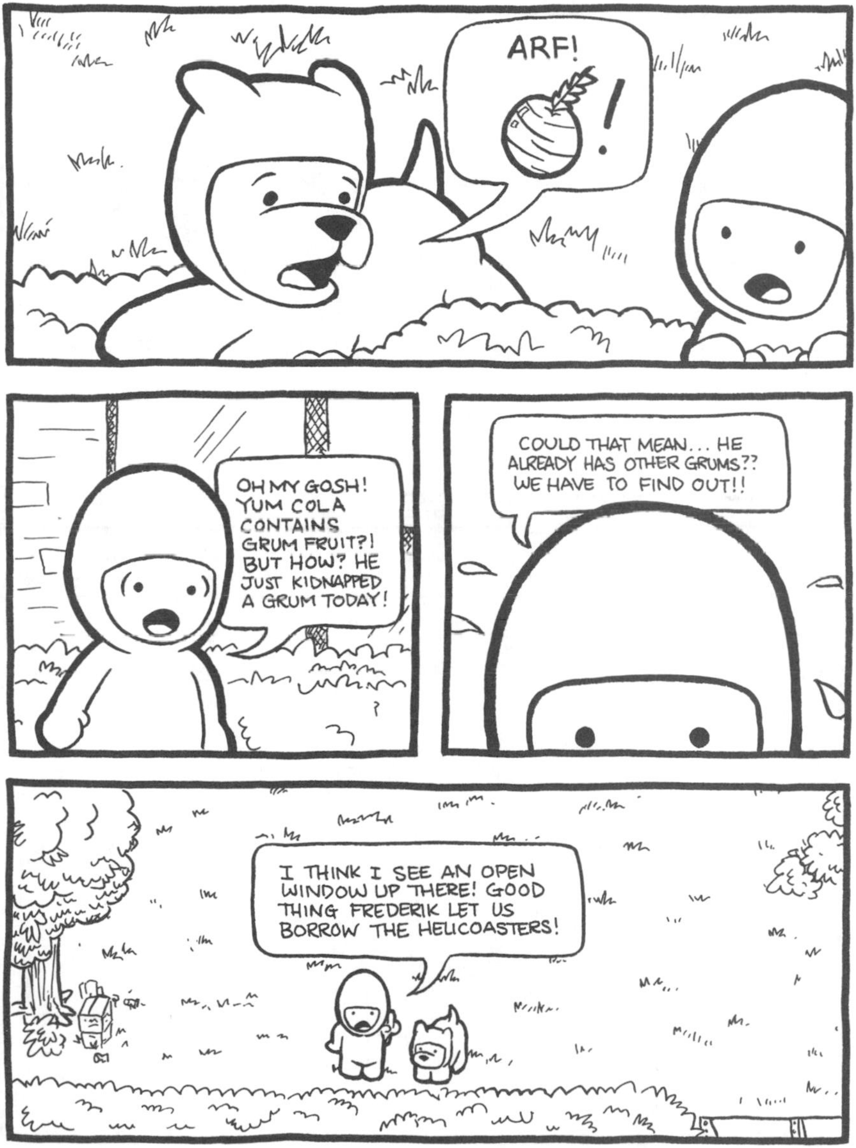
ARF!
!
OH MY GOSH! YUM COLA CONTAINS GRUM FRUIT?! BUT HOW? HE JUST KIDNAPPED A GRUM TODAY!
COULD THAT MEAN... HE ALREADY HAS OTHER GRUMS?? WE HAVE TO FIND OUT!!
I THINK I SEE AN OPEN WINDOW UP THERE! GOOD THING FREDERIK LET US BORROW THE HELICOASTERS!

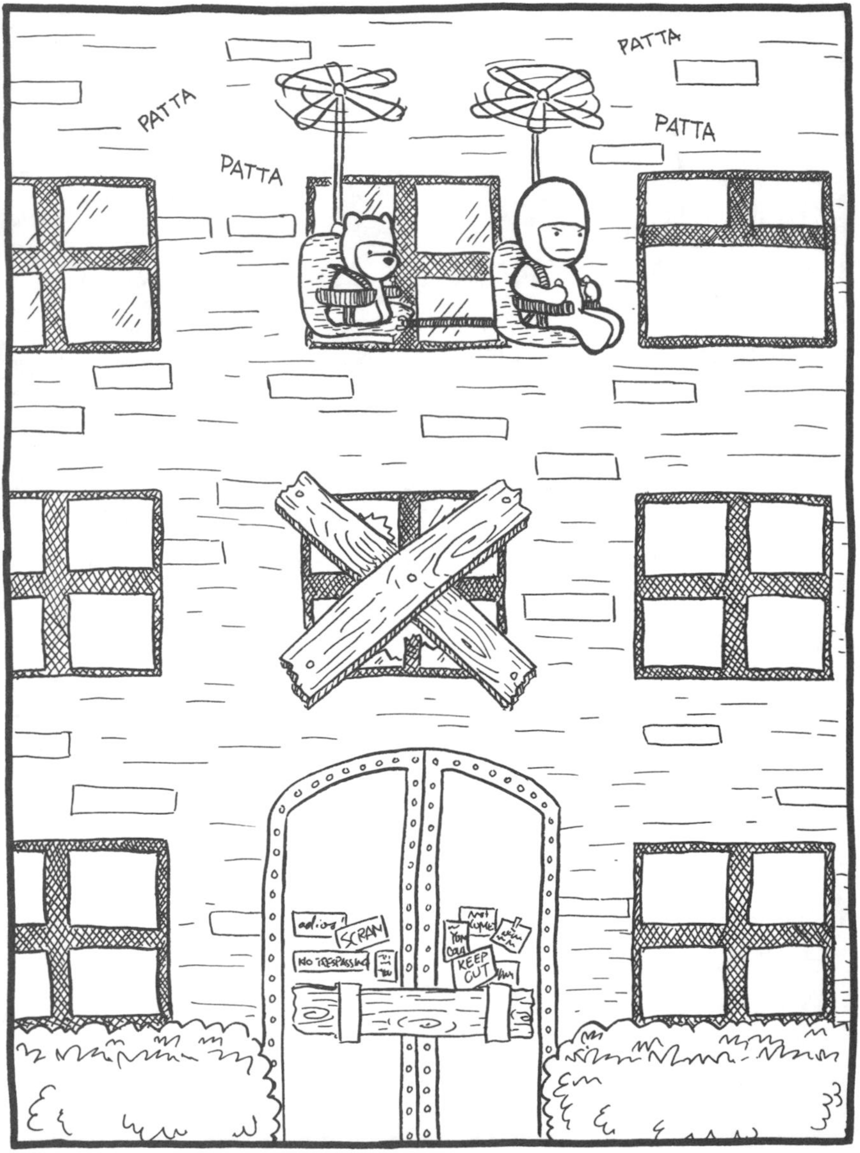
PATTA
PATTA
PATTA
PATTA
adios!
SCRAM
NO TRESPASSING
KEEP OUT

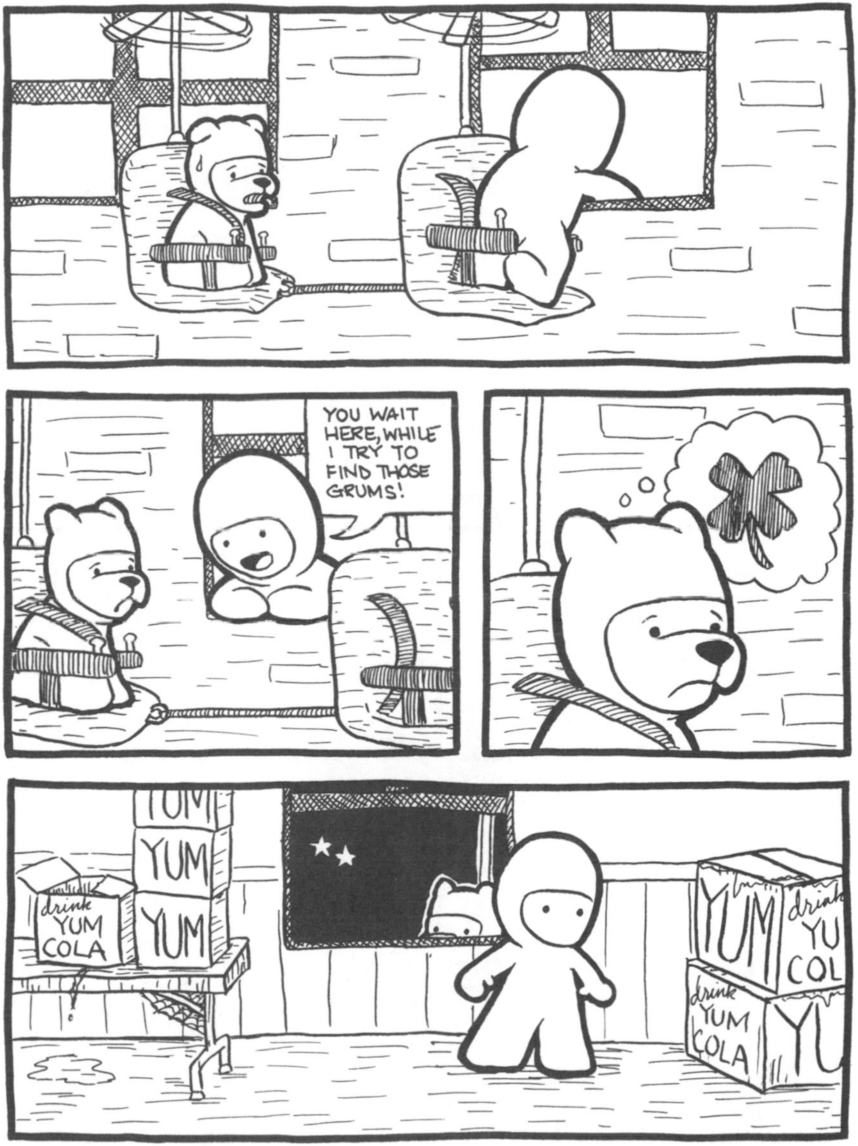
YOU WAIT HERE, WHILE I TRY TO FIND THOSE GRUMS!
YUM
YUM
YUM
drink YUM COLA
YUM
drink YU COL
drink YUM COLA
YU

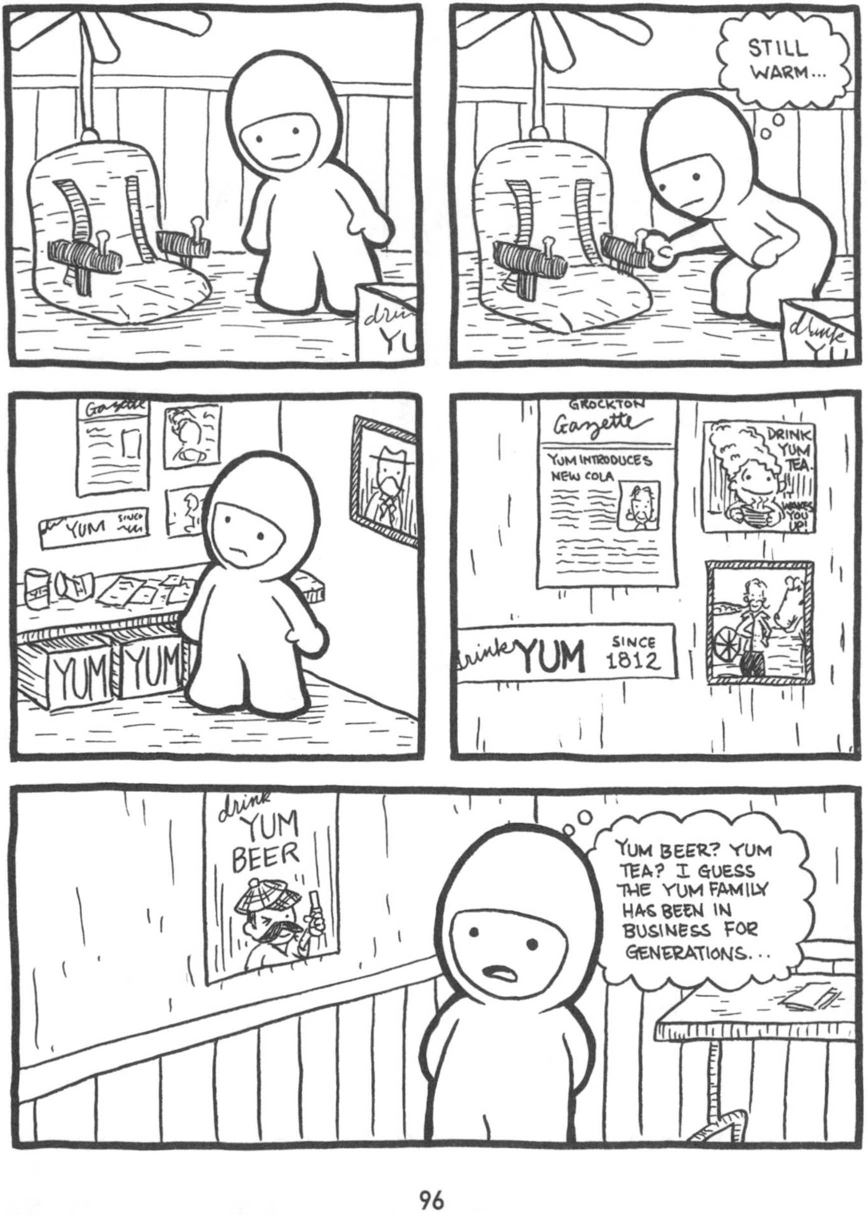
STILL WARM...
Gazette
YUM
YUM YUM
GROCKTON Gazette
YUM INTRODUCES NEW COLA
DRINK YUM TEA. IT WAKES YOU UP!
drink YUM SINCE 1812
drink YUM BEER
YUM BEER? YUM TEA? I GUESS THE YUM FAMILY HAS BEEN IN BUSINESS FOR GENERATIONS...

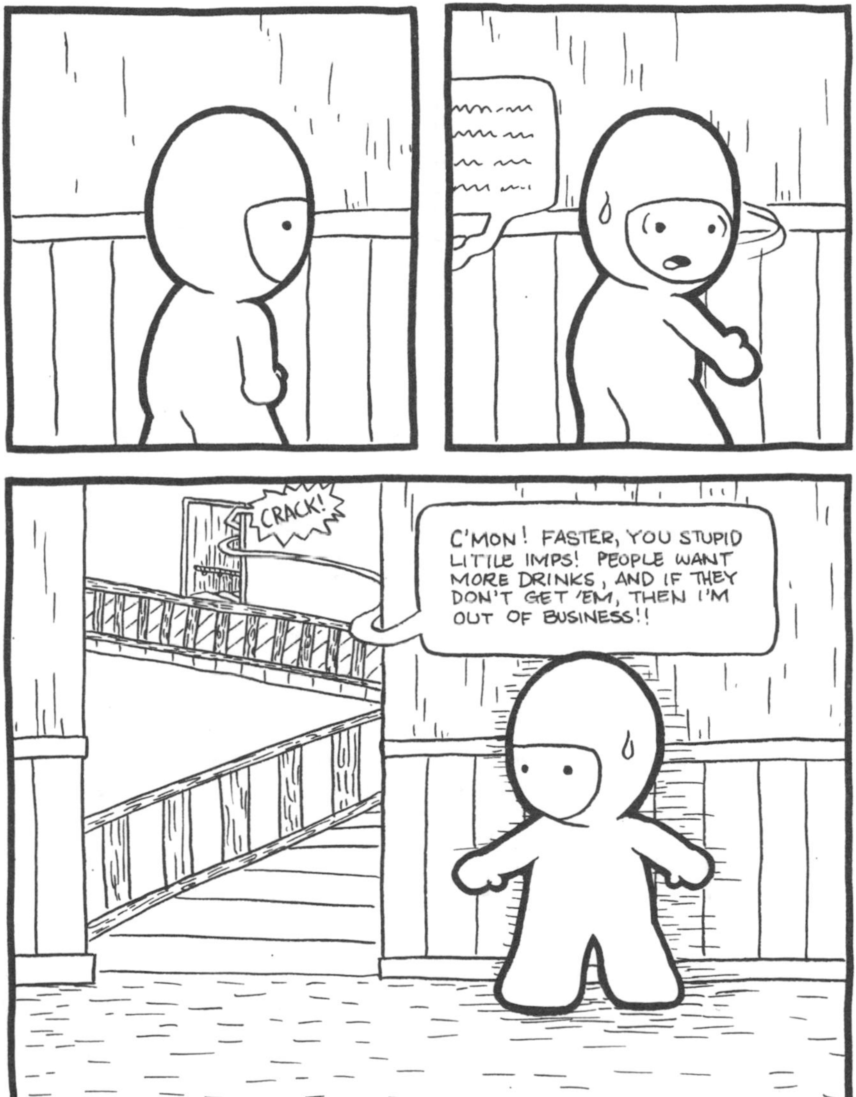
CRACK!
C'MON! FASTER, YOU STUPID LITTLE IMPS! PEOPLE WANT MORE DRINKS, AND IF THEY DON'T GET 'EM, THEN I'M OUT OF BUSINESS!!

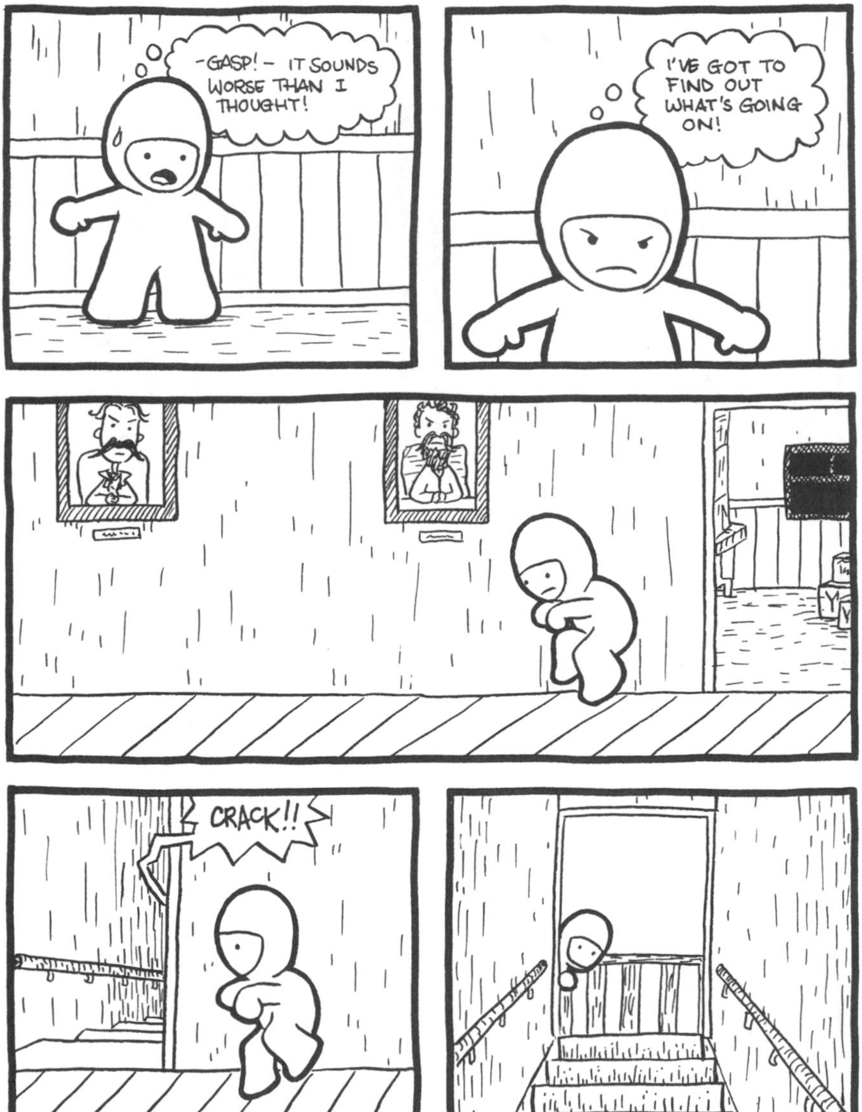
-GASP! - IT SOUNDS WORSE THAN I THOUGHT!
I'VE GOT TO FIND OUT WHAT'S GOING ON!
CRACK!!

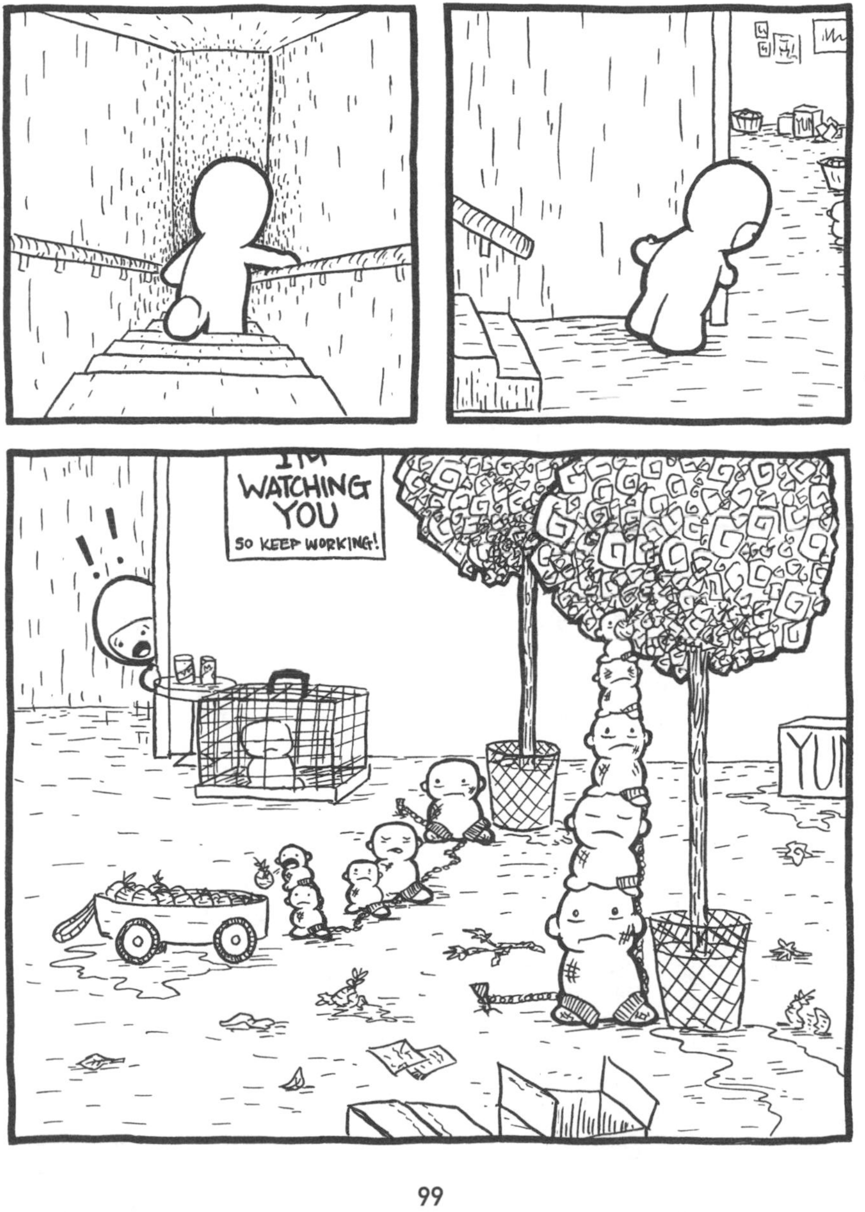
WATCHING YOU
SO KEEP WORKING!
!!

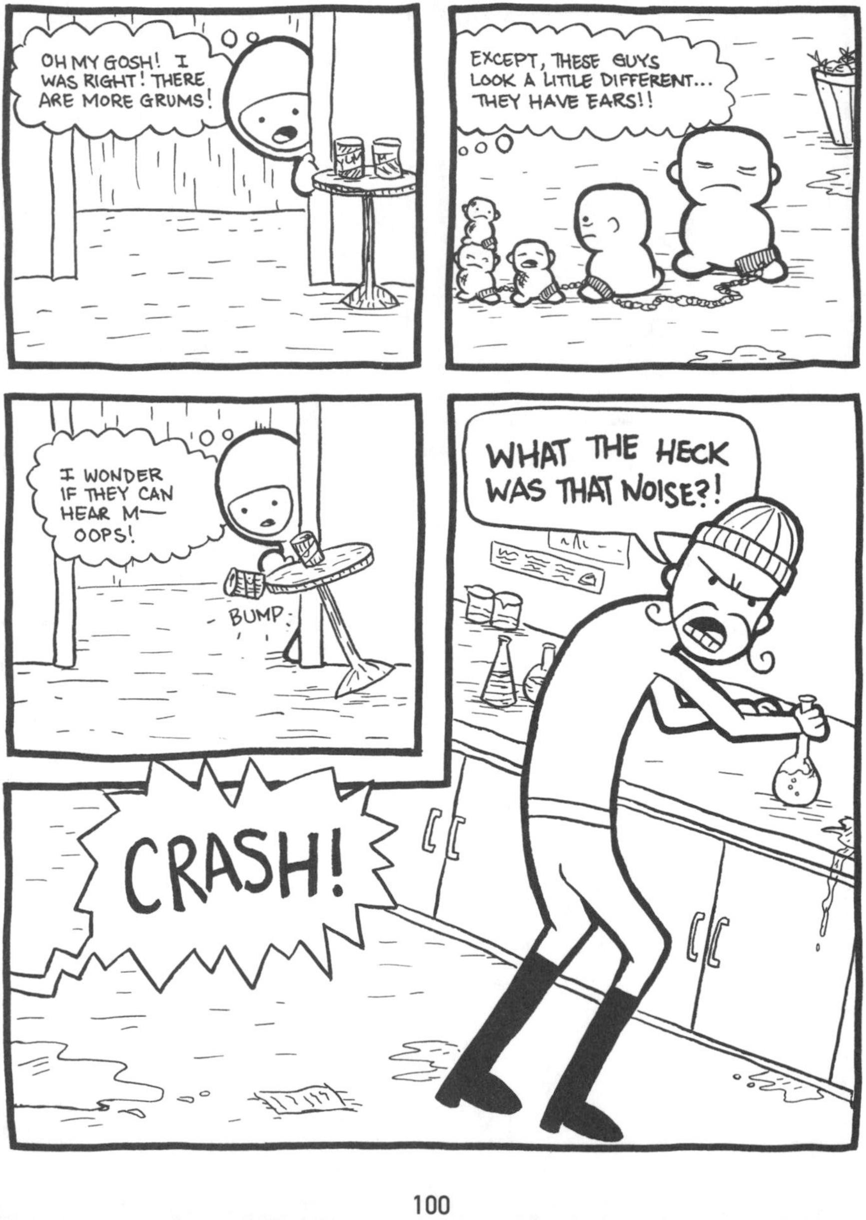
OH MY GOSH! I WAS RIGHT! THERE ARE MORE GRUMS!
EXCEPT, THESE GUYS LOOK A LITTLE DIFFERENT... THEY HAVE EARS!!
I WONDER IF THEY CAN HEAR M— OOPS!
BUMP
WHAT THE HECK WAS THAT NOISE?!
CRASH!

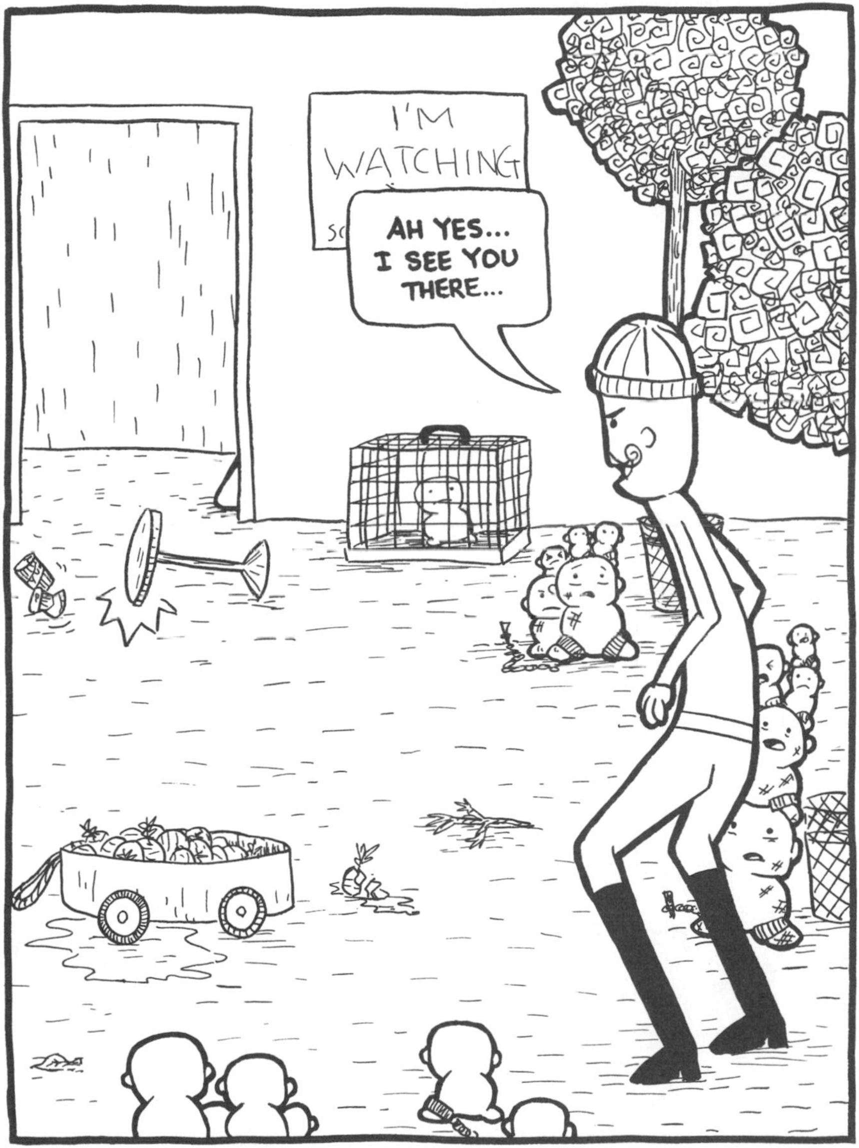
I'M
WATCHING
AH YES...
I SEE YOU
THERE...

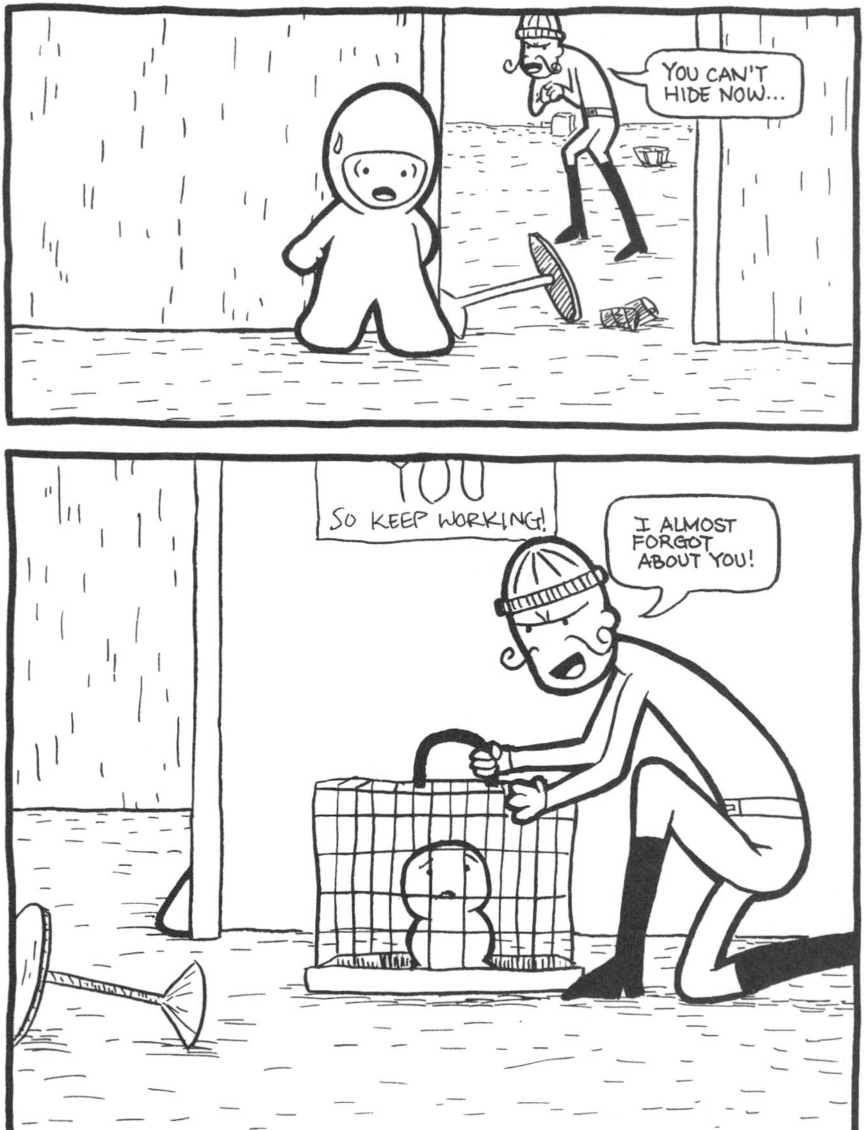
YOU CAN'T HIDE NOW...
YOU
SO KEEP WORKING!
I ALMOST FORGOT ABOUT YOU!

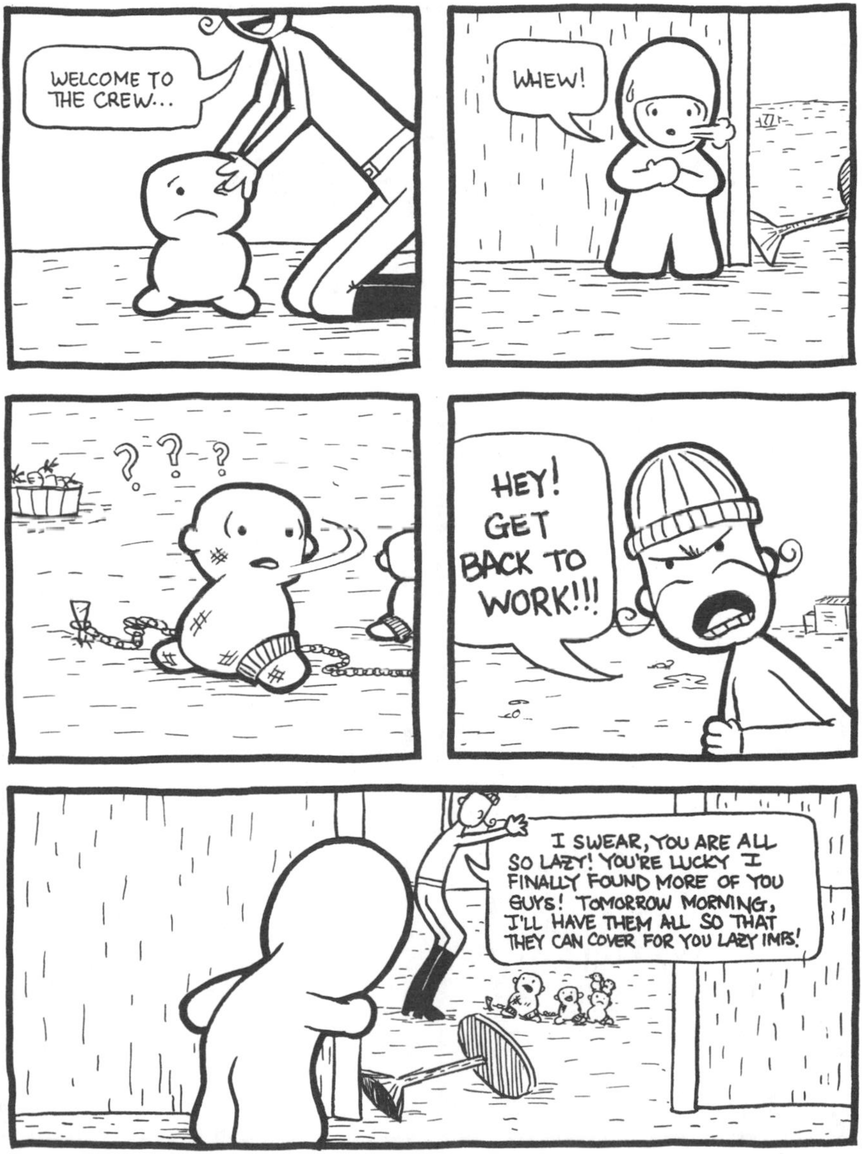
WELCOME TO THE CREW...
WHEW!
HEY! GET BACK TO WORK!!!
I SWEAR, YOU ARE ALL SO LAZY! YOU'RE LUCKY I FINALLY FOUND MORE OF YOU GUYS! TOMORROW MORNING, I'LL HAVE THEM ALL SO THAT THEY CAN COVER FOR YOU LAZY IMPS!

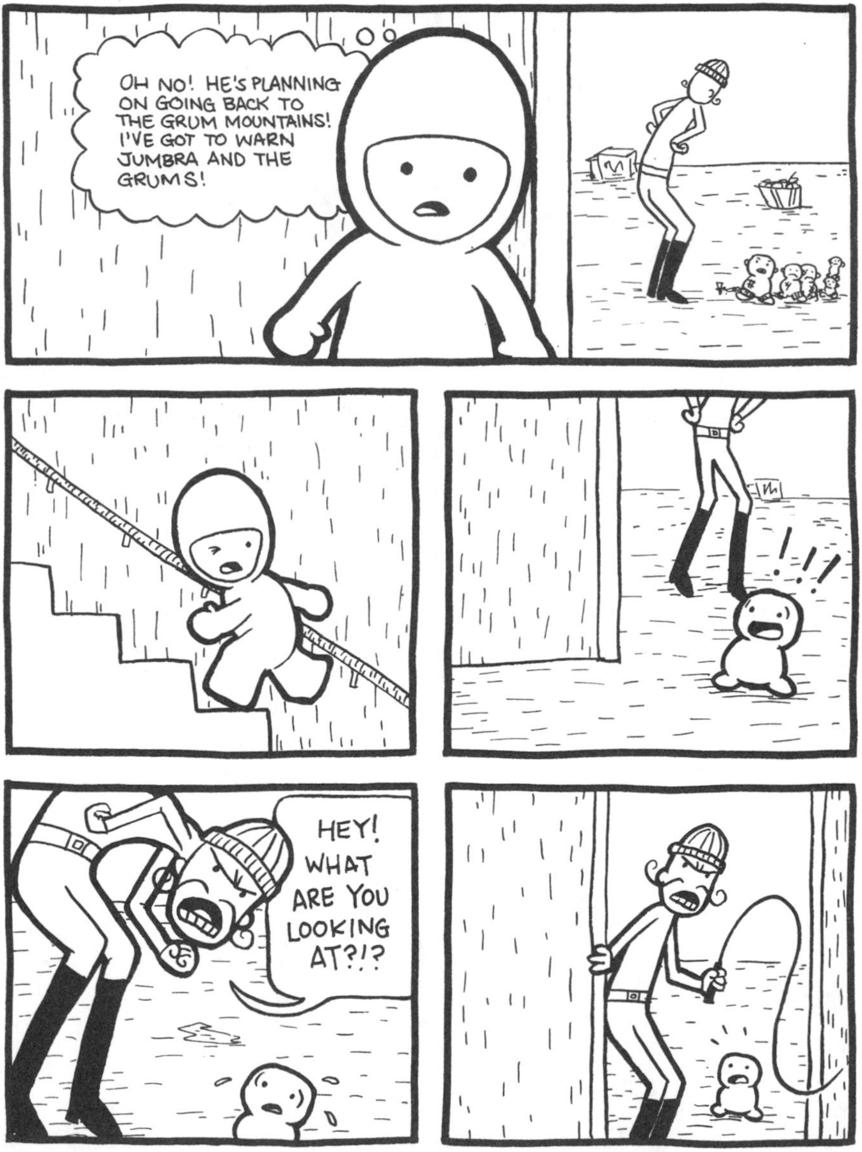
OH NO! HE'S PLANNING ON GOING BACK TO THE GRUM MOUNTAINS! I'VE GOT TO WARN JUMBRA AND THE GRUMS!
!!!
HEY! WHAT ARE YOU LOOKING AT?!?

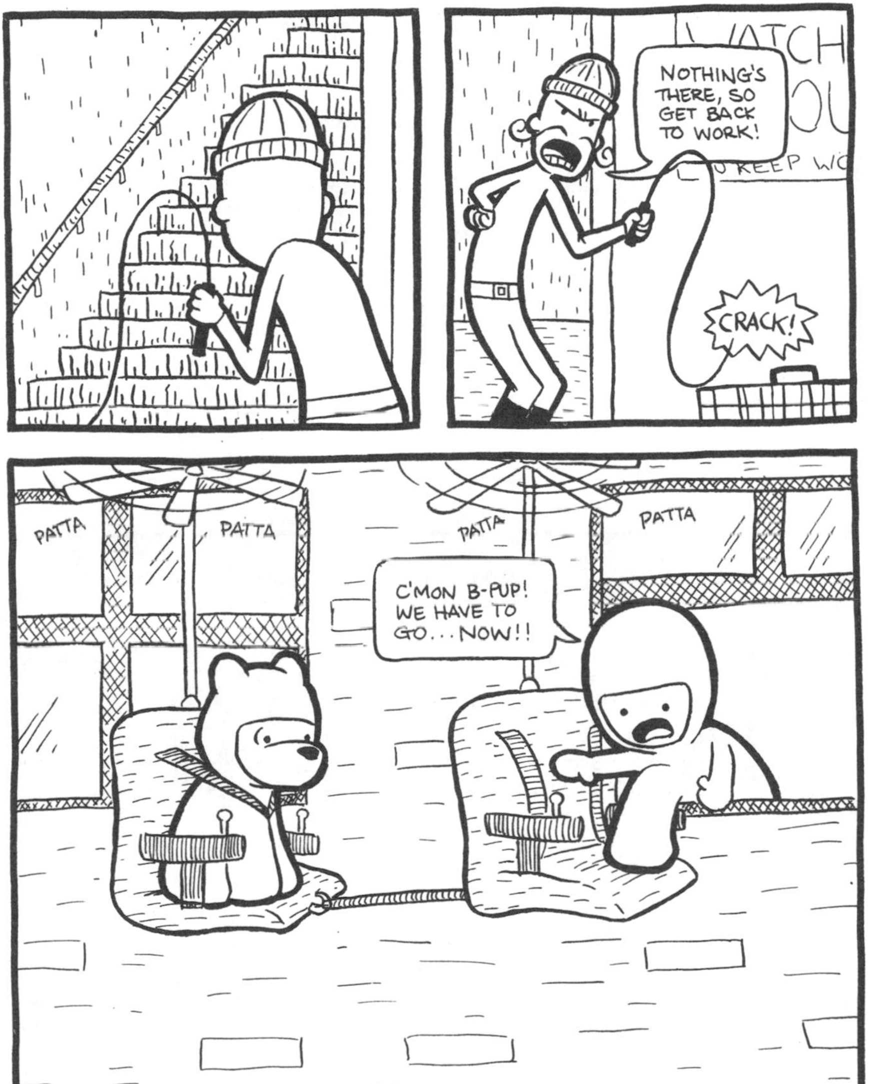
NOTHING'S THERE, SO GET BACK TO WORK!
CRACK!
PATTA
PATTA
PATTA
PATTA
C'MON B-PUP! WE HAVE TO GO... NOW!!

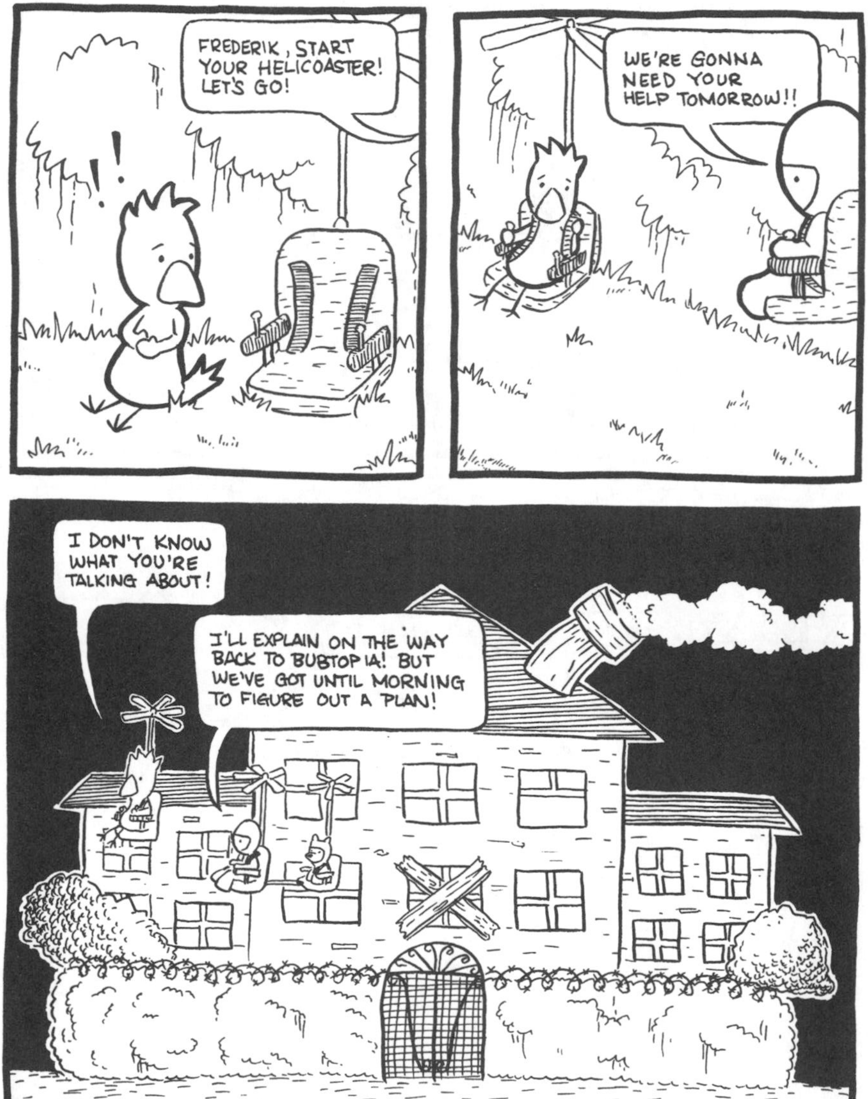
FREDERIK, START YOUR HELICOASTER! LET'S GO!
!!
WE'RE GONNA NEED YOUR HELP TOMORROW!!
I DON'T KNOW WHAT YOU'RE TALKING ABOUT!
I'LL EXPLAIN ON THE WAY BACK TO BUBTOPIA! BUT WE'VE GOT UNTIL MORNING TO FIGURE OUT A PLAN!

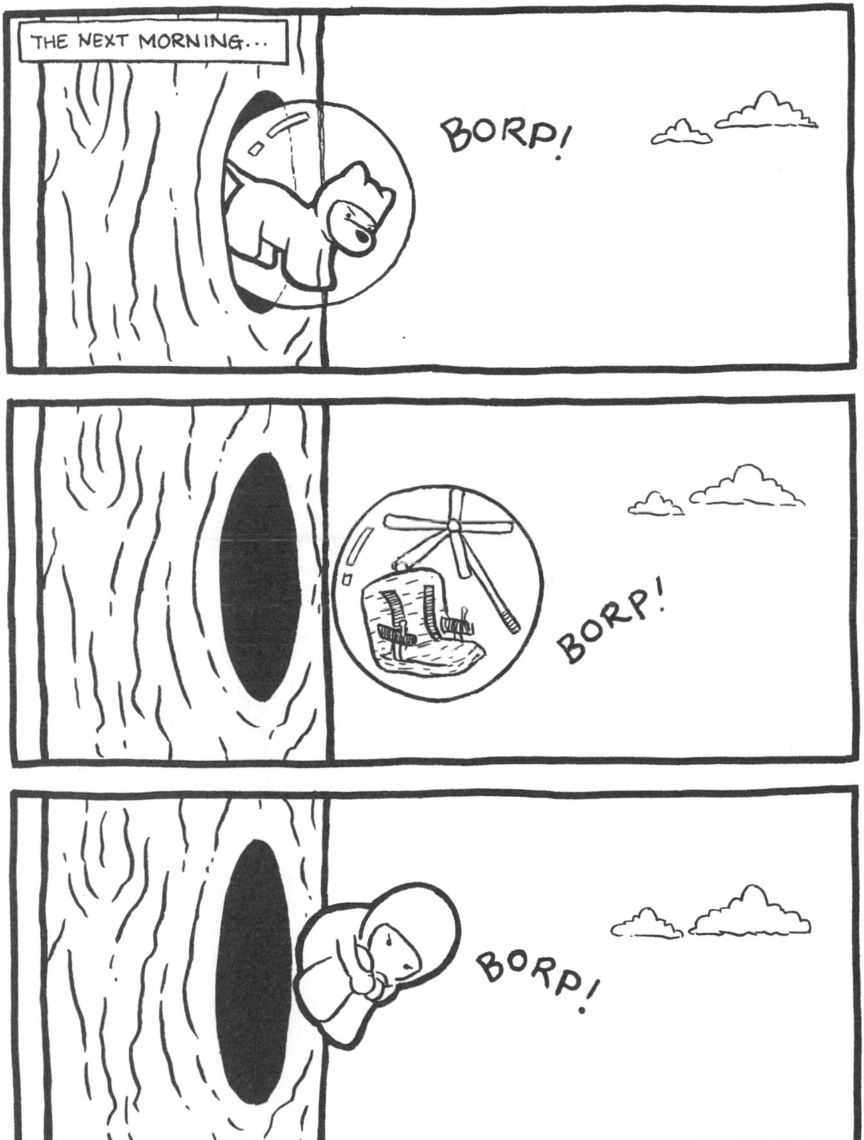
THE NEXT MORNING...
BORP!
BORP!
BORP!

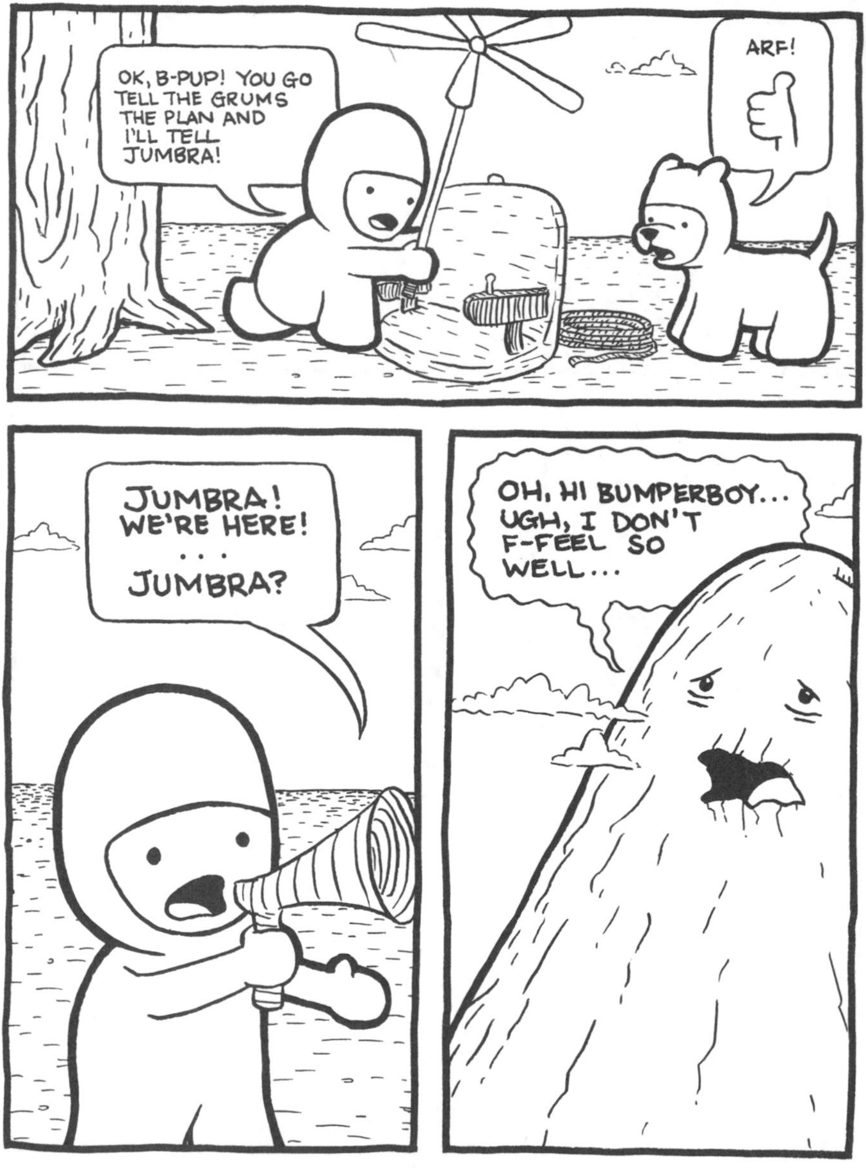
OK, B-PUP! YOU GO TELL THE GRUMS THE PLAN AND I'LL TELL JUMBRA!
ARF!
JUMBRA! WE'RE HERE! . . . JUMBRA?
OH, HI BUMPERBOY... UGH, I DON'T F-FEEL SO WELL...

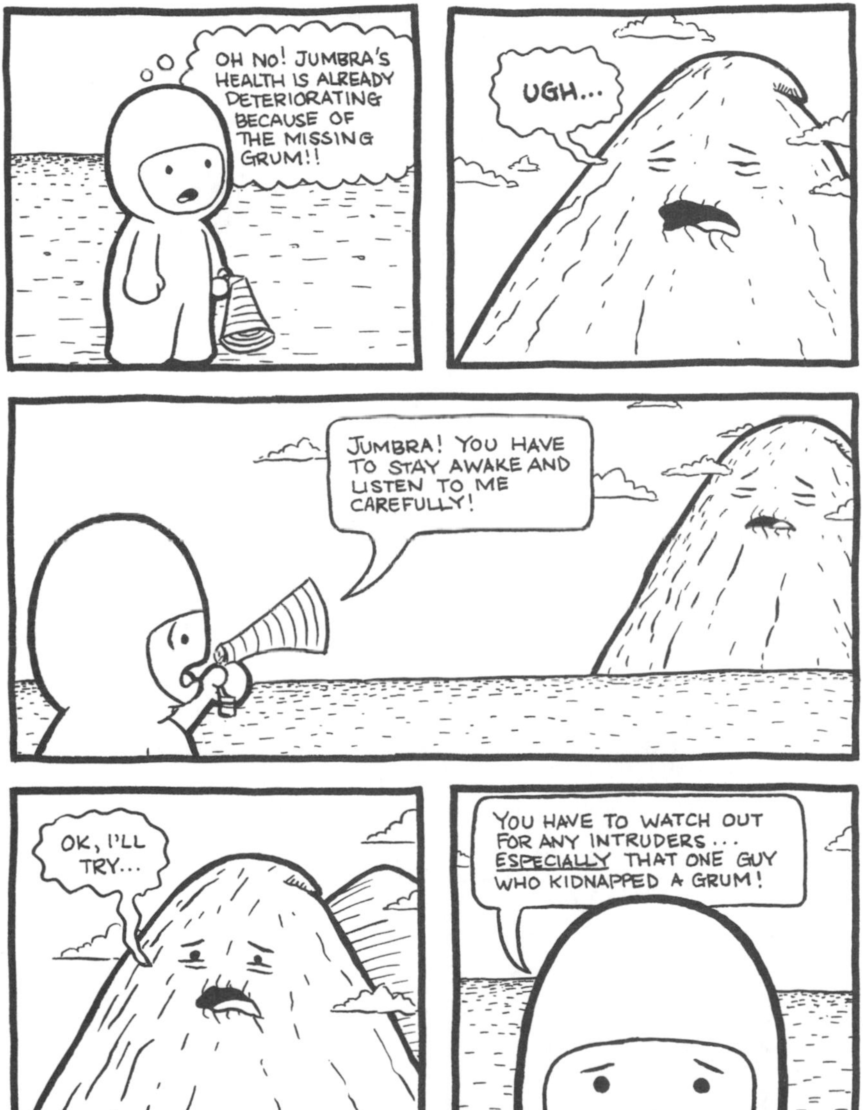
OH NO! JUMBRA'S HEALTH IS ALREADY DETERIORATING BECAUSE OF THE MISSING GRUM!!
UGH...
JUMBRA! YOU HAVE TO STAY AWAKE AND LISTEN TO ME CAREFULLY!
OK, I'LL TRY...
YOU HAVE TO WATCH OUT FOR ANY INTRUDERS... ESPECIALLY THAT ONE GUY WHO KIDNAPPED A GRUM!

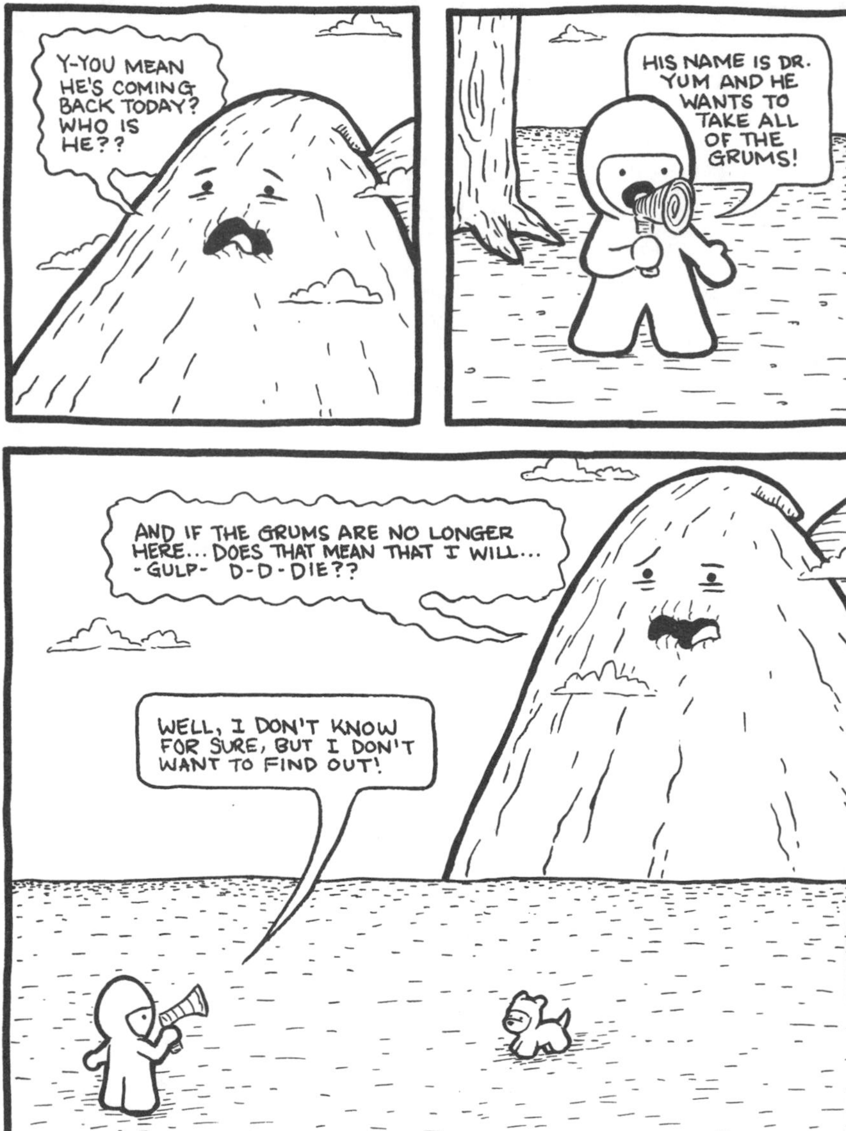
Y-YOU MEAN HE'S COMING BACK TODAY? WHO IS HE??
HIS NAME IS DR. YUM AND HE WANTS TO TAKE ALL OF THE GRUMS!
AND IF THE GRUMS ARE NO LONGER HERE... DOES THAT MEAN THAT I WILL... -GULP- D-D-DIE??
WELL, I DON'T KNOW FOR SURE, BUT I DON'T WANT TO FIND OUT!

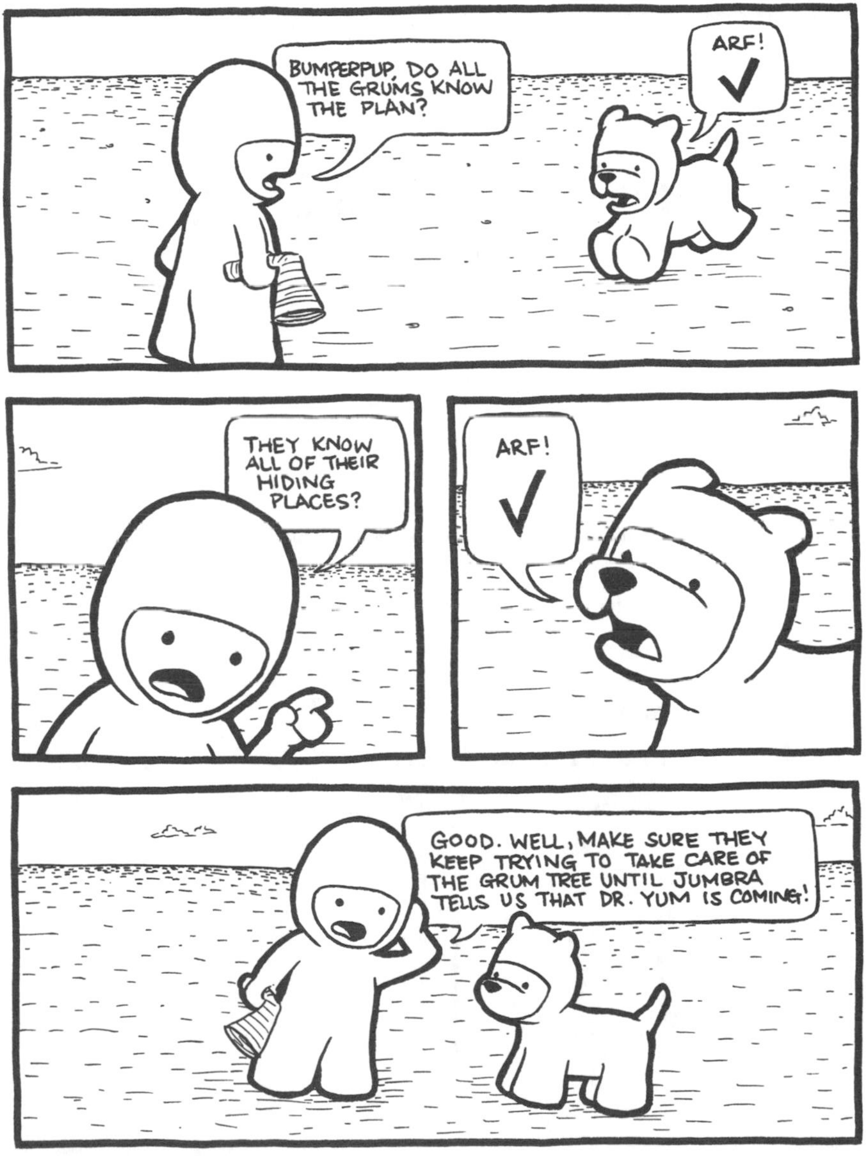
BUMPERPUP, DO ALL THE GRUMS KNOW THE PLAN?
ARF! ✓
THEY KNOW ALL OF THEIR HIDING PLACES?
ARF! ✓
GOOD. WELL, MAKE SURE THEY KEEP TRYING TO TAKE CARE OF THE GRUM TREE UNTIL JUMBRA TELLS US THAT DR. YUM IS COMING!

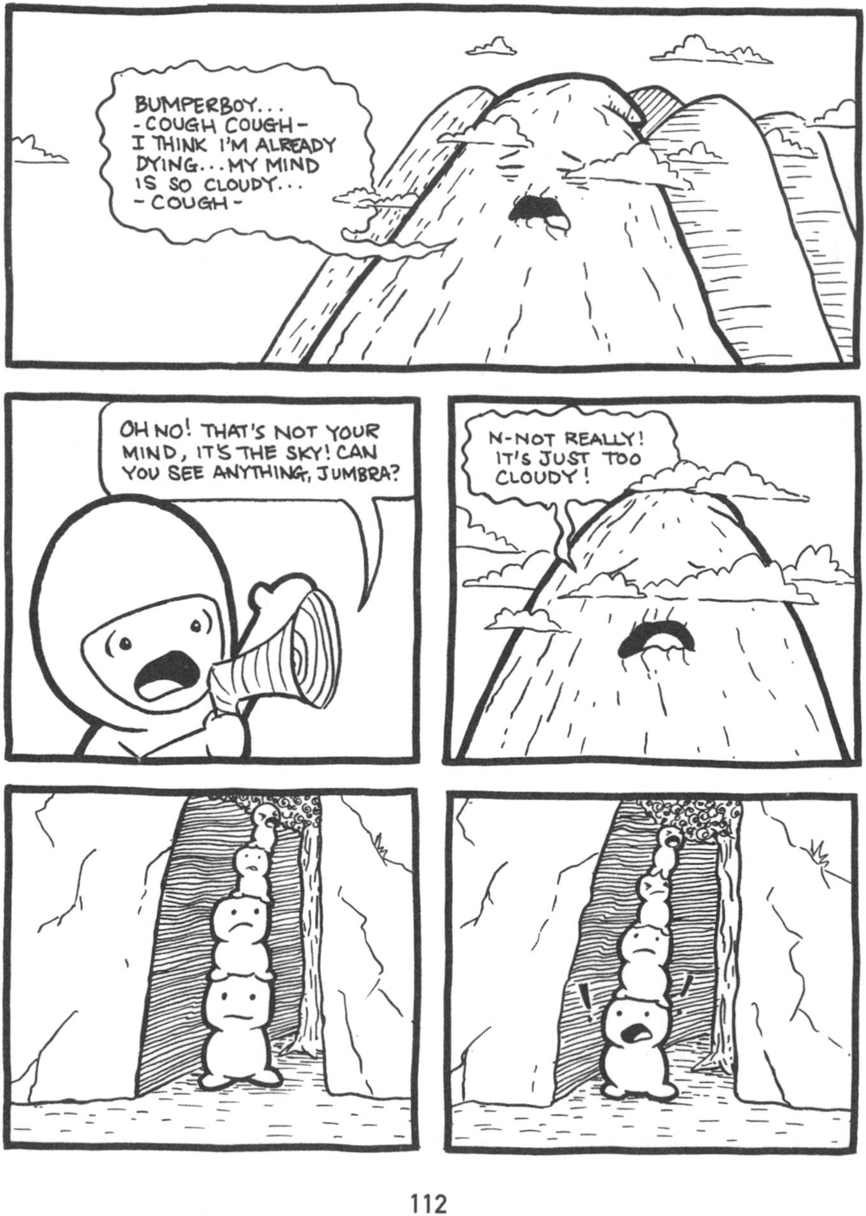
BUMPERBOY... -COUGH COUGH- I THINK I'M ALREADY DYING...MY MIND IS SO CLOUDY... -COUGH-
OH NO! THAT'S NOT YOUR MIND, IT'S THE SKY! CAN YOU SEE ANYTHING, JUMBRA?
N-NOT REALLY! IT'S JUST TOO CLOUDY!
!
!

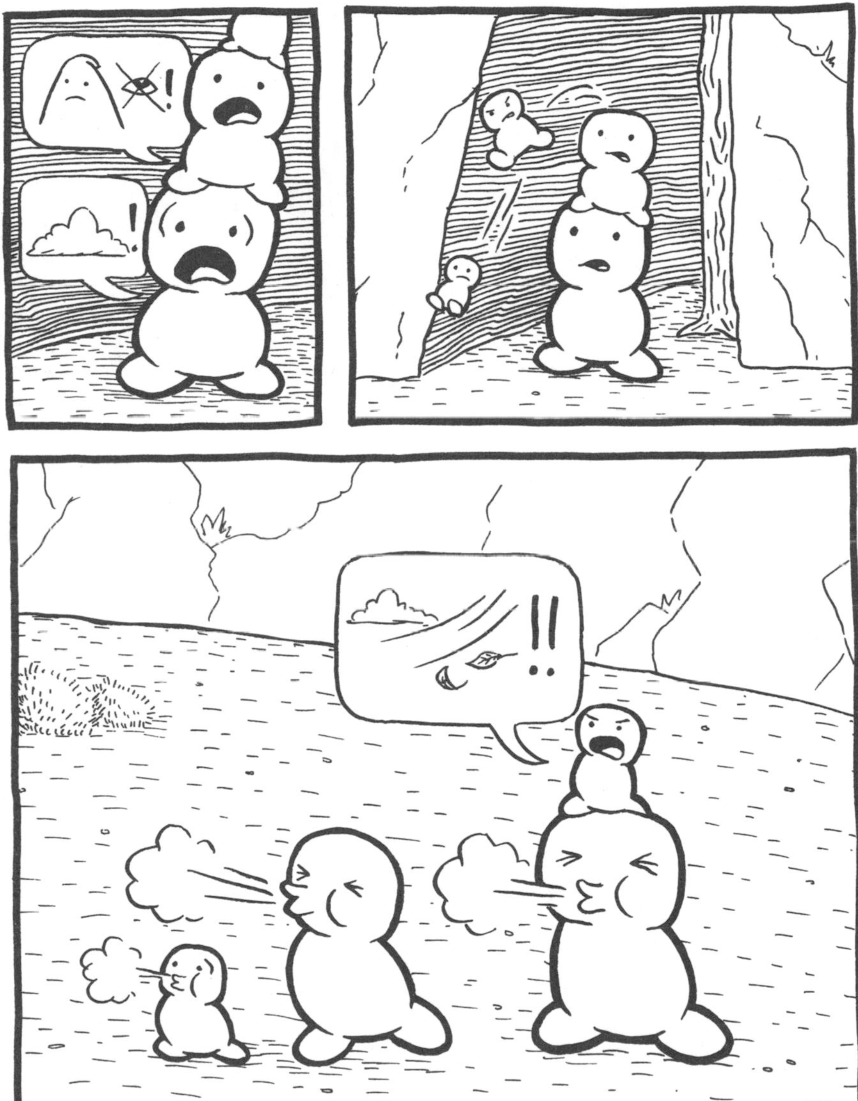
!
!
!!

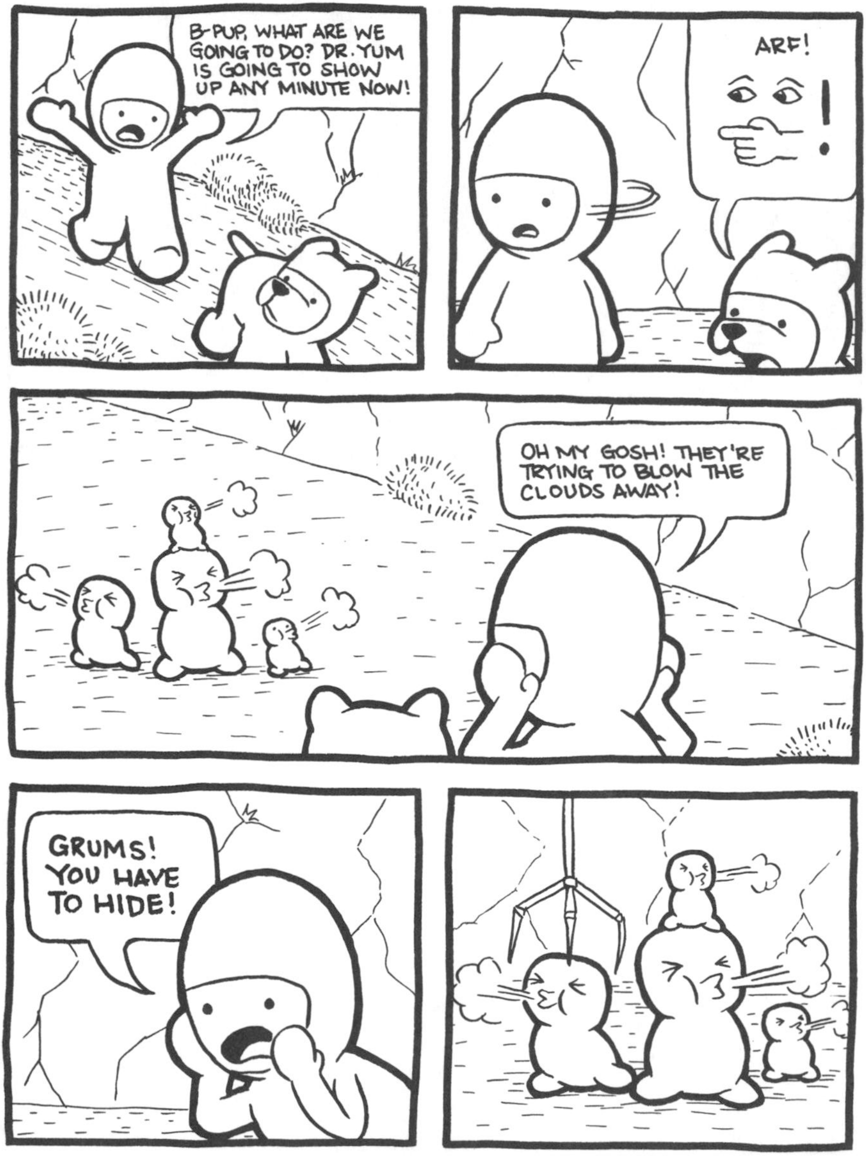
B-PUP, WHAT ARE WE GOING TO DO? DR. YUM IS GOING TO SHOW UP ANY MINUTE NOW!
ARF!
!
OH MY GOSH! THEY'RE TRYING TO BLOW THE CLOUDS AWAY!
GRUMS! YOU HAVE TO HIDE!

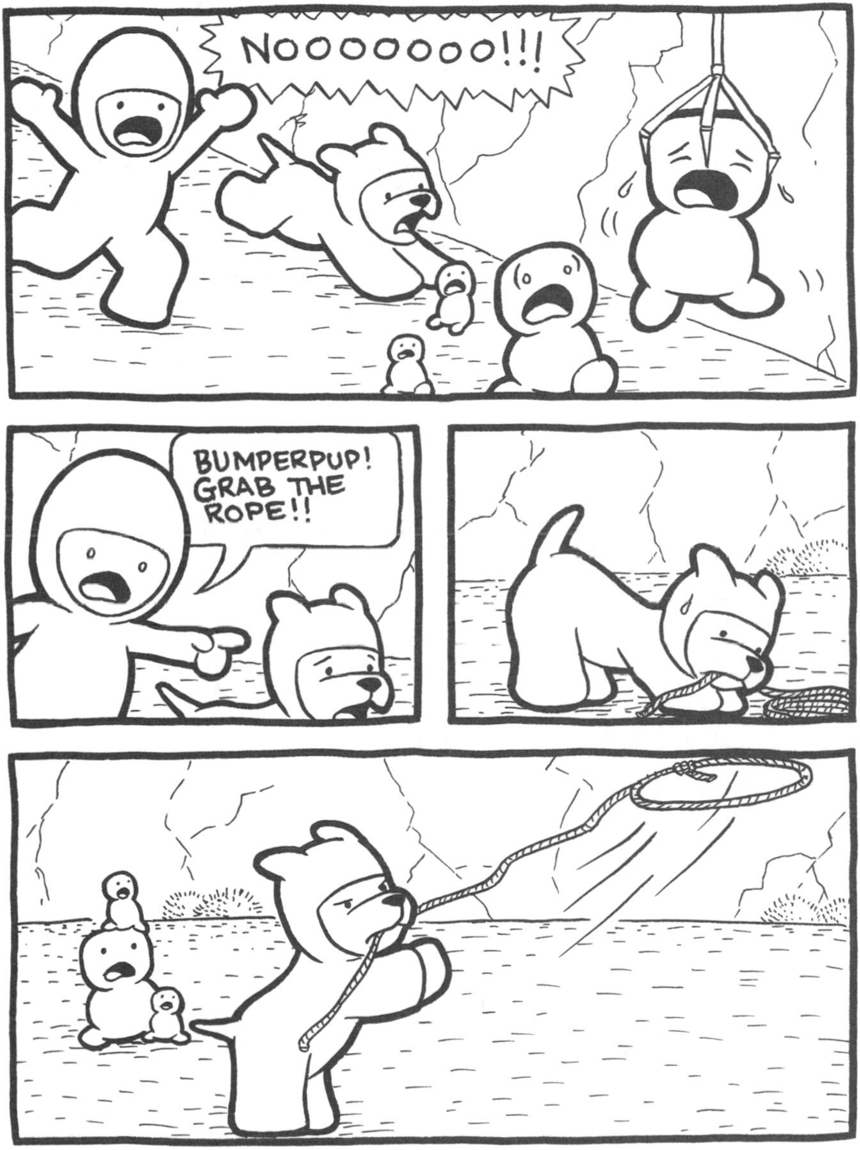
NOOOOOOO!!!
BUMPERPUP! GRAB THE ROPE!!

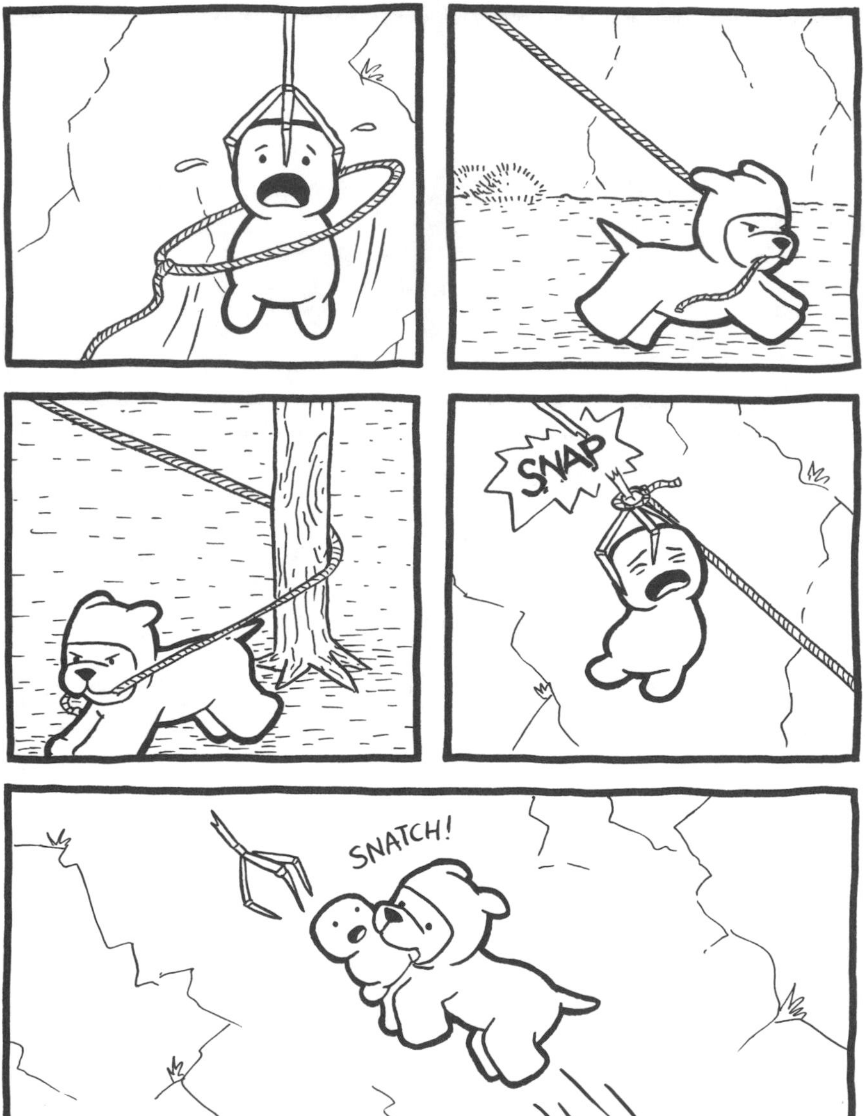
SNAP
SNATCH!

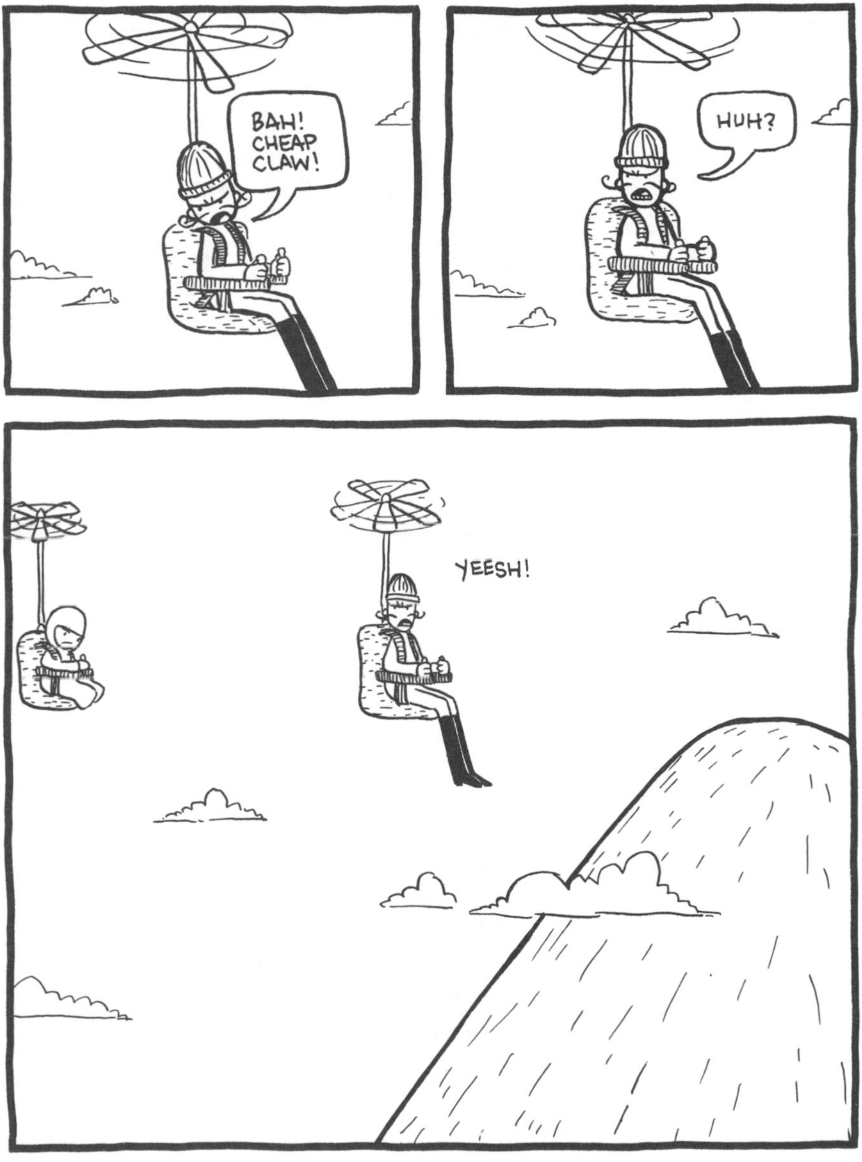
BAH! CHEAP CLAW!
HUH?
YEESH!

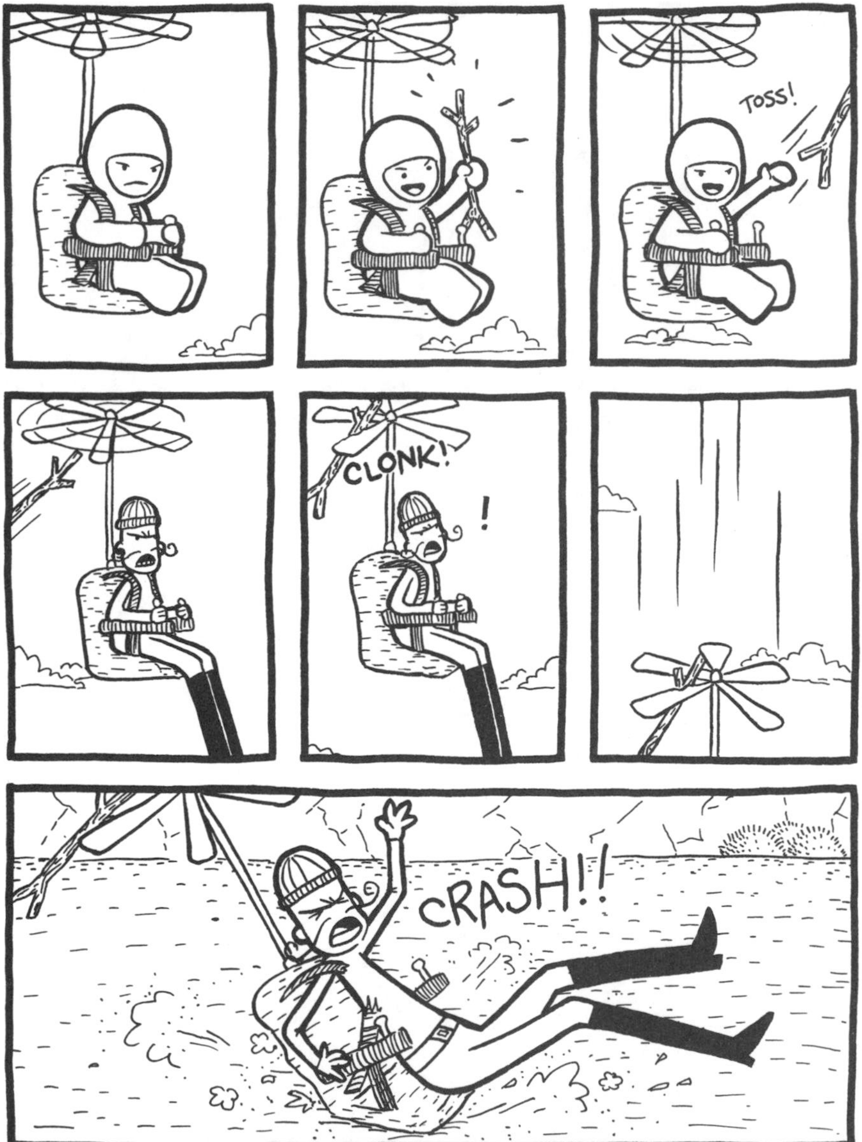
TOSS!
CLONK!
!
CRASH!!

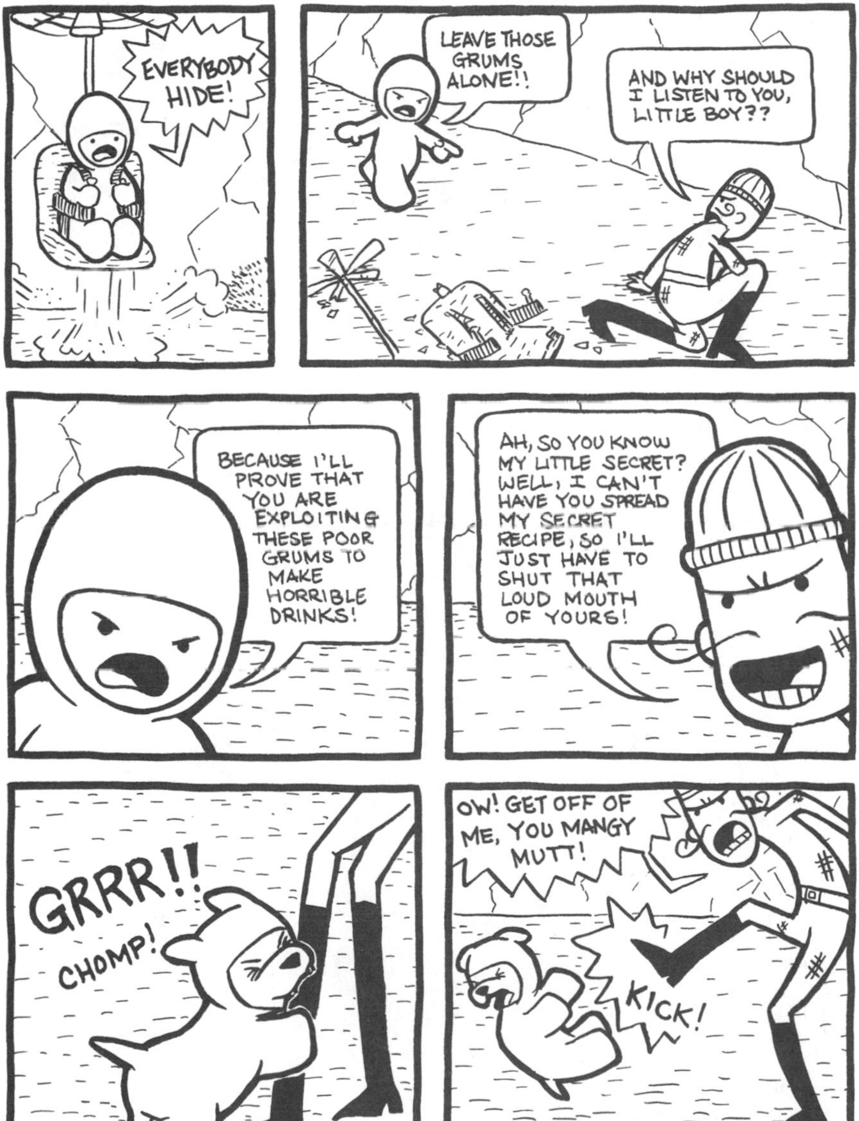
EVERYBODY HIDE!
LEAVE THOSE GRUMS ALONE!!
AND WHY SHOULD I LISTEN TO YOU, LITTLE BOY??
BECAUSE I'LL PROVE THAT YOU ARE EXPLOITING THESE POOR GRUMS TO MAKE HORRIBLE DRINKS!
AH, SO YOU KNOW MY LITTLE SECRET? WELL, I CAN'T HAVE YOU SPREAD MY SECRET RECIPE, SO I'LL JUST HAVE TO SHUT THAT LOUD MOUTH OF YOURS!
GRRR!!
CHOMP!
OW! GET OFF OF ME, YOU MANGY MUTT!
KICK!

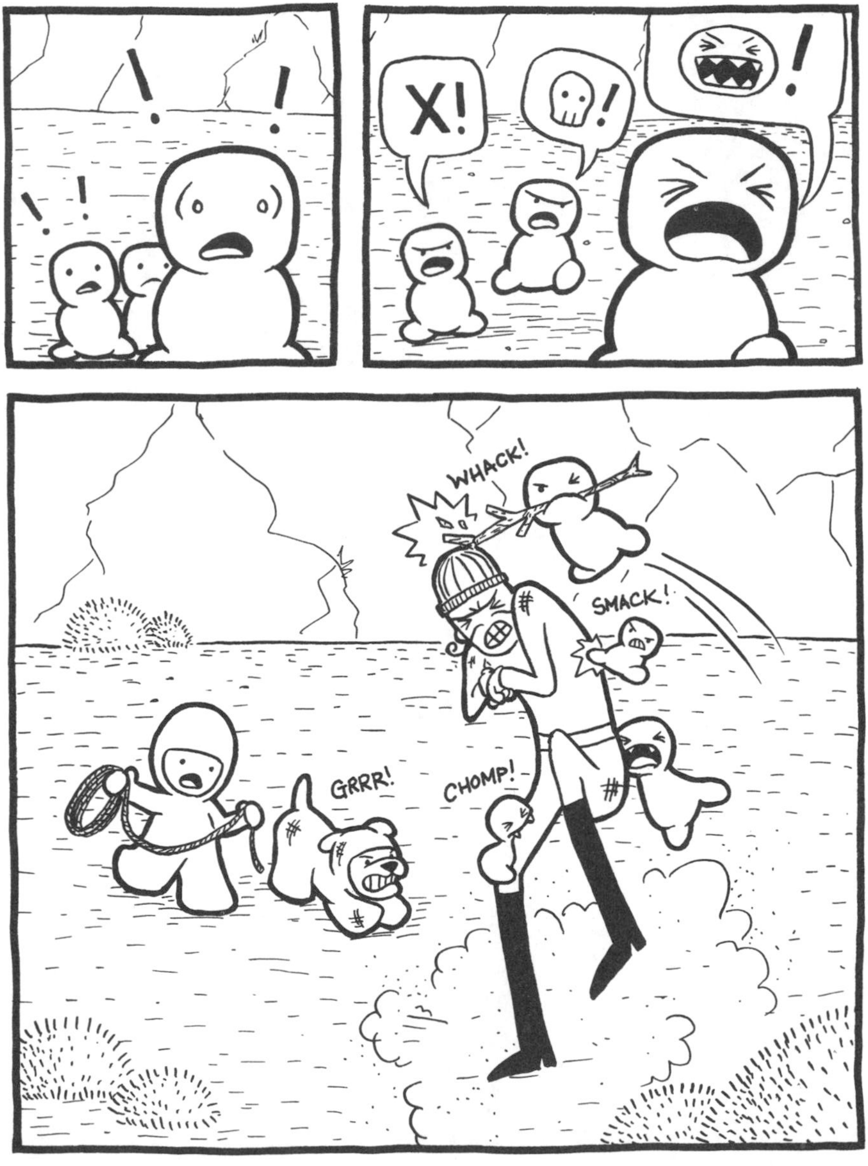
!
!
!
!
X!
!
!
WHACK!
SMACK!
GRRR!
CHOMP!

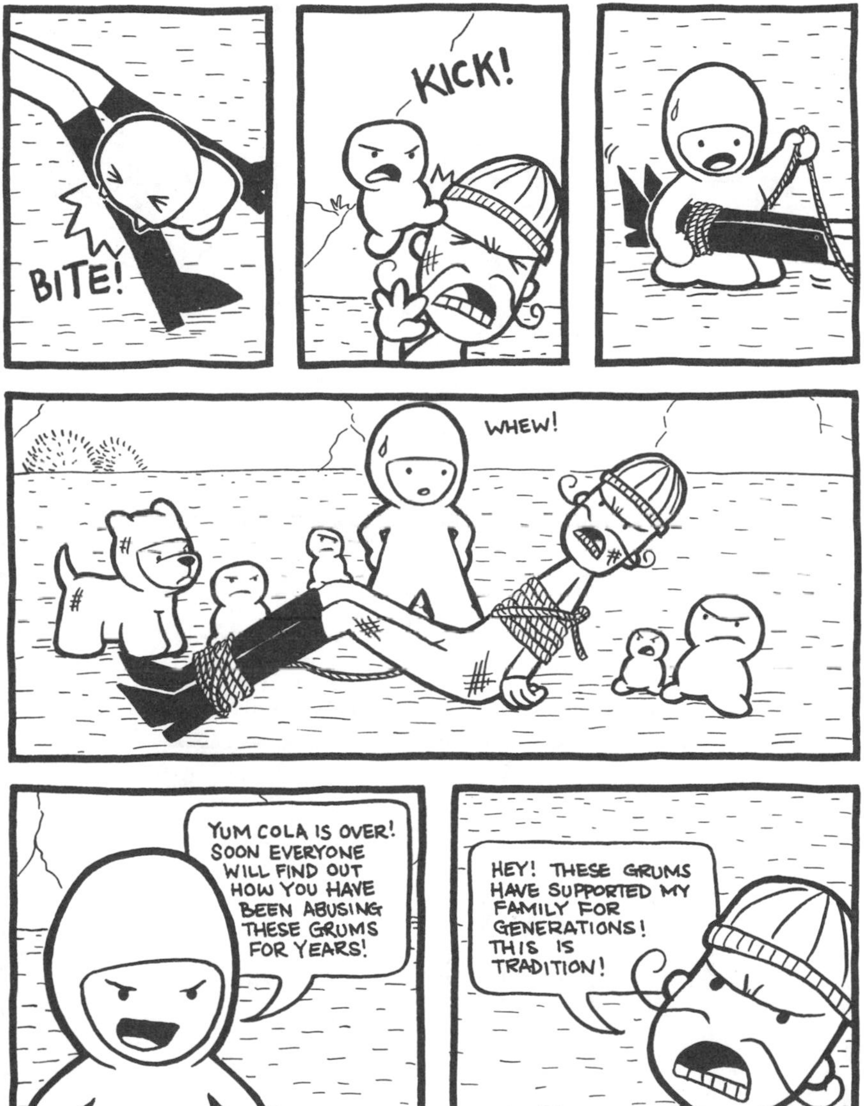
BITE!
KICK!
WHEW!
YUM COLA IS OVER! SOON EVERYONE WILL FIND OUT HOW YOU HAVE BEEN ABUSING THESE GRUMS FOR YEARS!
HEY! THESE GRUMS HAVE SUPPORTED MY FAMILY FOR GENERATIONS! THIS IS TRADITION!

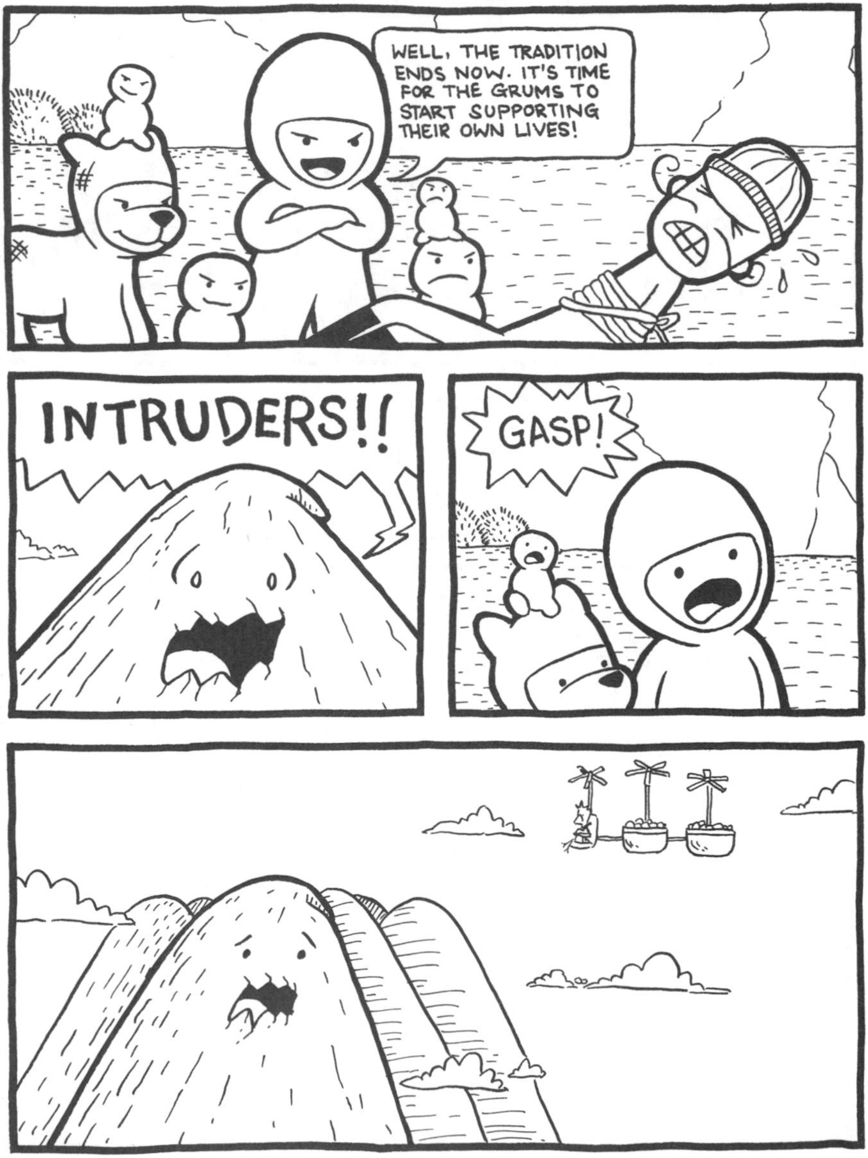
WELL, THE TRADITION ENDS NOW. IT'S TIME FOR THE GRUMS TO START SUPPORTING THEIR OWN LIVES!
INTRUDERS!!
GASP!

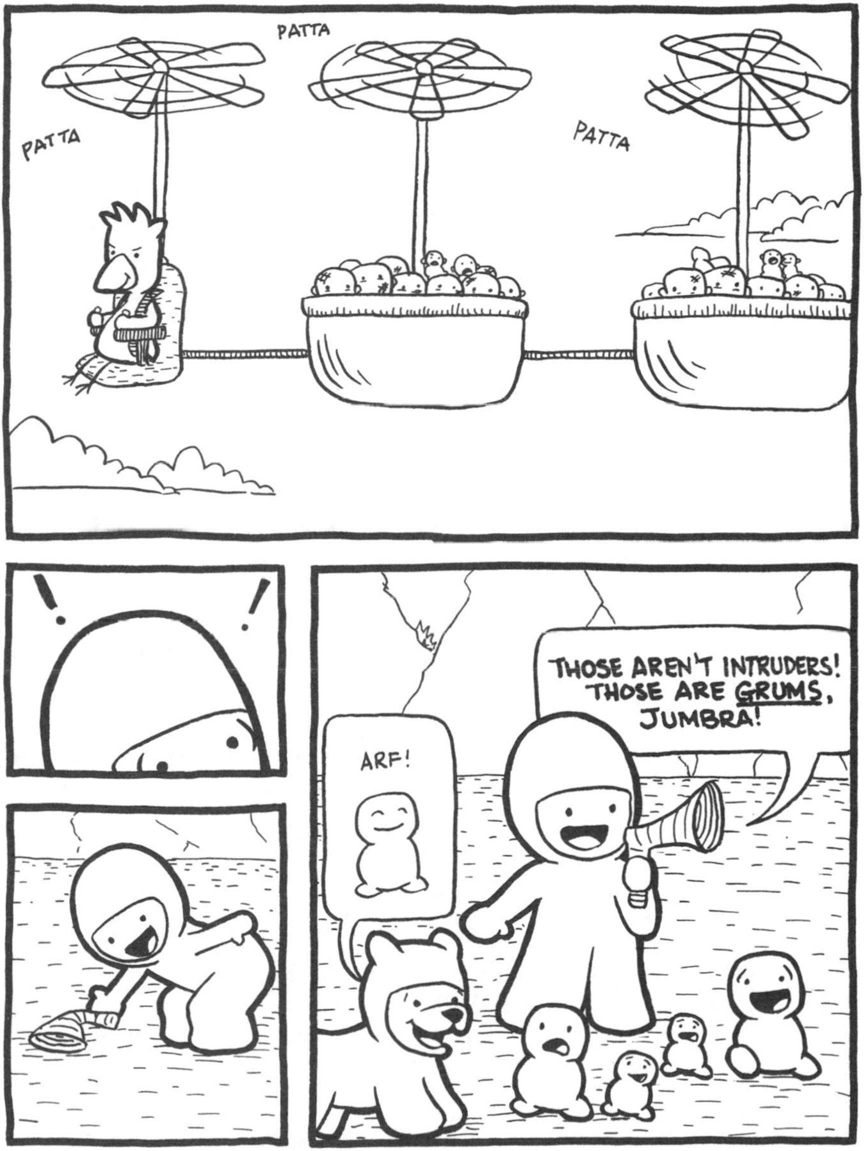
PATTA
PATTA
PATTA
!
!
ARF!
THOSE AREN'T INTRUDERS! THOSE ARE GRUMS, JUMBRA!

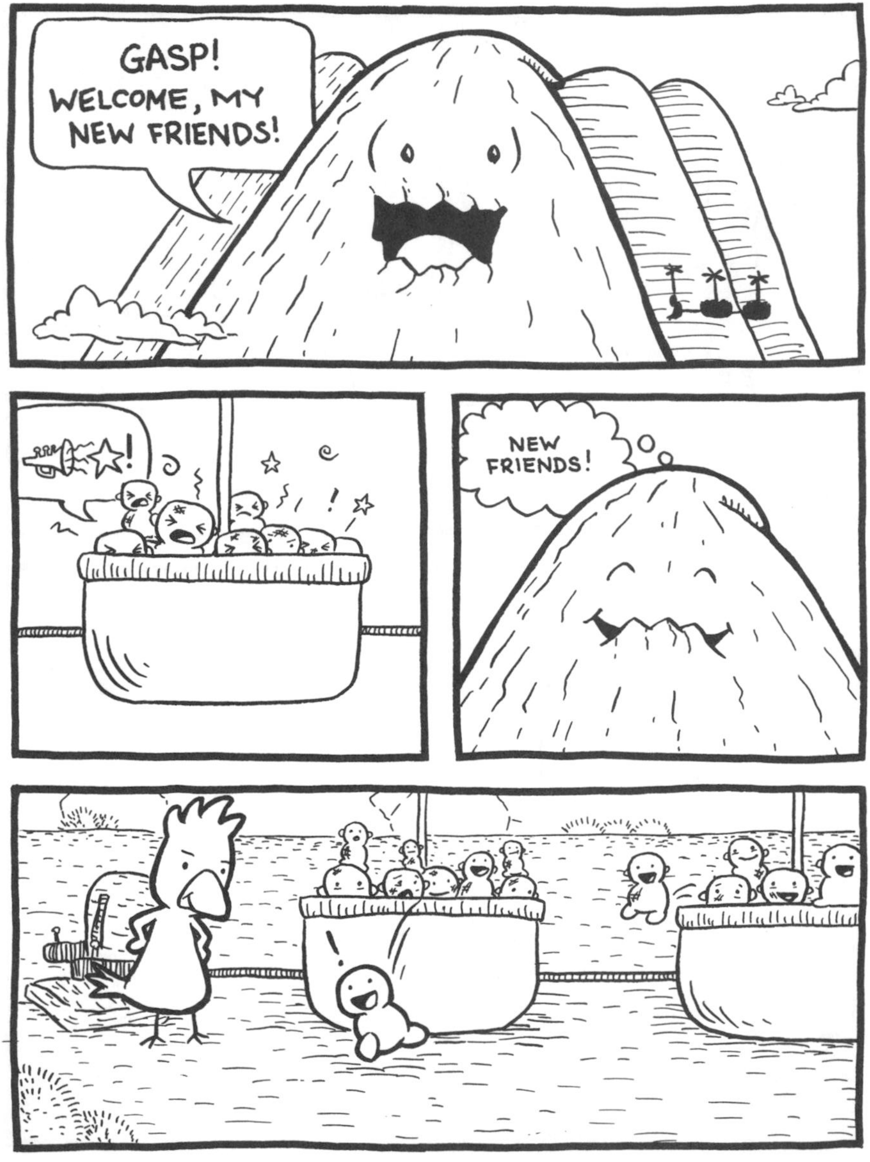
GASP! WELCOME, MY NEW FRIENDS!
NEW FRIENDS!

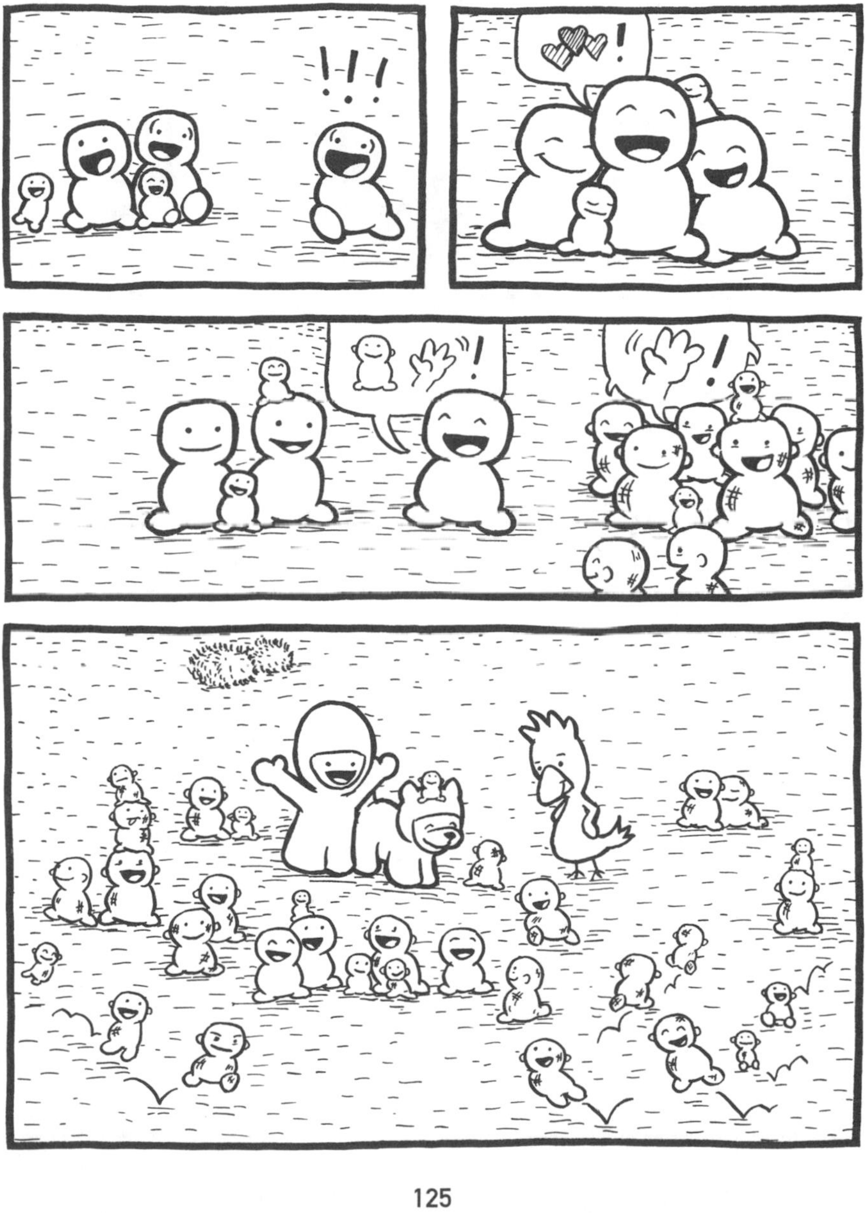
!!!
!
!
!

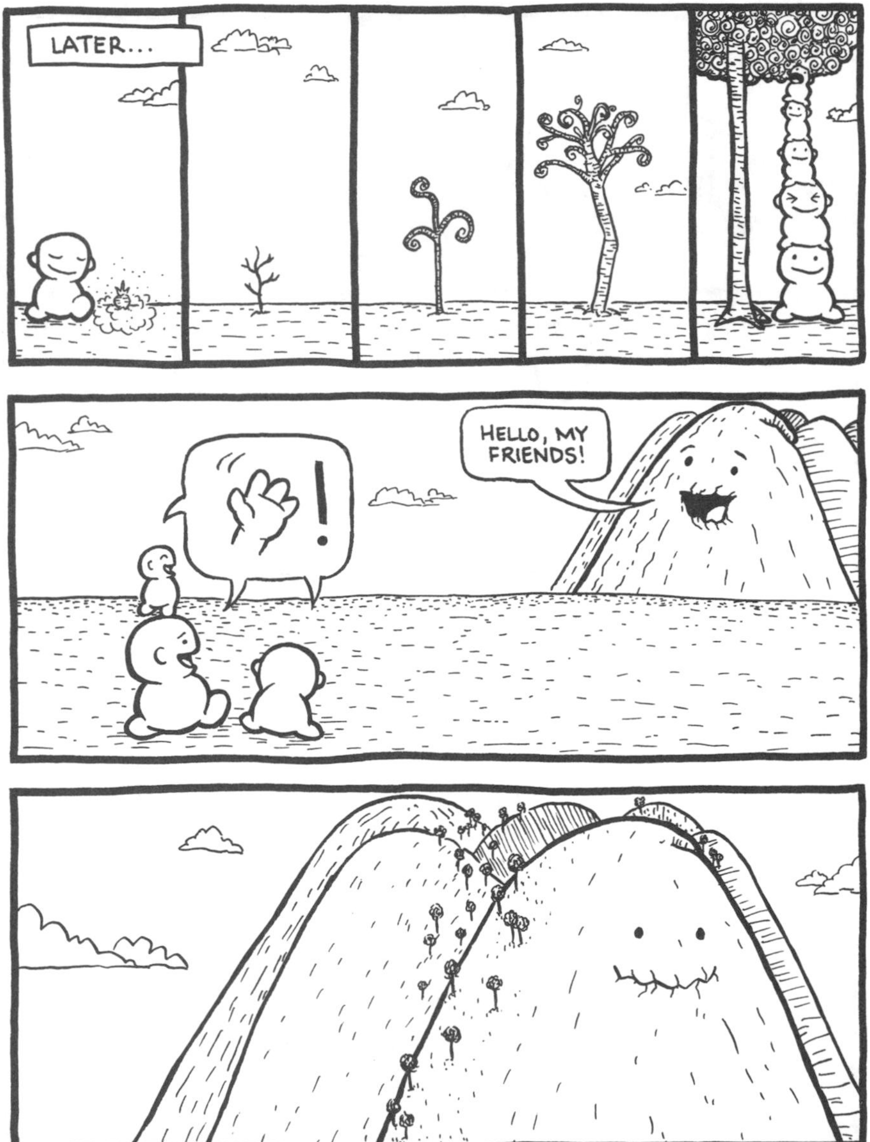

LATER...
!
HELLO, MY FRIENDS!

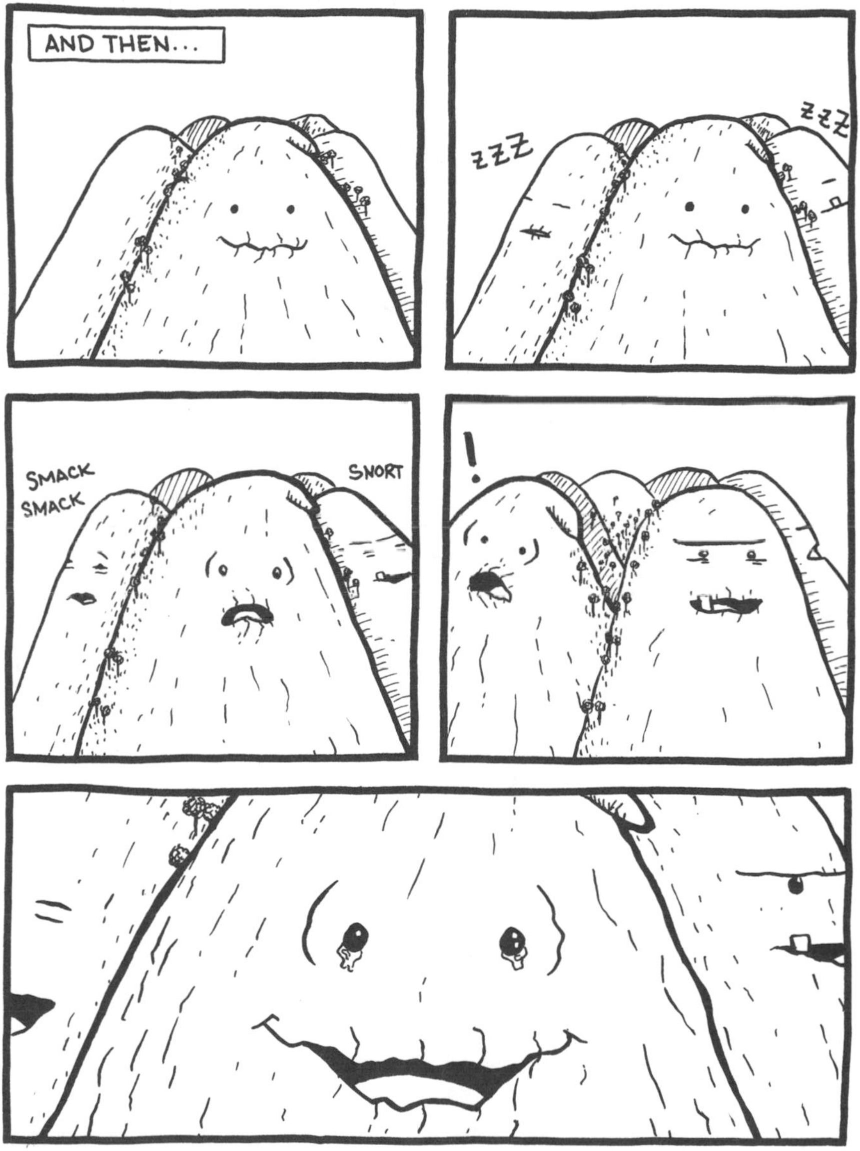
AND THEN...
ZZZ
ZZZ
SMACK
SMACK
SNORT
!

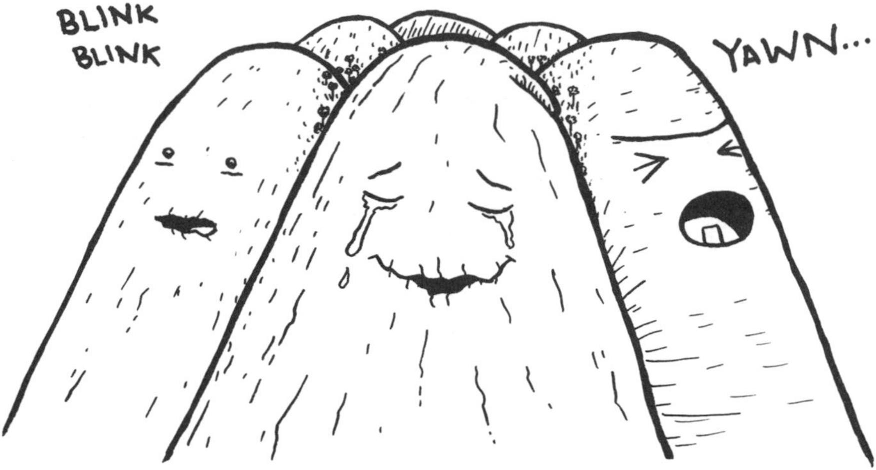
BLINK
BLINK
YAWN...

the end.